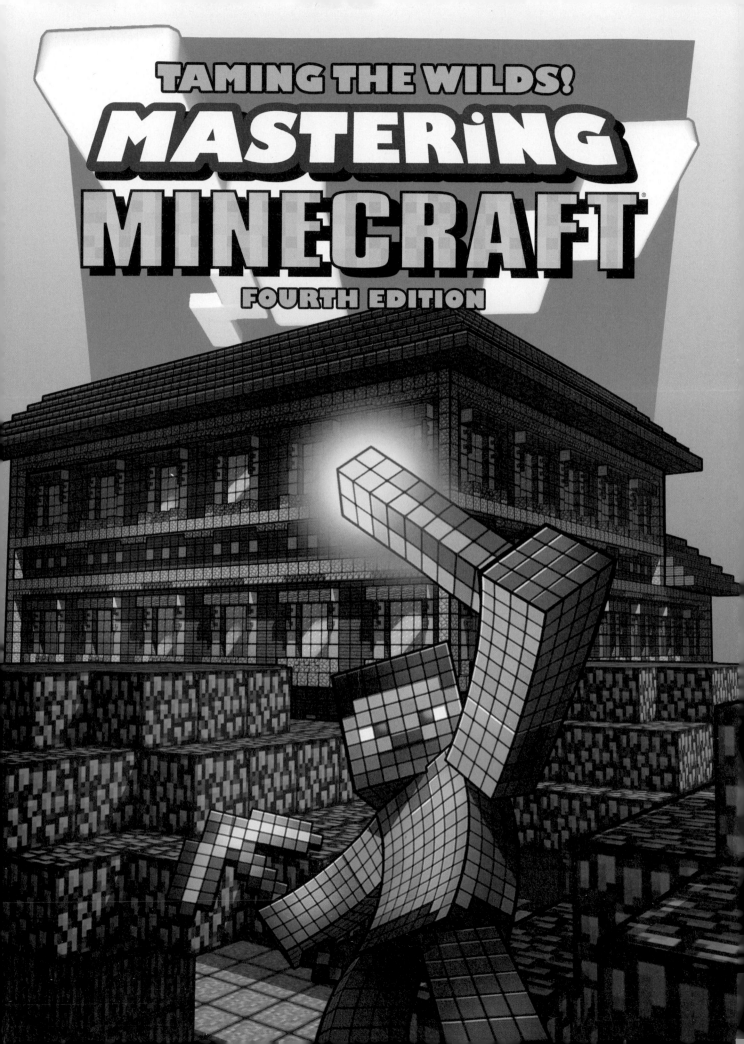

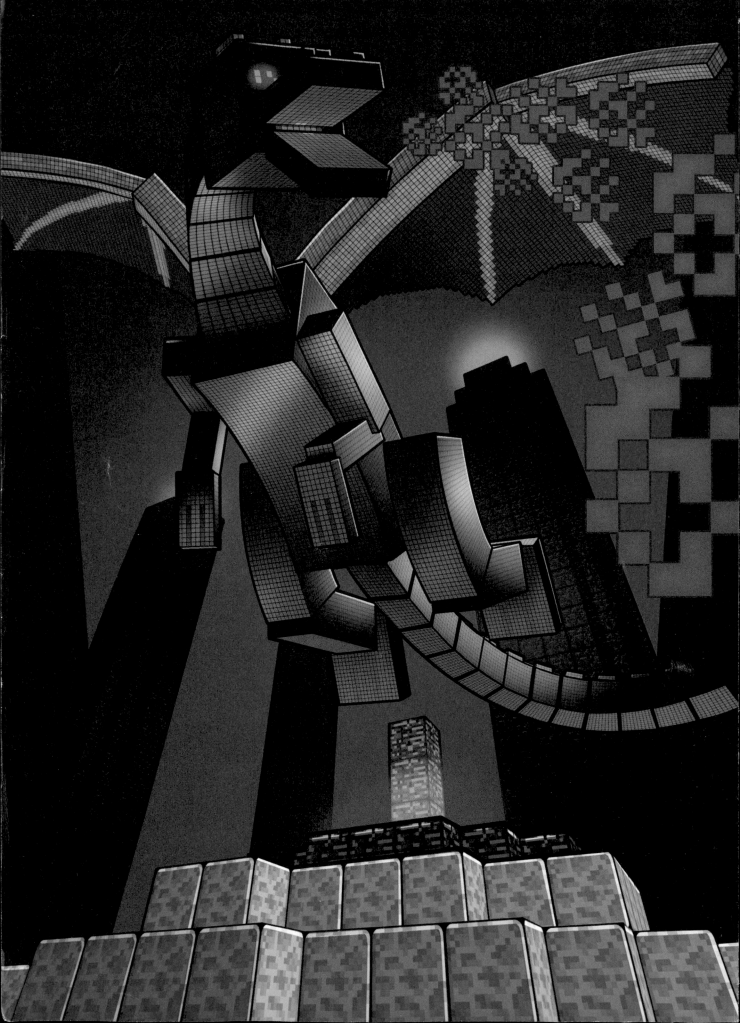

Welcome to Minecraft

Are you someone who likes to fight monsters, adventure through strange worlds, and come back laden with gold, riches, and glory? Or are you the type of person who wants to explore, build great castles, mine the depths of the world, and see all there is to see in the universe?

Either way, you should be very happy, because we have an entire book devoted to talking about *Minecraft*! Whether you're a fighter, explorer, builder, or dreamer, this game has something special for you.

Minecraft is an open-world game that doesn't hold your hand and tell you where to travel or what to work on. You're the one in charge, and you decide what happens. This book tells you how to play the game and what you might find out there, but we're really just giving you suggestions. If you want ideas on how to build, craft, fight, and thrive in this world, we're here to help.

This book covers every aspect of the game so that you can quickly find whatever you're looking for. This guide expands on our previous coverage and brings the book all the way up to the World of Color update.

In our first chapter (**Using This Guide**), we'll explain how to find everything you need so that you can easily locate the information you're looking for.

Using This Guide

If there's something specific you're looking for, this chapter lets you know where to search. Here are the chapters in this book, and a list of the subjects that they cover:

A BRIEF HISTORY OF MINECRAFT goes through years of this game's updates and shows when things were added.

BEFORE WE START covers *Minecraft's* controls, settings, etc. Beginners should go here first to find out how to move around, build, craft, and defend themselves.

LET'S BEGIN WITH THE BASICS takes your introduction to *Minecraft* a step beyond getting started. We guide you through the first few play sessions, giving you basic goals and tips on how to survive. Once you've mastered these, it's much easier to branch out and explore the world at your leisure.

YOU CAN DO ANYTHING WITH A LITTLE PRACTICE is an advanced chapter that covers the more complex systems in *Minecraft*. We get into deeper discussions about farming, mining, special locations, advancements to shoot for, enchanting, brewing, and more. When you're interested in learning all there is to learn, this is where you want to go.

TOOLS, RESOURCES, AND CONSUMABLES is a resource-heavy chapter. We give you a breakdown of every block type, item, and recipe in the game. Try this portion of the guide when you forget a crafting recipe, want to see the uses of a new item, or just feel the urge to browse through *Minecraft's* possibilities.

CREATURES BIG AND SMALL tells you all about the monsters and animals in the Overworld, the Nether, and the End. Everything in the game is discussed, so you can see how tough enemies are, or find out how to take care of friendly creatures.

BUILDING BIGGER AND BETTER PROJECTS is our last chapter. We show off a few tricky construction projects that are meant to involve many hours and produce large-scale changes to the terrain. It's fun stuff that brings together dozens of the various lessons that are spread throughout the earlier guide.

A Brief History of Minecraft

Minecraft, as we write this book, is the second best-selling video game of all time. It's sold over 122 million registered copies across many platforms, and continues to grow and expand. It has spawned its own convention (Minecon), and has fans all over the world. But where did it come from?

Minecraft started its alpha testing in 2009, and was released in full during 2011's holiday season. It's been many years since then, and we've seen a huge round of improvements to the base game. If you've ever wondered about the timeline for this, read on. We've gone back and catalogued everything that's come and gone in the past nine years. Let's see where it takes us.

PRE-ALPHA MINECRAFT

May 2009 – June 2010

Minecraft was in heavy development during 2009. People followed the introduction of a huge range of items into Minecraft. This is called Minecraft Classic. The first official version of Minecraft that we know of was 0.0.9a. This was a time when you'd see new types of blocks added constantly. Many of the items became core elements of gameplay that are still here today (e.g. Lava, trees, Sand).

Indev and Infdev came next. During late 2009 and the first half of 2010, we saw the introduction of far more complex items. Signs, Ladders, and Doors came into use. Cave systems became more complex. Minecarts, Spawners, and Dungeons were all added too. Things got a lot more dangerous out there in the night. Luckily, daylight hours were increased, so we had more time to build shelter before the nasties started knocking on our doors.

Survival Mode helped Minecraft grow from a building and exploration simulator into a full-fledged game of life or death. The burning hiss of Creepers continues to live on in our nightmares.

ALPHA

June 2010 – December 2010

Alpha took up the second half of 2010. Machinery was a major focus at this time. Levers, Buttons, Plates, and Redstone to power it all were given to us.

These made the game much more intricate. It wasn't just a survival game with cool building; you could suddenly make the game do things that didn't even seem possible without some serious forethought and planning. Automated systems started with doors you didn't need to open manually, basic traps, and so forth. Soon, they grew into automated farms, monster-harvesting rooms, and storage systems. People have made "hard drives" within Minecraft, and created computers that let you play Minecraft, while you're playing Minecraft. If that isn't awesome, then we've lost all perspective.

BETA

December 2010 – November 2011

Leading up to release, we got to fill out the world. Weather added considerable ambience, and also held a few surprises (what happens when various things are struck by lightning?).

Even more machinery was added, but there was also a large push for better player mechanics. Combat improved with critical strikes, the need to keep yourself properly fed for healing, and superior Bow fighting. Our sluggish heroes finally learned how to sprint and get around the world that much faster.

Speaking of the world, it too began to fill out. Villages, Strongholds, and other rare locations started popping up. *Minecraft* had more toys in its sandbox, which made exploration even more fun.

RELEASE

November 2011

The game released with a few new features that hadn't been part of the *Beta* (they were in the *Beta* 1.9 release that never came to be because they were rolled into the main game). These included Hardcore Mode, for people who wanted to really challenge themselves.

We also started seeing negative and positive status effects, such as Strength boosting, Poison, and so forth. Brewing was introduced, as was breeding. The End was added, as were Nether Fortresses, so we had a huge amount of new things to try and accomplish.

1.1 January 2012

We didn't have to wait long for a substantial patch. Major language support was added (try playing the game in Pirate Speak or Klingon sometime!). There were quite a few tweaks and adjustments made to improve general gameplay, but not too many major overhauls were done at that time.

1.2 March 2012

NPC Villages weren't too happy about this patch; it came with Zombie sieges. At night, Villagers had to contend with heavy monster attacks as long as there were players anywhere in the same chunk. This sometimes led to depopulation of entire towns. Pretty nifty, actually. Fallen Villagers become Zombies themselves, further adding to the chaos and destruction. Good times!

Biomes continued to expand, so world generation improved a decent bit after 1.2 was added.

1.3 August 2012

This was the first patch where Adventure Mode was available. Players could craft specific challenges and structures for others to explore, and this was possible because creating buildings was disabled. Fire and Bucket use were also restricted, so adventurers couldn't simply tunnel or burn their way through everything.

Villages continued to improve as well. Trading was introduced, so Villagers had a bit more purpose, besides being cool, to find and protect (or slaughter if you weren't such a nice person).

1.4 "The Pretty Scary Update" October 2012

Beacons and Anvils were added. Beacons were especially interesting because they're so hard to create, so they serve as yet another type of late-game goal for serious players to focus on. Speaking of endgame stuff, the Wither was included in this update. Being one of the nastiest things in the game, this boss is hard to summon and can be quite tough to kill.

We also got to meet Witches, Wither Skeletons, and Bats (not quite so scary as the other creatures in the list). This made for a really cool Halloween in *Minecraft* history.

1.5 "The Redstone Update" March 2013

Even more machines came into play with 1.5. Activator Rails, Daylight Sensors, Droppers, Hoppers, Redstone blocks, Comparators, and Weighted Pressure Plates were introduced. *Minecraft* machinery was always cool, but many more automations were doable after this.

1.6 "The Horse Update" July 2013

We already had Wolves and Ocelots in the game, but Horses were a necessary inclusion for many players. Exploration was even more fun now that you could take your animal friend along for the ride.

1.7 "The Update That Changed the World" October 2013

Our personal favorite was Patch 1.7. The improvement to world generation was extreme; biome additions and improvements made the world richer, so regions felt like they had much better differentiation.

1.8 "The Bountiful Update" September 2014

Mapmaking and Survival Mode both received updates and improvements in 1.8. There were also quite a few new types of blocks added to the world, which greatly enhanced the feeling that the underground wasn't just a huge slab of rock and special resources. New varieties of stones and ores added visual appeal to the underground areas, and also improved the ability to build interesting structures that had more stylish decorations.

Villages also became more robust. Villagers could be encouraged to breed through gifts of food, and adult Villagers gained distinct professions for trading.

The rest of the world became slightly happier and cuter with the inclusion of Rabbits. To balance all things good and evil, Guardians and Endermites were also included.

1.9 "The Combat Update" February 2016

Shields, Quivers, and left-handed items came into the game during the Combat Update. This improved the more tactical aspects of the game, and made fighting more skillful.

1.10 "Frostburn Update" June 2016

Improved desert and snowy biome creatures and features were added in this patch. These isolated areas used to feel a lot more desolate. Now they've gotten enough variety that they're even more fun to investigate.

1.11 "Exploration Update" November 2016

New Villagers and their unfriendly Illager cousins were added into *Minecraft*. Illagers are dangerous to players, and they have Evokers that act like another type of endgame boss to defeat if you can find one.

1.12 "World of Color Update" June 2017

In 1.12 the achievement system changed over toward Advancements. The goal for these is still to help guide new players through the various systems and goals that the game has to offer.

Also, colors in the game were given more saturation, and crafting items like Concrete and Glazed Terracotta came into the game. Another type of Illager (the Illusioner) also joined the monsters' ranks.

If you're completely new to *Minecraft*, it's useful to learn about the game's controls and options. We'll explain all of them in the next few pages; it's not as exciting as the material that comes later, but you get a good overview of what you can do with your character—and that's important for avoiding frustration further down the road.

THE MENUS

We'll start as the game loads. You first arrive in a menu that displays the title of the game and several options. If you don't want the game to display text in English, look at the button on the lower left (with a blue world icon on it). This controls the language displayed in the game. *Minecraft* has been translated into quite a few other languages, so you're likely to find what you need! Change this whenever you like; the language can be changed back in the same manner. You can even change the settings to display text in Pirate Speak. Yarr!

Next, look at the Options menu, toward the bottom. You can access this menu while you're playing or when you're just sitting in the menu. There are quite a few controls here, so we have much to cover. Some are mentioned elsewhere in the guide because of their relevance to different subjects, but we'll also talk about all of the options right now.

FOV

FOV stands for Field of View. This determines how much of the game world your character sees at a given time. Set this really high if you'd like to see a huge amount of the world around your character. Set it low if you want to look closely at things that are directly in front of you.

Because this isn't a game with much shooting, the default FOV works really well. It's a good balance of vision around your character.

Difficulty

Difficulty appears in the Options menu once you've loaded a world.

Choose between Peaceful, Easy, Normal, and Hard difficulties. These settings control the damage output of monsters and a number of additional factors as well. Peaceful difficulty turns off monster damage entirely. After that, raising the difficulty meter makes the game harder and harder. Damage on Hard is sometimes more than twice what it is on Easy.

DIFFICULTY CHANGES THE FOLLOWING GAME SETTINGS

- Chance for Villagers to turn into Zombies when slain by Zombies
- How often monsters appear with weapons (and if those weapons are enchanted)
- If monsters attempt to pick up dropped items
- If Spiders and the Wither cause status effects
- The rate at which Zombie Pigmen come out of Nether Portals
- Whether Zombies appear with additional Zombie allies
- How severe the Hunger penalty is on your character

Music and Sounds

Use this submenu to control the volume of various game elements. If you want music to be off (or quieter), come here. The same is true for weather noises, monsters, other players, blocks, the environment, and so forth.

If anything bothers you, slide these bars around to find out how to silence the sound that you don't like. Otherwise, you don't need to mess with this submenu.

Video Settings

Come to Video Settings if you want to tweak how much detail is rendered in *Minecraft*. You can control whether the game looks as pretty as possible or runs as quickly as you'd like. Very strong systems can run everything in *Minecraft* without sacrificing any quality, but people run this game on a wide range of systems and devices.

If the game doesn't feel like it's running quickly, turn down settings like Anisotropic Filter or Particles, and switch Graphics to Fast. You should also lower the Render Distance.

If your computer is running *Minecraft* wonderfully, then turn everything up and see if the game still runs well. Go ahead and enjoy the game even more!

Controls

The Control submenu is the most involved menu in the group. It lets you influence how you move your character, break blocks, build things, and so forth. You can flip the mouse so that it acts more like a joystick, turn on/off Touchscreen Mode, and switch the keys that control your character.

Because our book handles all versions of *Minecraft*, we don't know how you'll assign your keyboard controls, or if you're even going to use a keyboard! Therefore, we won't say things like, "Press Left Control to do this." Instead, we'll talk about the game's actual commands, like this:

"Sprint to get away from the Creeper."

"Break three blocks of Stone and look in your inventory after you pick them off."

"Stack blocks together until you're happy with how they look."

Because of this, it's very important that you learn what the commands are before going deeper into the book. See the following page!

COMMAND NAME	WHAT IT DOES
Attack/Destroy	Uses your hands or the object you're holding to hit anything in front of your character.
Drop Item	Drops the item that you're currently holding.
Pick Block	If you're looking at a type of block, this switches so that your character holds any blocks of that type that are in your inventory.
Sprint	Moves at higher speed, but causes you to get hungry much faster.
Use Item/Place Block	Places a block that you're holding on the ground where you're looking. Or tries to activate any Doors, Levers, or controllable objects in front of your character.
Hotbar Slot (1-9)	Switches what you're holding to the item located on your hotbar at the bottom of the screen. There are nine of these slots.
Inventory	Opens your inventory and shows you what your character is holding. Your hotbar slots are also shown there.
Take Screenshot	Grabs a picture of the game.
Toggle Cinematic Camera	Makes the camera move in a slower, panning fashion.
Toggle Fullscreen	Switches between a windowed view of the game and a full-screen display.
Toggle Perspective	Lets you decide whether to look at the world from a first-person perspective or from one of two third-person perspectives.
Jump	Causes you to jump; this also causes your character to get hungry faster.
Sneak	Lets you move quietly and slowly, preventing your character from falling off of ledges. Very useful!
Strafe Left	Walk to the left.
Strafe Right	Walk to the right.
Walk Forward	Go forward.
Walk Backward	Go backward.
List Players	See a list of the people who are playing on the same server.
Open Chat	Lets you type in anything you want, then shows the message to everyone on the server. "Hi guys!"
Open Command	Lets you type in a command to control the game world.

Language

This opens the same menu that you accessed from the world icon back in the game's front menu.

Multiplayer Settings

This submenu is primarily focused on the way text displays when you join multiplayer servers. To make the screen easier to read on those servers, you can always turn off Colors, Web Links, or even the entire Chat system.

Snooper Settings

Turn this off if you don't want the game to send information about your play to Mojang. Or turn this back on if you're cool with that. Leaving the Snooper Mode on does not influence gameplay in a major way, so there isn't a substantial downside to turning it on or off.

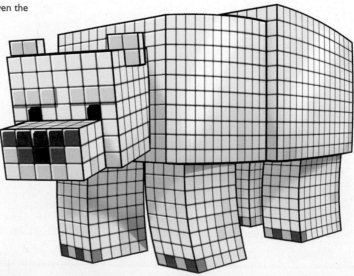

SINGLE-PLAYER

This menu lets you create a new world or return to one that you've already made. We'll walk you through that in the next chapter, and it's a very intuitive process.

MULTIPLAYER

When you first open the Multiplayer menu, there won't be any servers available. Instead, you have to go online and look up places to join. Search the Internet with your browser, and use "Minecraft Servers" to find lists of them. When you go, copy their IP addresses, and come back to the Multiplayer menu.

Now that you're here with an IP address, press "Add Server" and paste the IP you found into the empty bar. Press "Done," and then you can enter that server from the Multiplayer menu in the future without having to do anything special. The game even searches ahead of time to tell you how many people are already playing on that server.

You're free to add as many or as few servers as you like.

Minecraft Realms

This is a paid service that lets you set up multiplayer servers more easily. If you don't know much about multiplayer servers but still really want to have a world of your own for others to play in, this is an option. Just know that it costs money to use (with the cost scaling depending on the number of simultaneous players allowed on your server).

CONTROLLING YOUR CHARACTER

Once you're in-game, put the commands to good use by wandering around the world and messing with everything you find. Let's quickly explain what everything on the screen means and how to control your character.

Understanding the Interface

Minecraft has a fairly simple display, so it doesn't take long to understand. Most of the screen is taken up by a view of the game world itself. You can see what's in front of your character, and that's how you decide where to go and what to do. Easy enough.

At the very bottom of the screen are nine gray boxes. These represent your hotbar slots! Pressing the keyboard keys that are bound to those hotbar slots lets you switch between items quickly once you assign objects to the slots. For example, you can put a Pickaxe in "1," a Shovel in "2," an Axe in "3," and so forth. Doing this makes it easy to use all of your tools quickly and efficiently.

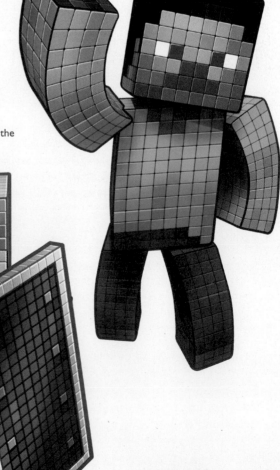

What to Put in Your Hotbar

By default, consider anything that you use the most. We suggest Pickaxe, Shovel, Axe, Sword, Torches, some type of food, a construction material (Dirt or Stone), and whatever else you need.

To change your hotbar assignments, go into your inventory and drag items to the bottom row. That's where your hotbar slots are located. Move items around so that similar tools are together and can be accessed without delay.

Above your hotbar is an experience bar. This fills as your character gets orbs of experience. These are gained by killing creatures, breeding animals, refining metals in a Furnace, gathering certain minerals, and so forth.

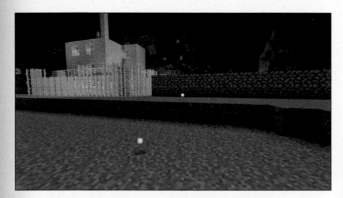

When the bar completely fills, your character gains a level. This doesn't raise any stats, like it would in some roleplaying games. Instead, levels are there so you can enchant objects later on. Your accumulated experience is also treated as a way to keep score between deaths. The more experience you get in a given life, the higher your score will be when you die. This lets you compare your survivability and progress between play sessions.

There are three sets of icons above your experience bar. The red Hearts display your character's health. As you take damage from fire, falls, monster attacks, Poison, or Hunger, the Hearts disappear. If all of them go away, your character dies and then respawns at either your starting point or the last Bed you used. In Hardcore Mode, even a single death is permanent, so you're gone forever.

The meat and bone icons represent your hunger meter. They deplete over time, as well as when you heal from damage or exert yourself by jumping and sprinting. Refill hunger by eating food. Characters regenerate health when their hunger meter is nearly full, so it's wise to keep your meter at nine or ten pips as often as possible.

The last icon set shows a number of shirts. They depict your armor. The more shirts there are, the better protection from monster attacks your character has. Craft leather or metal armor when you can, and wear that to protect yourself. If any of those shirts suddenly disappear, it likely means that a piece of your armor just broke. Replace it!

Movement

Now that you know the interface, try moving around. Walk forward, backward, left, and right. These commands are as basic as they come, so it shouldn't take long to understand them.

Double-tap the movement keys (i.e., press them twice in the same direction as quickly as you can). This tells your character to sprint in that direction. It burns through your food quickly, but sprinting can save your life when a Creeper is about to explode or when you need to get somewhere quickly. When night is falling and you're away from home, sprinting is often a good idea.

When you've mastered basic movement and sprinting, try jumping. Your character can hop up a single block's worth of height. If you have to go any higher than that, either dig through blocks that are more than one space above you, or build a ladder with Sticks to climb up vertical faces of mountains, trees, or whatever.

Breaking and Gathering Blocks

Once you're moving around the world, it's time to gather materials. Do this by hitting things until they break. The most basic gathering action is to walk up to a tree and attack it with your bare hands until the block of Wood breaks and falls to the ground in front of you. Collect these resources by walking directly over them; your character picks up items automatically if they're on the ground anywhere close to you. This creates a happy "pop" sound to let you know you grabbed something.

Use your hands to break easier materials, like Dirt, Grass, Flowers, Wood, and whatnot. It's not especially fast, but it works well enough in the early game. Once you do a little bit of crafting, you get to make tools that allow faster resource gathering.

Whether you're using tools or your fists, the basics of gathering never change. Approach the block that you want to gather, attack it with your hands or tools, and keep hitting the block until it breaks. Rinse and repeat. When objects are damaged by your attacks but not destroyed, they'll almost immediately heal. That's why you have to hold the Attack button until the job is done. Test this by hitting a tree for a couple seconds and then stopping. Notice that the cracks in the Wood disappear almost immediately. The same is true for Stone and other minerals.

If you try to harvest blocks that are really hard, you might not be able to break them. Or you won't be able to gather anything even when you succeed. For example, it's possible to break Stone with your bare hands. This takes a very long time, and then when the Stone breaks, no resources fall to the ground. That's because you need a Pickaxe to break Stone. You might even need specific types of Pickaxes to harvest certain resources. More advanced metals and minerals can't be gathered without Iron or even Diamond Pickaxes!

Placing Blocks

After you gather materials, such as Wood, the items appear in your inventory. Place them in a hotbar slot to make them easier to work with. Then switch to the hotbar slot in question by pressing the shortcut key that you bound in the Options menu.

Selecting a hotbar slot with an item essentially equips that item. If it's a tool or weapon, your character holds that up and gets ready to attack with it. Other objects are held but still act like regular fists if you attack anything.

Some materials can be placed back into the game world. Blocks of Wood, Stone, Planks, and various metals all fall into this category. Select these items on your hotbar and use the "Place Block" command to put the object directly in front of your character. This command is how you place furniture and building materials in the world.

Put Wood blocks down in front of your character. Look! You can make a basic wall like this. But that takes a long time. There must be a better way to get building materials, right? Let's talk about that.

Basic Crafting

You can now jump, sprint, move around, break blocks, look through your inventory, and place blocks around the world. Let's finish this puzzle. Crafting gives you the power to change materials and do thousands of interesting things.

In the PC version of *Minecraft*, you have a 2x2 space in your inventory. It says "Crafting" above it, so you know exactly where to look. To the right of the four crafting spaces is a single square where the output from your crafting appears.

To make an item, put materials into the crafting boxes and find the right recipes to produce what you need. Experiment as much as you want, but don't get worried. Our item chapter, **Tools, Resources, and Consumables**, lists everything you need to build all of the items in the game.

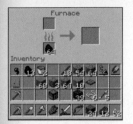

Also, we list common recipes again in some sections of the guide where they're especially important.

As a quick test of crafting, put a block of Wood into the crafting squares; it doesn't matter which of the four spaces you use. Behold! A Wood Plank icon appears on the right. Your regular Wood block is turned into four Wood Planks by this very simple crafting recipe. Highlight and grab the Wood Planks to put them in your inventory, and then use them as you see fit.

You can convert multiple items at the same time by stacking them on top of each other. For example, put ten blocks of Wood into the same crafting square. As before, the Wood Planks appear as a result. Click on them again and again to retrieve as many of the Wood Planks as you need.

Press Shift and click on the results to craft as many items as possible instantly. Shortcuts like this allow you to craft quickly and efficiently when making huge stacks of specific items.

MODIFYING YOUR GAME

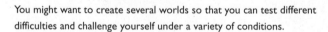

Even the best games sometimes need a few updates to remain exciting, especially if you play for years on end. That's why *Minecraft* has implemented quite a number of ways to customize your game, how it's played, and how you see it. Here are some of the ways to spice things up when you want to try something new.

The Options Menu

Before you do anything radical to modify your game, try out the basic options that are available to everyone.

Knowledge Required	None
Potential for Problems	None

You can modify the game's difficulty at any time, moving it from Peaceful all the way up through Hard. All of the non-Peaceful settings determine the damage output of monsters. It's a fairly impressive spread, but the change between Easy and Hard is very noticeable. If you're into Survival Mode challenges, pushing the difficulty higher and higher is a big way to keep things fun.

You can test out different difficulties dynamically by using the /difficulty console command. If you need to do that, bring up the command prompt and type /difficulty 1, 2, or 3.

You might want to create several worlds so that you can test different difficulties and challenge yourself under a variety of conditions.

If you find higher difficulty to be frustrating, it's possible to dial back the settings whenever you like. There is literally no risk or downside to experimenting with this setting—unless you're playing a Hardcore character, in which case you already know what you're getting into. At worst, your character gets killed.

Skins

Knowledge Required	Low
Potential for Problems	Very Low

Search for "Minecraft Skins" if you'd like to alter the appearance of your character in-game. Sites that host these skins let you download them to your computer or directly upload them to Mojang so you can add them to your account and use the skins in the future.

Skins don't change anything except the look of your character, so they're fairly risk-free. There are many, MANY skins available, and they can change your character's gender, race, or even species.

Resource Packs

Knowledge Required	Moderate
Potential for Problems	Moderate

Minecraft gives players the ability to modify the textures, sounds, and functionality of their games through Resource Packs. These are available online at a wide range of sites. Search for "Minecraft Resource Packs" using your Internet browser, and look for places with free content—you can use most of them without cost!

Follow the instructions for installing each pack. Once they're on your system, go into the Options menu, select the Resource Pack that you want to activate, and proceed from there. You can almost completely reinvent *Minecraft* by getting the pack that's right for you.

Once you have Resource Packs installed, it's relatively simple to switch between them. Go with your mood and change the game at your leisure. Sometimes, updates to the game engine make a Resource Pack non-functional or semi-functional for a while, and you have to stop using it until the Resource Pack gets an update. This is the most common type of problem.

If you can't run your Resource Pack, go back to regular *Minecraft* (the default) and stick with that while you check your favorite Resource Pack website for updates.

For the maximum effect, use a Resource Pack and a Shader Mod to crank *Minecraft*'s visual beauty to the limit. The change is huge! It's like seeing an entirely different game.

Game Mods

Knowledge Required	High
Potential for Problems	Somewhat High

If you want to go deeper than most Resource Packs go, search for "Minecraft mods" instead. People like to push further into the game engine with mods, making it possible to do all sorts of things: minimaps, engines, pumps, spaceships, more monsters, and so on. There's a lifetime's worth of content to check out.

To use mods, you need to download and install them. Each mod should have a guide to help you get it working. You may need to get additional downloads to help with launching mods, so it's not a quick process the first time you try one. Be patient, though, and you'll be impressed.

Game mods are the trickiest things to work with. They can mess with your game and cause enough disruption that you might not be able to play without reinstalling the game. Be aware of these risks from the outset. If you aren't comfortable enough with computers to back up your *Minecraft* saves, then mods probably aren't for you yet. There's a ton to learn. It's worth the time, but only when you're ready and excited to invest hours getting familiar with everything.

Let's Begin With the Basics

Minecraft is easy to play once you've gotten used to it. But it takes a little while to get through the first part of the game without running into trouble. When you don't know how to create a safe home, grow food, or build the items you need, life can be hard!

This chapter takes you through the first 30 minutes of the game, after you've created a new world. Although you normally have a different starting point every time you play, there are common techniques that are essential for survival against monsters, starvation, and other hazards.

We'll talk about these survival techniques and give you goals to work toward, so you can use each minute as productively as possible until you've mastered the basics that are so important to your life in *Minecraft*.

If you have any trouble getting things done as quickly as you'd like, don't be afraid to start over and try again. Your first time going through these techniques will be *much* harder than the second time. So have fun and keep trying these tricks until they become second nature to you.

Once you finish with that, we'll explain how to join your friends for online play. It's smart to get the basics down on your own so that you have more confidence in your skills when you join other people.

CREATING YOUR FIRST WORLD

Log in to the game using whatever version you own. Select Single-Player from the Main menu, and then pick "Create New World" from the menu that appears.

You arrive in a new menu. Name your world anything you'd like here; we've chosen to name ours "Minecraft 101!"

Next, choose a Game Mode: Creative, Survival, or Hardcore.

WHAT DO GAME MODES MEAN?

Creative	No risks, easy building, fly around, and do whatever you want
Survival	There are monsters, resources are limited
Hardcore	Monsters are more dangerous, and death is permanent! (Not an easy choice for beginners)

We suggest that you try Survival from the very beginning. Creative Mode is fun for making massive projects to show off to other people, but the challenges of Survival are quite engaging. They keep you invested in the game more than playing without a specific goal in mind.

Hardcore Mode is an even greater challenge, but it's probably better to wait on that until you're more experienced with the game. Dying and losing everything can be frustrating if you don't have the basics down pat.

More World Options

If you want even more power when creating your new world, select "More World Options" and toggle some of the settings in there.

Generate Structures is turned on by default. This lets the game world have Villages, Dungeons, Abandoned Mineshafts, and other cool features.

World Type lets you try out extreme biome conditions. In other words, you can have your world create larger biomes—this makes it harder to gather multiple resource types as quickly, because travel is a greater investment. Amplified biomes make your regions more extreme. It's pretty wild, so that's another option that we don't recommend for beginners.

Allow Cheats if you want to use various commands to make the game easier, or to test out specific things. You can see monsters that are normally restricted to specific places, or just goof around.

The Bonus Chest is a feature that *is* beginner-friendly. If you're having any trouble with the game, go ahead and turn this on to begin your journey with a few extra items.

WHAT'S IN THE BOX?

The Bonus Chest has a few Torches surrounding it. The Chest itself contains a little bit of food and some Wood. This gets you started on your construction even faster than usual.

Once you've set the options exactly the way you like, create the world and wait a moment while the game puts it together. Soon, you'll begin your journey.

IS THIS WHERE YOU WANT TO LIVE?

As soon as the screen clears and you can look around, see what's near your character. Let's create a checklist to see if you have what you need to survive!

Checklist for Survival

- ■ Are there trees in your line of sight?
- ■ Do you see or hear any animals?
- ■ Can you find a location that would be safe for building a house or a cave?

Wood

The three items in the preceding checklist are your immediate priorities. You need trees for Wood. That's essential for your survival, because you need Wood for construction, basic tools, and for fire. It's your lifeblood during the earliest parts of the game. If you can't see any trees at all, either restart or move quickly in any direction to find an area that does have trees. You can survive without Wood, but it'll be much tougher because you won't be able to use any tools for a little while.

Animals

Many animals that you can see and hear during the day are useful to you. These creatures give you food, Wool, Leather, and other nice items for crafting. In the early game, edible animals are the best because they provide food much sooner than farming. We've sorted many common animals in the following list from most useful to least useful for a starting hero.

Cows	Drop multiple pieces of meat and can be milked once you find a bit of Iron
Chickens	Easy to raise, drop meat when killed
Rabbits	Have Hides, meat, and can drop a Rabbit's Foot (for brewing Potions of Leaping later in the game)
Pigs	Drop meat when killed
Sheep	Drop Mutton when killed and have Wool for Beds
Horses	Not very useful in the early game (greater later on)
Llamas	Help you carry around items because you can equip them with Chests

Safe Housing

You can build a house darn near anywhere, but some locations are easier and faster to work with. Open, flat ground works well if you want a freestanding house that looks nice. If you're interested mainly in survival, you're better off scanning the area for a hill or mountain. Building into existing Dirt or Stone lets you create a defensive location quickly, because you don't need to put down many blocks of Wood or Stone to secure yourself. Instead, hollow out a small space and you'll be good to go in almost no time at all.

Final Decision

Now that you know what to look for, is your area a good enough starting point? For a total beginner, we recommend you demand at least trees and either a safe area or animals. You don't need to have all three right there in front of you, but going for two out of the three starting items is a good compromise.

If you're really nervous about the spot you've been given, go ahead and return to the Main menu. Delete that world (or come back to it later), and create a new place to check out. This doesn't take very long, and it's better for new players to start somewhere that feels just right.

HOW TO SPEND YOUR FIRST DAY

You've got ten minutes of daylight to work with after the game begins. It's likely that you won't get attacked by anything in this first day because monsters spawn at night, and none of them have had a chance to appear. As long as you avoid big caves and dark places, you should be fine for a while.

Set goals for yourself and quickly get a series of tools and shelter so that you can deal with the coming evening.

Goal #1: Harvest Three Blocks of Wood

Run toward the nearest tree and attack it. You have only your hands to work with, so breaking through the bark will take a few seconds. Hold down the Attack command the entire time. If you stop at any point, the damage you did to the Wood disappears and you'll have to start again.

ATTACKING

Your hands, tools, and weapons are all used with the same controls. Anything that you currently hold in your hand is used to interact with objects when you use the Attack command. This command is used when you punch trees for Wood, attack animals for food, defend yourself, or mine for minerals.

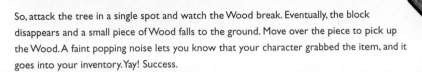

So, attack the tree in a single spot and watch the Wood break. Eventually, the block disappears and a small piece of Wood falls to the ground. Move over the piece to pick up the Wood. A faint popping noise lets you know that your character grabbed the item, and it goes into your inventory. Yay! Success.

Do this again for two more pieces of Wood, so you have three total pieces to work with.

Goal #2: Make an Axe for Yourself

Go into your inventory and put the three pieces of Wood into your crafting area. Notice that a new item appears on the right side of the screen. The displayed item represents the results if you choose to craft those pieces of Wood. Every piece turns into four Planks of Wood. Turn your three pieces of Wood into 12 Planks right now.

You then need to craft several items with your new Planks. Fill the entire crafting box with Planks (one in each slot, as shown). These four Planks are turned into a Crafting Table. Put that into one of your hotbar slots at the bottom of the inventory screen.

Leave that screen and use your appropriate hotbar command to ready the Crafting Table. Place that item down someplace where it's easily visible. These tables allow

you to work with a far greater variety of items. When you interact with a Crafting Table, it brings up a larger interface, so you can put up to nine ingredients into your crafting. Other versions of the game simplify this, but they still require you to use a Crafting Table to make most of the items.

Next, put two Planks into your crafting slots (use the Crafting Table or your normal inventory interface for crafting). Putting two Planks together, one above the other, lets you make Sticks. Sticks are required for a huge number of tools.

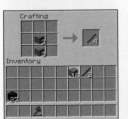 

Look at the next picture to see how to create a Wooden Axe. Two Sticks and three Planks go together to make this happen. Now that you have a Wooden Axe, it's much easier to chop Wood. Get several more pieces of Wood now.

Goal #3: Make a Pickaxe and a Shovel

Many tools are made almost exactly the same way, so use your new supply of Wood to make a Pickaxe and a Shovel. They require a similar setup, with two Sticks to form a handle, and then some Wood to complete the tool, depending on what you're making.

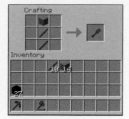

Once you have a Wooden Pickaxe, Shovel, and Axe, put all three of them on your hotbar. You can then start the next phase of your project. We're going to hunt for Stone!

Goal #4: Find a Source of Stone and Harvest at Least Six Pieces

Select your Shovel and dig into the Dirt until you find Stone (usually a few spaces down). If there are deposits of Stone nearby—in a cliff or wherever—then go ahead and rush over to those instead. The general rule is that if you can't find Stone, start digging downward. It'll be there.

Once you hit Stone, stop using your Shovel. Switch to your Pickaxe and hit the Stone just like you hit the trees with your Axe and the Dirt with your Shovel. Harvest at least six pieces of Stone as soon as possible, and then return to your Crafting Table.

If you dug down into the earth to get your Stone, you might not be able to get directly back to the surface. If that happens, carve a crude set of steps out of the blocks around you. Your character can jump as high as a single block, so cut the blocks around you until you can jump up one block in front of your character. Then cut until you can do that again and again until you're back on the surface. There are ways to make nicer steps that don't require these big jumps, but you're on a schedule and don't need to worry about that just yet.

Also, when digging down, it's wise to dig in front of your character (not under your own feet). This lets you see what's below you before you hop down into the hole. Usually it's more Dirt, Stone, etc. However, there are caverns all over the place, and you might fall to your death if you dig directly down and break through into one of these deep caves.

Goal #5: Switch to Stone Tools

Use your Crafting Table and recreate your Pickaxe, Shovel, and Axe; this time, use Stone and Sticks instead of Wood and Sticks. The final products are Stone tools. These last longer and are faster at their tasks compared to Wooden tools, so this is a big upgrade without having spent much of your time. After this point, you can stop using Wooden tools entirely; they have practically no value to you. However, hang on to yours for the moment—you'll use them for fuel in the Furnace you're about to build.

Goal #6: Make Shelter for the Evening

Use the remaining time in your day to build shelter for yourself. Dig into a rock face, a hill, or use a tunnel into the ground at the base for your evening's home. Or, if you have more time than that, build a Stone or Wood structure around yourself. This takes more resources and time, but it's 100% possible if you work quickly before nightfall.

PUT A ROOF ON THAT!

If you build a shelter outside, *always* remember to put a roof on it either three or four blocks high. If you leave your house open to the sky, Spiders can climb into your home at night and attack you. You do not want this to happen.

Once you have your shelter, make a Crafting Table to put in there, so you can keep making items during the evening. It's possible to chop down your old table with an Axe and bring it inside, but that often takes too much time.

Using a full box of Cobblestone (as shown in our picture), you should also make a Furnace. These are major items to help keep you alive. You can cook food in them, such as any Raw Chicken, Beef, or Pork that you gather from animals in your area. Furnaces also get you Charcoal.

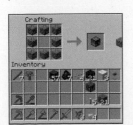

If there isn't Coal Ore mixed in with the Stone in your area, you'll need some Charcoal tonight. So, let's talk about how to get some!

Goal #7: Setting Up Your Furnace, Door, and Light

Place your Furnace near the Crafting Table, and throw your old Wooden tools into the lower slot of the Furnace. That's your fuel. The tools won't burn for long, but they'll get the job done. Use Wood blocks in the Furnace's upper box. That's the item you're trying to cook. Burn through several pieces of Wood (using your old tools as fuel), and collect the Charcoal created. Charcoal is efficient fuel for your Furnace, so you can now cook plenty of other items during the late afternoon and evening. Burn Wood when you need to get more Charcoal. Also, cook any meat that you harvested today. Don't eat raw meat because it's not as filling for your character, and sometimes it's even dangerous (raw meat can poison your character).

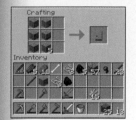

Furnaces light the area while they're cooking, so you can see in the dark or even underground while this is going on. Take six Planks of Wood to make a Door for your house. Block off the rest of the entryway so there's only a narrow space one block wide and two blocks high leading into your shelter. Put the Door there to keep enemies from walking in. Alternatively, you can wall off the entire house from the inside and cut your way out in the morning.

The finishing touch is to use Sticks and Charcoal to craft a few Torches. Once you make them, these simple devices keep your home and area well lit. That's important for getting around, but it's also great for keeping monsters off your back. Monsters only appear in dark areas. As long as you keep your home lit, nothing horrible will appear there, even when your character is away. Monsters can still come after you, or walk through open Doors, but they can't magically appear anywhere that's properly lit.

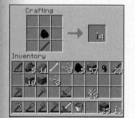

Put Torches on your hotbar, and hang them on walls inside and around your house. Don't worry; they won't burn anything down! They also won't need to be replaced or reset. Torches burn forever.

SURVIVING THE NIGHT

Once the sun goes down, the light levels fall dramatically. It's hard to see if you walk around outside, and monsters can spawn almost anywhere. Zombies are the most common, and they're easy to outrun. They moan frequently, and are easy to hear or spot. But Creepers are quiet and very deadly. They explode if they sneak up on you, dealing potentially lethal damage and destroying anything nearby.

Until you have weapons, armor, and more practice, you're better off hiding during the nighttime hours.

If you check your clock, phone, or watch, you'll find the evening lasts ten minutes. Later, you can craft a Clock in-game to tell time more accurately.

As evening passes, be productive. Carve down into the earth and gather more Stone. You're going to need many, many pieces throughout your career. While mining, you might find Coal, Flint (in Gravel), or Iron. Iron is the best of the resources you find in the earth's upper layers. To spot this metal, look for Stone blocks that have a lightish metal embedded inside them. Once mined, you refine these in your Furnace to get Iron Ingots, which are quite useful. Make Pickaxes with them so you can harvest Gold, Redstone, Diamond, and other rare materials in the deeper levels of the world.

Goal #8: Forging a Sword

Take a break from your mining at some point during the night. Use your Crafting Table to make a weapon for yourself. One Stick and two pieces of Wood, Stone, or metal make a Sword. For now, a Stone Sword is perfectly adequate, but an Iron Sword will be much better later on. Always keep your Sword in the same slot on your hotbar so you get used to switching to it quickly. Monsters can jump you while you're wandering outside, mining, or whenever. Even when you think you're safe, there are sometimes moments when you get surprised. Practice switching to your Sword quickly and comfortably. The better you get with it, the longer you'll live.

Expand your home and your mines until morning. Look through the holes in your Door to see if it's light outside, or carefully wander outside if you're feeling brave. Just be ready to head back through the Door if you see trouble coming.

TSSSSSSSSSSS, BOOM!

There's a thin line between brave and reckless in *Minecraft*. If you go outside at night, accept the possibility that you could die. Quickly. And even if you don't, a Creeper explosion has the potential to tear the wall out of your home if you're standing close by. Be extremely alert.

Also, watch your back in the morning when you go outside. Sunlight kills many monsters, but not all of them. Don't be surprised by late-partying monsters that may still be near your home.

THE NEXT DAY

As time passes and you get ready for the next day, you may notice that your hunger meter is falling—that's the series of drumsticks on the lower-right portion of the screen. Your character can't heal from injuries unless your hunger meter is almost full. If it ever goes down to zero, you lose almost all of your health (or can even die if you set the difficulty all the way up).

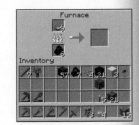

Goal #9: Gather Enough Food to Keep Yourself Full

So, eating is a good thing. It'll take days to get a good farm ready, so you need something to snack on before then. You can hunt Chickens, Pigs, and Cows, and then cook their raw meat. That's a great way to survive in the early days, and it's good later, when you breed these animals as well. But there are many options.

Ways to Stay Fed

- Cook raw meat from nearby animals.
- Leave your local area and wander around until you find more distant cattle or livestock to eat.
- Make a Fishing Rod with Sticks and String, and then fish in any body of water.
- Plant Seeds for a Wheat farm, and hide somewhere safe for about half an hour while it grows.
- Spiders and Zombies drop Spider Eyes and Rotten Flesh; these aren't good for your health, but they can be eaten.

- Chop down leaves from trees and hope to find Apples—this is not very effective, but it's an option.

MINE, EXPAND, AND THRIVE

Once you have enough food to get by, it's sensible to expand your mining operation. Gather more Stone and keep searching for Iron. If you have enough Iron, it's possible to make armor for your character. This makes it much harder for monsters to hurt you. Leather and Iron both are used for armor, so hunting enough Cows early on can get you decent armor long before you can spare the Iron for defensive purposes.

Goal #10: Make a Tunnel Down to the Bottom of the World

When you're digging down into the earth, don't go randomly in any direction. Instead, make a single path that leads down into the depths. On the PC, you can press F3 to see how deep you are. About 30 blocks up from the bottom, you start getting a chance to find Gold. Fifteen blocks from the bottom, you can find Diamond, the real prize!

Torch

You won't want to spend minutes getting to these lower levels every time you go down there. One way to keep this process fast and efficient is to mine a set of steps that leads from your house all the way to the bottom. The straighter your tunnel, the less time you waste getting down there.

Next, make Stone or Wood Stairs. Adding these to your downward tunnel makes getting around faster, especially during the climb back to the surface. Also, Stairs reduce the amount of Hunger you incur from this trip. Jumping back to the surface takes a great deal of energy; climbing the Stairs isn't nearly as bad. So, the sooner you make real steps, the better off you are.

Here's a picture of the recipe for Stairs—use whatever material works best for you, depending on whether you have more Wood or Stone.

As you grow more comfortable with the game, start reading our next chapter about more advanced techniques. You can build water systems, railways, and other transportation routes to improve your mining efficiency. For now though, it's fine to simply dig deep and start making tunnels until you find good ore. Just remember a few rules:

Mining Tips and Warnings

■ Most good minerals are found in veins; if you see one piece of Iron, Coal, Gold, or another good material, there are probably more! Dig out the entire area around each special mineral to make sure you get everything.

■ Always bring food, Wood, Torches, a weapon, and tools on your mining expeditions.

■ If you hear bubbling Lava or monster noises, you're likely getting close to a dangerous cavern; proceed slowly and carefully.

■ Never dig straight down unless you have a death wish; one day, you will fall to your death or drop into Lava.

■ Don't dig up every single block to find ore. Make lots of narrow tunnels to maximize your search area.

■ Leave precious ores and materials in Chests that you keep inside your home. Don't carry everything with you, or you might lose it all if your character dies.

■ Once you have a Bucket, keep some water with you at all times (for putting out fires, cooling Lava, etc.).

■ Always put Torches on the same side of a new tunnel. If you get turned around, you'll always know which direction leads toward home.

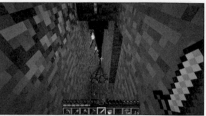

KNOW WHERE YOU ARE

Start to get a feel for the resources in your current biome. If there aren't animals, specific flowers, plants, or other goodies that you need, look up these items and find out where they naturally spawn. For example, if you want Sugar Cane, look it up to learn that Sugar Cane is common in sandy areas, near rivers or deserts. Make sure you gather all the valuable items in your area, and start stealing useful items anywhere within close range of your base.

LOOK AROUND

Goal #11: Make a Landmark So You Can Find Your Home from a Distance

It's nice and safe to stay near your home, but you can't thrive by remaining in one place. Make landmarks so you can see your house from a good distance away. A massive tower of Dirt is one of the fastest, cheapest ways to accomplish this task. We talk about ways to create more landmarks in the next chapter.

Once you've made it easier to find your way back, start exploring the surface. There are other biomes within easy reach if you're brave enough to walk a minute or two in any direction. This opens the way toward more animals, plants, and blocks.

Always secure your rare items in Chests at home before you venture too far out. If you die and can't make it back to your body, you don't want to lose anything important!

MOVING ON

Goal #12: Survive and Build!

As you get better and better at the game, you should add new tricks to your exploration and mining. The next chapter talks about many ways to improve your play: enchanting, brewing, combat techniques, using the Nether and the End, and so forth. There's still so much to learn, but you now have enough information to survive your first few days in *Minecraft*. With that, it's not much harder to build a house and use it as a base of operations for everything else you do. It all gets easier from here.

JOINING YOUR FRIENDS

Minecraft is great when you're alone, but it's even better if you find a place to play with your friends. There are many ways to do this, if you're interested. There are servers online at all hours of the day, and you can join them without any trouble. You can also play locally with friends on the same network as your computer. For an even larger group of people to game with, you can set up a server for yourself and anyone who wants to join over the Internet!

We'll explain how to do all of this, and then we'll discuss *Minecraft* etiquette, so you know a few of the common dos and don'ts of playing the game with other people.

Getting Onto Other Servers

The simplest way to play with other people is to join an existing multiplayer server. Launch *Minecraft*. Next, make sure you have the information for the server on which you'd like to play. If you have no idea where to go, then let's take a moment to find out!

Use your favorite Internet browser, type in something like "Minecraft Servers," and then search. Your search results should provide a decent list of sites that spread information about *Minecraft* servers.

The sites that share this information usually have blurbs about the type of community to which its server caters. Are they PvP (Player vs. Player) servers?  Playing to build? Survival? Look for an indicator that these people are interested in the type of gameplay you seek. Also, check to see how many people are logged in to the server. If it's too empty or too full, then maybe it's not a great choice for you. Personal taste takes priority here, so look for whatever you like. Maybe a small server is more your style. Or maybe you enjoy having tons of people to interact with.

What Do the Terms Mean?

It's tough to figure out where to go when you have no idea what people are talking about. Let's break down the types of *Minecraft* servers so you have an idea what you're getting into. Some servers use their own terms or have unique styles of play, but the following list should give you a fair idea of what to expect.

Survival	Mostly non-PvP-focused, standard rules
Freebuild/Anarchy	Unrestricted
Creative	Building servers, no combat, no risk
Roleplay	For creating a character, a story, and playing your role
PvP	Player versus player; combat between players, but there may be rules
Hardcore PvP	Player versus player; anything goes, at any time
Faction	PvP in teams
Hunger Games	Competitive PvP
Prison	Work your way up and out
Challenge/Mini Games	Specific goals are set forth
Economy	Build, trade, and expand
City	More rigid about where you can build; often involves heavy trade

Once You Choose Where You Want to Go

Look up the IP address of the server that interests you. The sites that discuss these servers almost always provide this information. Highlight the address itself, and then copy it (Control + C, or write it down). Go back to *Minecraft*, select Multiplayer, and then "Add Server." Paste the address (Control + V, or type it all in) that you copied into the Server

Address bar and proceed. You can now get to that server whenever it's online.

Make sure your login information is accurate. If you type in your user name incorrectly, the game won't let you join multiplayer servers. You must have a valid Mojang account to do this.

Local Play

You don't always need to hang out with 300 people to enjoy *Minecraft*. Maybe you're in the mood to host some of your friends visiting your home. Local play is easy to do in *Minecraft*. Have one person in your house start a regular, single-player game. Once they're in, hit Escape and then select "Open to LAN" to make the game multiplayer. Other people on your network will soon see the game pop up in their Multiplayer menus, and they can join.

Write down the port that the game is being hosted on. If anyone has trouble automatically detecting the game, they'll need to add that port number when they sign on. To do that, select "Direct Connect" from the Multiplayer page. Type in the IP address of the hosting computer, and then add the port that you just wrote down at the end of it. Here is the syntax:

"IP Address: Port Number" 192.168.1.102: 52088

Console editions of the game let people join in for split-screen local play. That's pretty neat too, as long as you have a good TV to play on.

Creating Your Own Server

For the best of a few worlds, you can create your own server and have friends and strangers come through to enjoy *Minecraft*. Note that this is very involved stuff compared with playing on someone else's server. Hosting is quite a commitment, so don't get into this unless you're extremely excited about messing around with the ups and downs of server management.

We don't go into this in-depth, because some of the routing challenges, security issues, and other complexities go far beyond the scope of this book.

Interacting With Other People

Now that you're ready to go online and have fun, take one more minute to stop and read. The following are a number of tips that help you avoid trouble with other people. Let's talk about etiquette, so you can be one of the cool folks everyone likes to have around!

Griefing Is Bad!

There's a time and place for trouble. If you want to wreck people's houses, attack their characters, slaughter their animals, and ruin everything you see, go to a Hardcore PvP or an Anarchy server, a place where this behavior is tolerated. This is perfectly fine—just make sure you end up playing with other people who want the same thing! Combat rocks. It's nice to compete and hunt people down, if they're cool with that.

Don't go into regular Survival servers or other cooperative modes and try to ruin things for everyone else. This is griefing (also called toxic, bad manners, etc.). It'll get you kicked off of the server sooner rather than later, and there's just no point. Treat people the way that you want to be treated, and everything will go fine most of the time.

Griefing includes:

- Attacking other players unless the server is PvP-focused, or the other player says that they're interested in fighting
- Stealing from other players' Chests or taking things from their homes
- Damaging other players' property with Lava or TNT, removal of light sources, destruction of walls, leading monsters to them, and so forth
- Inappropriate speech or text

If it seems like a server has a ton of people griefing and causing trouble, find a new server. Keep searching until you discover a place that has cool people. Why bother playing online if you don't like the players you bump into, right?

The Things People Say

Try not to overreact if people are a little bit rude from time to time. It's the Internet. It happens. Ignore the person who's being a pain, and focus on the players you like spending time with.

That said, report people to the server's administrator or moderators if you start seeing really nasty stuff. Anything hurtful, cruel, or upsetting should not be tolerated. It's totally fine to stick up for yourself and others!

If you're worried about saying anything wrong around other people, go by a simple rule: pretend that your parents and your younger siblings are in the same room.

Don't do anything online that you wouldn't do when they are listening in. Following this guideline prevents quite a few "Oops, I didn't mean to upset you," moments.

You Can Do Anything with a Little Practice

By the time you begin this chapter, you should understand how to control your character and survive in the wild, while crafting basic tools and structures. This chapter takes those minimal goals and extends them considerably. By the end, you should know how to build large structures, harvest any type of material, defeat monsters in all three of *Minecraft*'s worlds, and so on. All major concepts are dealt with here in detail.

HOW TO CRAFT

We've already talked about the very basics of crafting in *Minecraft*, but now we'll delve all the way into the heart of the matter. Crafting is an important skill for any player. You can't do much of anything without it, so knowing how to access all recipes in the game is vital.

Your basic character can always craft any recipe that requires only the 2x2 crafting grid. This is

accessed from your inventory at any time. To use more complex recipes, you need a Crafting Table. This is made by putting a Wood Plank into each slot of the 2x2 crafting grid. You then deploy your Crafting Table somewhere nearby and start working.

For this reason, we always suggest that players carry around either a Crafting Table or at least a decent number of Wood Planks so they can make a table without much delay. Having Wood Planks is great for many reasons, because they're also vital for Sticks, which are key components of almost every tool. So, you'd be crazy not to keep spare Wood around.

With access to a Crafting Table, you can work on any recipe that you have the correct ingredients to make. Learn which ingredients you need by searching through **Tools, Resources, and Collectibles**.

Certain basic ingredients are so common that they're great to keep on hand. We already mentioned Wood, but you also want to have some Cobblestone and perhaps Iron Ingots as well. A supply of these base materials can yield quite a bit of what you need. With just Wood Planks and Cobblestone, you can set up a convenient, safe base anywhere in the world. Make a Crafting Table, Furnace, block yourself into a room, add a Door, and you can work in peace for as long as you like. Add Chests as needed to store things there for the future.

It's often smart to place Chests near your Furnaces and Crafting Tables, because these three household features work together. Keep ingredients in the Chests, smelt them in the Furnace, and use your Crafting Tables to make more advanced products. You don't want to run around your house wasting time going to each station. Having these things in the same area is extremely convenient!

Consider placing Signs near your Chests once you have more than a few of them. Organize the contents of these Chests to make sure you know where your items are located and can access them quickly without having to look around for minutes.

Several shortcuts allow you to craft more comfortably. If you put enough crafting ingredients in their slots to make multiple items, hold down the Shift key and click on the final product to make as many as possible instantly.

Another trick is to grab a stack of items you're working with and slide them over several slots in your inventory. Do this when you need to divide items into multiple stacks. For example, if you want to divide your Wood Planks in half for making Sticks, roll your stack across two spaces while holding the button. Release the button when you have the proper number of stacks, and watch the items divide evenly. Quite nice!

SOMETIMES THINGS BREAK (I.E., DURABILITY)

Consumable items are those you use once before they're depleted. You eat a piece of Bread and it's gone. You blow up your TNT, and that's that. Certain items are reusable but can't be used forever. This is usually the case for tools, such as Axes, Shovels, armor, and so on. Items like this that rely on durability break when they've been used too many times. Armor loses durability when you take hits, and tools lose durability when they finish either dealing damage to a target or harvesting a block. You don't lose durability for swinging tools in midair or carrying them around.

Watch the bars that appear underneath items after you use them. Those bars reflect the items' remaining durability. Once they get really low, you know the item in question will soon break (and be completely destroyed). Before that happens, you have the option of repairing the object with an Anvil or simply preparing a substitute tool, so you still have something to work with when your primary one breaks.

NUMBER OF USES FOR TOOLS, BY MATERIAL

Wood	60
Stone	132
Iron	251
Gold	33
Diamond	1562

BREAKING TOO QUICKLY

If you use tools for the wrong function, they break much faster. Each improper use of a tool costs two or even three points of its durability.

Using Pickaxes, Axes, and Shovels as weapons costs twice the durability. Using a Sword to break blocks works the same way. Using your Fishing Rod against monsters, to pull them around, costs triple durability.

We strongly advise that you carry multiple tools of your favorite types. In the early game, this is a lifesaver because Wood and Stone tools break very quickly. Keep two or even three Pickaxes and Shovels so your digging isn't disrupted for long.

Tools that see less use aren't as big a deal. You certainly don't need three Hoes every time you head out; one is more than enough. Or you could leave the Hoe at home and grab it only when you're in the mood to farm.

GENERAL GUIDELINE FOR TOOLS

TOOL	NUMBER OF TOOLS TO CARRY
Pickaxe	2-3 (very important)
Shovel	2
Axe	1-2
Hoe	0-1
Sword	2
Shears	1

If you know you're about to focus on a specific activity, like chopping more Wood, adjust your tool count accordingly.

Make a few extra Axes before you go to harvest Wood. The same is true for Shears if you're chopping through heavy forest.

Each time you leave your base of operations, think about the activities that you have planned. Take what you need the most, and do what you can to maximize your free inventory space so your character isn't loaded down with crud you won't use. The more free space you have, the more treasure you'll return with!

Anvils and Enchanting

When you get further into the game, it's sometimes useful to save tools that are especially valuable. Enchanting lets you turn your character's levels into special properties for weapons, armor, and tools. Imagine a Pickaxe that can harvest multiple minerals per block and mine faster and last longer. You'll get one of those at some point! If it's a Diamond Pickaxe with those traits, you'll be happy every time you use it. This means you won't ever want it to break.

Repairing items is possible, though it's costly. Don't repair standard tools that aren't enchanted. It's not that important, because you can make replacements quickly and without much cost. Save repair jobs for things you love that aren't easy to come by.

To start a repair, make an Anvil. These expensive items take a pile of Iron to complete, but you won't need to make many of them. Keep an Anvil in your primary base, and leave it at that.

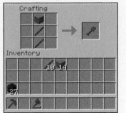

Your smaller bases and mining stations won't require something this impressive.

Once you have an Anvil, interact with it to bring up the repair interface. Use the item's base material to restore its durability. Thus, Diamond tools require Diamonds to repair (ouch).

Items cost more to repair if they have extremely high durability (e.g., Diamond tools). They also cost more to repair if they're enchanted, and if you've already worked on them previously. At some point, you have to give up on even the best items, because they cost way too much to repair.

Don't Rely on Damaged Tools

Tools that are almost out of durability should be treated as trash. Bring an extra tool of that type when you leave your base to account for the imminent destruction of your current tool. Or simply throw the badly damaged item into your garbage bin and stop worrying about it.

Do not keep damaged tools in Chests for the rest of your game. It's annoying to have a backlog of useless, damaged tools that you're never going to mess with again. Use them until they're destroyed or throw them away.

FARMING

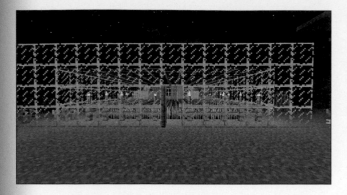

Once you have a few supplies and the basics squared away, farming is the way to go for food. You can hunt for meat, but eventually all the nearby animals will be gone. So why not spend some time learning how to plant and harvest fruits, grains, and vegetables? They're easy to grow, can be replanted, and fill up your hunger meter quite well. Some of them can be used later in things like Potions. So let's play in the dirt!

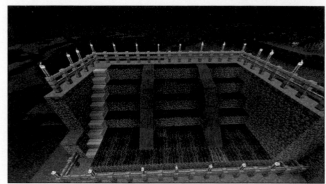

Setting Up Your Field

At the most basic level, farming is about planting seeds in wet Dirt with access to lots of light. You can start a farm on the shoreline of a lake, by the sea, or you can get a Bucket and make your own little puddle surrounded by Dirt blocks. One Water block can keep four Dirt blocks in any direction damp, so you can create a trench for the water to flow through with Dirt on either side, or dig a pit in the middle of the field for the water. You can even get fancy and create terraces of Dirt with a waterfall!

Seeds and Edible Plants

- **Wheat:** the staple of the farm
- **Carrots:** pointy, orange, delicious
- **Potatoes:** nutritious, but sometimes produce Poisonous Potatoes
- **Watermelons:** the long-term crop
- **Pumpkins:** gourd of many uses
- **Sugar Cane:** used in making Paper and Sugar
- **Cocoa Beans:** used in baking and dyes
- **Beetroot:** used for food and dyes

Wheat

You can get Wheat Seeds from any tall grass, so chop away at nearby patches. Don't worry too much if you don't find many, or if you start your game in an area without much in the way of grassy fields. Not every patch of grass drops Seeds, but harvested Wheat usually drops more than one Seed in addition to the Wheat itself, so you can replant and grow your farm from even the smallest beginnings. If you have plains nearby, you're in Wheat heaven; the large amount of tall grass there helps you gather Seeds by the handful.

Ripe Wheat is a golden-brown color. When harvested, the crop produces 1 Wheat and 0-3 Seeds. If you harvest too early, you get only Seeds and no Wheat.

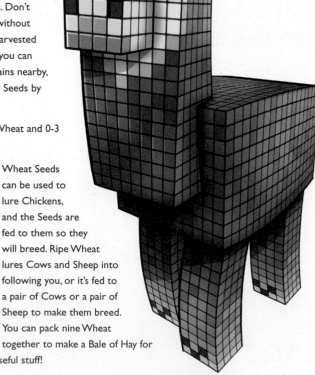

Wheat Seeds can be used to lure Chickens, and the Seeds are fed to them so they will breed. Ripe Wheat lures Cows and Sheep into following you, or it's fed to a pair of Cows or a pair of Sheep to make them breed. You can pack nine Wheat together to make a Bale of Hay for Horses, or use three of them to make Bread for feeding yourself. Wheat is useful stuff!

Carrots

You can find Carrots growing in Villager farms, so be sure and dig them up if you get the chance. Zombies also occasionally drop Carrots. Once planted, a single Carrot grows into as many as four more when ripe. You know Carrots are ready to be harvested when you see four of them poking out from the ground.

Carrots can be eaten directly out of the ground or replanted. They can also be used to attract Pigs and Rabbits or to make them breed. If you have a Saddle and want to ride a Pig around, make a Carrot on a Stick to get the Pig to go wherever you want!

Potatoes

Like Carrots, you can find Potatoes growing in Villager farms, and you can harvest them. Zombies also rarely drop Potatoes, so it may take a while before you can start enjoying delicious Baked Potatoes. A raw Potato planted in the ground grows into a group of Potatoes. You know they're ripe when the tops pop out of the ground.

Potatoes can be replanted immediately to increase your farm. Once you have enough that you can cook some, stick them in a Furnace to make Baked Potatoes, which are very good for satisfying hunger. You can eat them raw, but they won't fill you up nearly as much.

THE POISONOUS POTATO

When you harvest potatoes, there's a tiny chance that some of them will be Poisonous Potatoes, which can't be cooked or planted. You can eat them, but you probably shouldn't (because of the Poison).

Watermelons

Watermelons are found growing wild in jungle biomes. Break them into slices and turn those slices into seeds! You can also find Melon Seeds in Chests in Abandoned Mineshafts, or you can trade for them if you find a Farmer Villager.

Once planted, a Melon Seed turns into a stem. Once the stem matures, it tries to grow a Melon next to itself. The Melon will grow only if there's a free space for it, so don't crowd them out with other crops. Once the Melon bears fruit, harvest it, but save the stem! If you leave the stem, a new Melon will soon grow, saving you the need to replant. Melons can be broken into numerous slices. Each one fills the hunger meter only a tiny bit, so they're good for keeping your bar topped off.

Glistering Melons

Melon Slices can be combined with Gold Nuggets to make Glistering Melons. These are a key ingredient in making health Potions, which you learn about later in this chapter.

Pumpkins

Pumpkins grow naturally on grassland and can be crafted into Pumpkin Seeds. Like Melons, Pumpkin Seeds require some space as they grow into a stem. Once the stem matures, it needs an adjacent free block to grow a Pumpkin. Ripe Pumpkins can be harvested whole, leaving the stem behind to continue the cycle of growth.

If you're hungry, use some Eggs and Sugar with a Pumpkin to make a tasty Pumpkin Pie!

The Amazing Pumpkin

Pumpkins have lots of uses! They can be worn as helmets to keep Endermen from attacking when you look at them. They can be crafted into Jack-o'-Lanterns, which are brighter than torches and even work underwater. Want a Golem? Put a Pumpkin on top of some Snow or Iron blocks to make a defender for your bases.

Sugar Cane

Sugar Cane can't be eaten by itself, but it's still a useful crop. Search river areas and deserts for this tall plant, and chop it down. A full-sized plant of Sugar Cane is three blocks tall and thus gets you three pieces of Sugar Cane to plant.

Create a full line of Sand or regular Dirt, and then dig a ditch beside it to fill with water. Sugar Cane is very thirsty and needs to have immediate access to water just to take root.

Give Sugar Cane time to grow. Harvest it by cutting down the upper two blocks of each plant. Leave the base of the Sugar Cane untouched so it can continue to grow for as long as you like. In this way, you can get a huge amount of Sugar Cane without much effort after the initial planting.

Cocoa Beans

Cocoa Beans are found only in jungle biomes, where they grow as pods on the sides of small jungle trees. Unripe pods are green, but they turn a golden-brown when they are ready to harvest.

Making a Cocoa Bean farm is slightly more challenging than some other types of farms. It's more of an orchard. Cocoa Beans don't require water, but they do need Wood, and only Wood from jungle trees will do. As you go through the jungle gathering Cocoa pods, chop down a few jungle trees. Take the Wood from the trees back to your farm, set it down where you want your orchard, and put the pods on the Wood. A fully harvested Cocoa pod gives 2-3 Cocoa Beans.

Two pieces of Wheat and one Cocoa Bean make eight Cookies. Delicious! Cocoa Beans can also be used to dye items brown, which is an extra benefit.

Beetroots

Search Villages to find Beetroots. Once you get some of their seeds, you can start a fairly standard garden with these items. Once harvested, turn six Beetroots and a Bowl into Beetroot Soup, or turn individual Beetroots into Rose Red Dye.

Time to Dig in the Dirt!

You've got Dirt, Seeds, and Water. Now you need to prepare the ground for planting. This is the job for the Hoe. A Wood or Stone one will work just fine, so you don't have to use any of your precious Iron, Gold, or Diamonds unless you really want to dig in style.

Use the Hoe on the ground to change the Dirt into tilled land (a Farmland block), ready for planting. If you look closely, you can see the blocks of tilled land nearest the water start to get darker, which means they're getting nice and damp. You might also see them going back to normal Dirt, which means they are too far away from the water and are drying out. This also happens if you jump on your tilled land, so don't hop around in your garden.

SAVING SPACE

Because you need only a single block of Water to irrigate a large area, it's possible to plant a 9x9 farm with only one block of Water in the center. If you're measuring ahead of time and want to wall off the area, make an 11x11 set of walls, and put your water pit in the center of that hollow space.

Planting

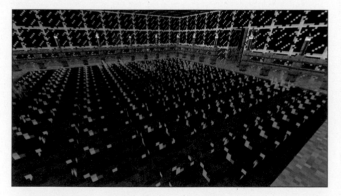

Now that the ground is prepared, use your Seeds (Potatoes, Carrots, and so forth) on the Farmland. Look! Tiny green shoots appear. That lets you know the plants are growing. Give them time and light, and soon they'll be ready for harvest.

Light makes your plants grow and ripen. Sunlight works fine, but Torches are a great addition because they keep monsters from spawning in your garden. They also let the plants keep growing at night. You can even make an underground farm using Torches! If you don't have any Torches handy, be sure to sleep as soon as it starts getting dark. The plants don't grow if there is no light, and sleeping prevents monsters from spawning and trampling your nice farm.

Protecting Your Crop

Creepers are a big threat to growing plants. If they explode, they'll blow up hours of hard work in a single moment, destroying lots of Seeds in the process. Torches help keep Creepers from spawning in the middle of the garden, but they can still wander in at night unless you protect your Farmland. Fences or Stone Walls are a great way to keep the plants safe, but you can also make a complete building with a nice Glass roof to let in the light. If you want to work in the garden at night, a building can be used to protect yourself from Spiders and Skeletons. That way, you don't have to watch your back constantly.

Harvesting

Finally, it's time to reap the benefits of farming. You know that Wheat is ready when it turns brown. Potatoes and Carrots poke out of the ground. Pumpkins and Melons grow fruit. Hit ripe crops to pop them out of the ground. Walk over them to collect these goodies. Use an Axe to break Pumpkins and Melons, because they're tougher to smash.

Often, ripe Wheat gets you more Seeds than it took to plant, but there is no guarantee. Potatoes and Carrots get you anywhere from one to four plants when harvested, and you can choose whether to eat or replant them. It's generally a good idea to plant a new crop as you harvest the old one, so you can keep the cycle going without accidentally eating all your future produce.

If you've enclosed your farm with walls, a fun trick when harvesting is to take a Bucket of Water and flood your field. Then use the Bucket to pick up the Water source block. The ripple of water uproots all your crops at once and pushes them to the walls. This makes it super easy to pick up everything at once. Flooding a field will always uproot Seeds, so it's useful when everything is ripe at the same time. However, it can be annoying if some of your crops aren't ready yet (once they get uprooted, they lose any progress they made). Make sure to let everything fully ripen to get the greatest benefit from this method. If only half your field is ready, either wait longer or pick the ripened crops by hand.

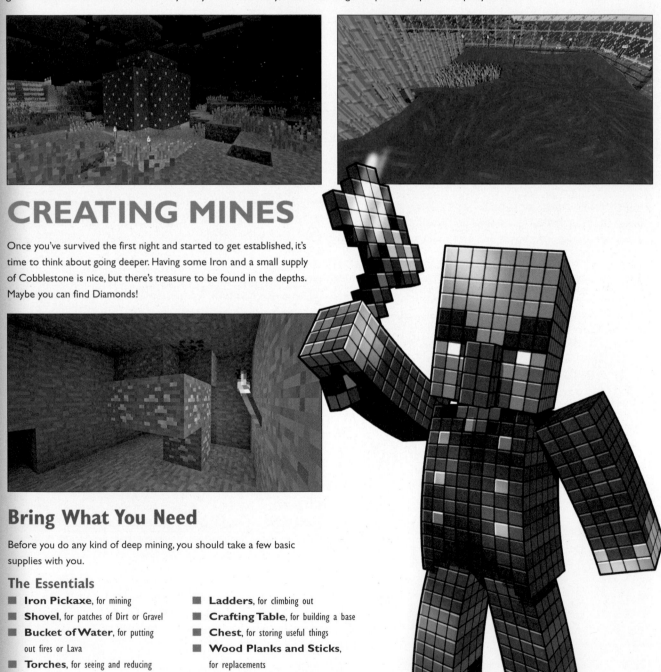

CREATING MINES

Once you've survived the first night and started to get established, it's time to think about going deeper. Having some Iron and a small supply of Cobblestone is nice, but there's treasure to be found in the depths. Maybe you can find Diamonds!

Bring What You Need

Before you do any kind of deep mining, you should take a few basic supplies with you.

The Essentials

- **Iron Pickaxe**, for mining
- **Shovel**, for patches of Dirt or Gravel
- **Bucket of Water**, for putting out fires or Lava
- **Torches**, for seeing and reducing monster spawns
- **Ladders**, for climbing out
- **Crafting Table**, for building a base
- **Chest**, for storing useful things
- **Wood Planks and Sticks**, for replacements
- **Food**, because everyone gets hungry

Iron Pickaxe and Stone Shovel

Stone Pickaxes are great when you're starting out, but Iron is extremely useful once you start any sort of large-scale digging. You have to use resources to get resources, because you can't get Gold, Redstone, and Diamond without using an Iron Pickaxe or better. Take one along so you don't leave behind a cluster of Diamonds.

Take a Stone Shovel or two as well, so you can clear Dirt and Gravel without wasting any time.

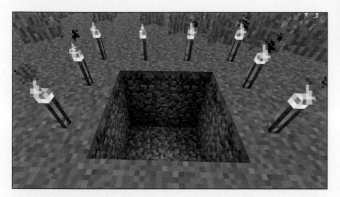

Bucket of Water

As you go deeper into the earth, Lava starts to be a concern. Lava pools can be a real challenge! You might see some great resources on the walls and ceiling around a Lava pool, but going after them risks you or the materials you want falling into Lava. We'll cover how to get them a bit later, in a section titled "Lava Mining."

There's usually a way around, but if you don't feel like walking around Lava, you can use your trusty Bucket of Water to turn large swathes of it into Obsidian. Simply pour it out near the edge and then immediately pick up the source block. The ripple of water turns all the nearby Lava into Obsidian. Lava is so hot that you can catch on fire just by being near it. The Bucket of Water is great for putting yourself out if that happens. Just pour it out and hop in!

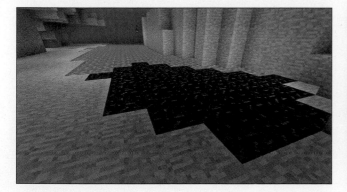

You can also use water when you're faced with a ravine or giant cave. If you tunnel out in the middle of a cave wall with empty space below you, use the water to create a waterfall that you can swim down. It's much better than jumping, and you can swim back up the waterfall when you want to get out.

Torches

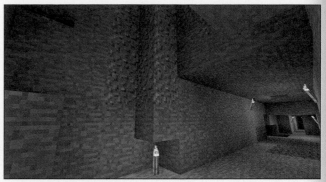

The world's deep places tend to be dark. Torches keep your mines illuminated, so monsters don't spawn and you don't miss patches of resources. Also, use them to track your exploration in cave systems to see where you've been and where you came from.

Gravel can be an annoyance in any sort of large-scale mining work. Blocks of it drop down and get in the way when you mine the block supporting them. When you confront a wall of Gravel, dig underneath the supporting block and put a Torch on the ground underneath the stack. Then mine away the block supporting them; instead of falling down, the Gravel hits the Torch and breaks.

Ladders

What goes down eventually wants to come up again. Ladders create an easy way to get from your central base to the bottom of your mineshaft, without having to risk jumping or building Stairs. Take Ladders with you when you create the original shaft to set up a quick way home.

Exploring caves can be risky, especially large ones with sharp drops and high ledges. You can use mined blocks of Stone and Dirt to create pillars, but Ladders are quicker and more useful. They also make handy landmarks to important places!

Crafting Table

The first thing you should do when creating a large underground mine is set up a secondary base camp. This is where you can go to drop off resources without having to return all the way up to pick up something you need, like food or a new tool.

Taking a Crafting Table ensures you can adapt to any changes or difficulties. If you break a tool, you can make another. Build Furnaces to smelt your raw materials. You can also make things like Signs, Doors, and Chests to organize your resources and keep from getting lost.

If you need to save inventory space, bring tons of spare Wood Planks and make a Crafting Table on the fly. They're cheap and simple.

Chest

Storage is always a priority when creating a mine. The last thing you want is to have all your precious things on you when a Creeper sneaks up and defeats you, or a gang of Zombies overpowers you, or you fall into Lava. It's heartbreaking when the last thing you see is a dozen Diamonds burning in a puddle of Lava, or when you realize you have no idea where you (and all of your stuff) were when those Skeletons came and took you out.

Accidents happen to even the most careful miners. Avoid pain and mental anguish. Put spare items into your Chests, and leave those Chests by your secondary bases. Don't collect the goods until you're ready to head back to the surface!

Wood Planks

Spare Wood is essential. Unless you've created an underground tree farm (and if you have, that's fantastic!), there won't be any trees in your mine. Wood is useful for Torches, new tools, Signs, and plenty of other essential goods. Don't go down into the mines without a substantial supply of Wood Planks.

Doors and Signs are great additions to an extensive mining operation. Use Doors as barriers to keep monsters from wandering into your safer areas or as visual cues that you're close to places you've already developed. Signs can point the way home, warn you (or others) about hazards or particularly rich areas, or label Chests when your storage increases. When you find yourself rummaging through all of your Chests to find a single item, then it's time to make a few Signs and do some sorting!

Food

The last essential inventory group when you start a mining operation is food. Returning home every time you get hungry slows everything down. It's also dangerous to be hungry and unable to run when you encounter a group of monsters. You need to keep your health at max, because there are falls and hazards everywhere. A single Heart can make the difference between surviving and losing all of your hard work.

Don't just avoid starvation, either. Keep your hunger meter maxed out so your character heals quickly from wounds. Don't be stingy with your food while you explore caverns; too many things can go wrong.

Types of Mining Operations

After you gather your essentials, it's time to mine. Now you have to decide what kind of mine to make. Will you explore a cave? Dig down to the very bedrock? Follow a pool of Lava? You might find yourself doing all three, or coming up with a new system!

Cave Exploration

Caves are great access points into deeper areas. They spare you from having to create your own mineshaft. They can be ideal mining locations, especially if you start near one. The main challenges in cave mining are getting lost, fighting monsters, and getting to the resources you want.

Caves can be really big, in some cases going from the surface all the way down to bedrock. They sometimes branch off in multiple directions, at multiple heights. You can easily get lost if you don't take care to mark your exits and keep a trail of Torches. Signs, Doors, and Torches are essential to track your progress and find the way out.

Getting what you want is tricky when you see resources high up on a wall. Ladders and Dirt pillars are great ways to reach higher ledges, but be extremely careful of Skeletons. Getting knocked off of a ledge by an Arrow is a good way to plunge to your doom.

CROUCHING ON THE EDGE

Crouching keeps you from falling off edges and lets you reach really far without fear of suddenly dropping. When you make a bridge to a patch of resources or across a chasm, crouch down and walk backward. You won't fall, and you can place a block, then walk to the edge of that block and place another. Before you know it, you're safely across.

Navigating Caves

Illuminate everything you can so monsters don't constantly surprise you. Use Cobblestone walls to partition large caves and ravines. Smaller areas prevent you from being overwhelmed with monsters. You might even want to seal up areas too big and dangerous to deal with. Caves are full of nasty ambush spots, with Skeletons shooting you off ledges or attacking from places you can't reach. You also face Zombies and Spiders dropping from higher ledges, and Creepers sneaking up on you in the darkness. If you find yourself dying and getting frustrated, seal off the entire area. Make a giant wall with an Iron Door that monsters can't get past. Be careful, get armor as soon as you have the resources for it, and always be ready to cut and run.

You have to think in three dimensions with big cave systems, because you often go up and down. Signs are helpful; even something as simple as an arrow pointing the way back to your base camp can save time and energy. Use Torch patterns to mark out special places, like putting triple Torches around the corridor that leads home, or to the cave you're currently exploring. For the big ravines with lots of vertical height, consider making pillars or intentionally creating Lava flows by carving out a hole high up and putting in a Lava source block. Lava flows make nasty puddles on the floor, so plan them out carefully and surround them with a wall of Dirt or Stone. Lava pillars provide light, landmarks, and a trap for monsters!

You can always explore a tough cave again later, when you have more food and armor!

Deep Mining

Mineshafts are great for getting down to the lower levels. These are different from exploring a surface cave, as you are going deep into the earth and creating your own tunnels. You may run into caves or Lava pools, but sometimes it's very quiet down there. You might go a long time without seeing any hazards or monsters.

The easiest way to start is by digging a 4x4 hole in the ground. You may want to create a separate room or special area for the dig, so you don't fall into it by accident, and so you can find it again later. Take your essentials with you and start digging downward. *Never* mine the block directly beneath you. That's a certain way to fall into unexpected caves or Lava pools. Mine around yourself first, and move onto the newly revealed blocks to keep accidents from happening. Place Torches on the wall and use Ladders to get back to the surface.

If you keep going straight down and don't break into a cave, you eventually hit bedrock. Though you can start mining near this level, it's easy to break into Lava pools. It can actually be safer to build back up ten blocks or so from the bedrock. Staying at this level (roughly "Y" 10-12) lets you come in above most Lava caverns.

Once you finish the mineshaft, make a temporary base and store everything you don't want to take with you. Consider using some of the Cobblestone you've mined on the way down to build a few Furnaces. Smelt any Iron you found on the way to make spare tools. Dig out the area to give yourself room for future expansion.

Quick Trip Down

You need your Ladders for the way back to the surface, but a little pocket of water makes your downward trips very fast. Put a hole at the bottom of your shaft and fill it with water. In the future, leap down the shaft and land in the water to safely shorten your ride to the bottom. As long as you don't have dangerous ledges in your shaft, this method is safe and fun.

From the bottom of your shaft, pick a direction and start mining. Go as far as you want, but be sure to keep Torches at regular intervals. As always, you don't want to mine the ground directly beneath you; falling into Lava is a terrible way to lose everything. Keep the corridors straight so you don't get lost.

Once you've made a central corridor, start creating branches at regular intervals to the left and right. These can be as long as you want and should be well-lit. If you don't go up or down, you don't have to worry about Lava suddenly coming from the ceiling, or falling into it. If you happen to break into a Lava pool, you can explore it or seal it off. If you find a patch of resources, mine them fully!

Navigating Your Corridors

Because everything in the corridor contains right angles, telling which corridor leads back to your base can get confusing. You can solve this by using Doors to the branches and Signs pointing the way home. A little preparation and organization keeps you from getting confused and wandering your own system in circles.

Lava Mining

Because Lava pools form deep underground, Lava mining often comes into play at some point. To brave the danger, follow the Lava pools and mine the edges and ceilings of these caves. Let the Lava be your light source as the caves it creates reveal Gold, Redstone, Lapis Lazuli, Iron, Coal, and Diamonds. Large Lava lakes also tend to lead to other large lakes, letting you repeat the process. It's a useful technique when you don't want to spend much time in little corridors, but you also don't want to deal with huge caverns full of monsters.

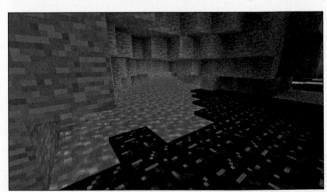

Lava mining has one big danger: the Lava itself. Just standing near it can set you on fire, and falling in can be deadly and burn up all your stuff. So, the first thing to do is respect the Lava and learn how to handle it with a degree of safety.

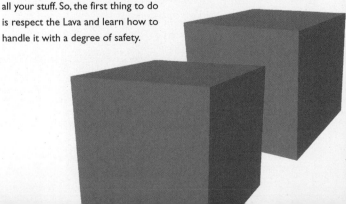

Everyone Falls In

At some point, everyone falls into Lava. It can be by surprise when you mine a block beneath you, or when you rush ahead while mining and walk straight off the edge. Maybe you'll break through a wall or ceiling and it flows on top of you; that's common in the Nether. It might happen when a Skeleton shoots you off a cliff's edge!

So, why not get it over with? Leave all your stuff in a Chest, make sure you've slept, and then hop right in! You'll get to see firsthand what happens, at a time of your choosing. Try getting out to see how difficult it is.

This is the best way to practice surviving a fall into Lava. You don't have to try this if you don't want to. But it's a great way to learn how nasty Lava is without the stress of trying to save your resources from burning up.

Lava Safety Tips

There are three types of Lava to watch out for: the flowing kind, the surprise kind, and the kind that sits around in pools. Small Lava streams are common in caves. The large pools tend to occur deep underground, close to the bedrock. You may see some Lava pools on the surface as well, particularly in mountain biomes.

When you come across a small Lava flow, the first question to ask is, "Can this help me?" Caves and ravines are really dark, and having a large light source is helpful. Lava pools are also nice to have around as navigation aids. It might be better to put up a wall at the Lava's edges and keep it around!

If you want the Lava gone, remove it by taking away the source block. A Bucket does the trick, or you can put Dirt or Stone into the source to block it off. Pouring water over the Lava flow also works, though this creates Obsidian (which is hard to mine).

Central Heating

Lava, like Coal, can be fuel for a Furnace. If you need to smelt a lot of raw ore, why not put a Bucket of Lava to good use? It burns for a long time! Plus, you get your Bucket back immediately, so there's no loss of resources.

If you mine a wall, ceiling, or floor and suddenly find a Lava flow you weren't expecting, then congratulations! You've found surprise Lava!

Act quickly. Grab a Stone block and swiftly fill the hole you just mined. This blocks the Lava and cuts off the flow before it starts. You can also back away, let the Lava spill out, and then carefully brick it up again.

This type of surprise Lava is more frequent in the Nether, which is filled with all sorts of fire. Lava flows more quickly there, so it's easy for surprise Lava to spill out and cover an area. It's often easiest to retreat, set down a Cobblestone wall to block the incoming flow, and then work your way back to the hole from which the Lava originated to stop it up.

If you mined a block underneath you and fell into Lava, you might be able to knock out a block beside you and get out of it. But there's a good chance you'll burn up and lose all your stuff. Never, ever, ever mine directly beneath yourself! We've mentioned that before. And you know what? You'll still do it at least once and regret it. Almost everyone does.

A telltale sign of surprise Lava is sets of glowing drips from the ceiling. They indicate that Lava is directly above you, separated by only one block. Unless you really want Lava, don't mine when you see those drips! You can also hear it bubbling when it's nearby, so be extra careful until you locate the source.

Keep a Bucket of Water handy to extinguish yourself if you catch on fire or manage to escape the Lava. Speed is always essential, because Lava takes away huge chunks of your health. Use the Bucket above the Lava so the water flows over your character *and* the Lava below, turning it to Obsidian.

Large pools are safer than flows or surprise Lava, because they don't go anywhere. The dangerous part comes from falling directly into them, as they tend to be several blocks deep, making them almost impossible to escape.

Making Lava Work for You

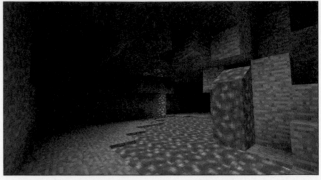

Lava is really bright—this means that Lava pools don't spawn monsters, and mining nearby doesn't require much in the way of Torches. The caves that the pools create reveal all sorts of resources. The largest Lava lakes can create gigantic, interconnected caves that are brightly lit and *full* of precious things.

If you're careful, you can make this work for you with Lava mining.

Start at the nearest edge and make it safer by mining out a two- or three-block ledge to stand on. Keep mining around the edge, but progress slowly. The last thing you want is to break through the wall into another pool and then rush off the edge.

When you see something good on the ceiling, use Stone to make bridges, or use your Bucket of Water at the edge of the pool to convert the Lava into Obsidian. Because Gravel drops down, it can also be used to make bridges. It hits the bottom of the pool, and a few Gravel blocks stack into a bridge.

As you go, look at the bottom edges of the blocks at the Lava lake's edge. Some of them have an orange strip at the bottom, which means there's more Lava underneath them. Even if a Lava cave seems entirely cut off and isolated, you can sometimes follow the small channels that go under the walls to find more caves.

Don't rush for valuable minerals. Always stay calm and go slowly when you mine around Lava. Excited miners often become dead miners.

One key to safety is to mine blocks while you're standing still. Go to the wall and start mining. When the block breaks, keep holding the Attack button to mine the next block, and the one after that, and so on. This creates a small hole you can look into to see if there's another big Lava lake on the other side. Once you make your small hole, widen it into a corridor that you can pass through. Keep water handy, and take a trip back to your Chests to drop off resources when you get them. Respect the danger!

Navigating the Pools

One of Lava mining's benefits is that the large pools are easier to navigate than a giant cave system or branching corridors. There is plenty of light, the lines of sight are nice and clear, and you can get from point to point around the Lava's edges or create Obsidian or Stone pathways straight across. Mark the exits toward your base camp to avoid confusion. An easy way to do this is to set up a Cobblestone archway around the corridor and then line it with Torches. Signs are also useful to point out the way to a fresh pool, but keep them away from the very edges of the Lava, or they'll burn up.

BUILDING UP AND OUT

Not all of *Minecraft* is about going down to the inky deeps. There are plenty of occasions where going up is the answer. Learning to build up and out is an essential skill, whether you want to build a new level for your house, cross a ravine to reach some fresh resources, or you come across a giant tree and really want to build a fort up high. Just because you start on the ground doesn't mean you need to stay there!

To the Sky!

Take a look at your house. Wouldn't it look better with a second story? You could put an Enchanting Table up there. You could make a storeroom to organize all the resources you've mined. Maybe put a Nether Portal on the roof! It's time to build up and learn how to make things taller.

The first thing to do is bring all the resources you need, plus a little extra Dirt to get yourself into position. In the case of building a new level on your house, you need tools to dismantle the roof and turn it into a floor, unless you built a flat roof in the first place. You also need material to make new walls, plus Stairs or Ladders to connect the upper floor with the bottom level. Bring all of this with you, so you don't have to go back for it later. In the case of building your house, getting more stacks of Wood or Stone is pretty easy. However, when you build a larger project farther away (like building up to some Diamonds high on the wall of a cave), running out of building material halfway through can be quite inconvenient.

Expanding your house upward uses the same basic principle of putting one block on top of another to get you where you need to be, and then making a new structure there. The easiest way to start climbing is to make a pillar at the base of the thing you want to modify: in this case, your house. Put down a Dirt block and hop on top of it. Then, while standing on the Dirt block, look down at your feet, jump, and place a block at the same time. It's easier than it sounds, because you can simply hold down the buttons! You wind up on top of the newly placed block, higher off the ground. Keep jumping and placing blocks until the pillar of Dirt reaches the top of your house. Because you built the pillar next to your house, you can step straight onto the roof.

GET LOW FOR SAFETY!

Crouching down keeps you from falling off ledges and lets you safely go out to the edges. It's not perfect, because monsters can still knock you off, but it really helps for construction.

Dismantle the roof or flatten it out, since you'll use it as flooring for your new level. When you start placing blocks for the walls, crouch and move to the edge to avoid falling off. Lay down the wall's lowest blocks around the edge to give yourself a pattern to follow. Once the new wall's base is laid out, hop on top, crouch down, and work around the perimeter. Place new wall blocks and hop on top when it's nearly complete to finish placing the last few blocks. Keep repeating until the wall is high enough to accommodate whatever needs to fit in the new room. Now that you're standing on top of your newly built wall, you can jump into the room and make a ceiling, or you can do it from the top of the wall by building outward.

Building Bridges

Building out is the technique of building into empty space. Crossing a chasm with a bridge is an example of building out. Another example is starting from a small ledge high up and turning it into a larger structure. If you want to make things up in the air, you have to get comfortable working on the edges.

First things first. Crouch! Always crouch when you're building out. A simple experiment shows the reason why. If you're still on the roof of your house, you might want to come down first via your Dirt pillar. Now, place a block on the ground. Hop on top of it and see how close to the edge you can go before you fall off. It's pretty easy to fall! Next, get back on top of the block and crouch down. Now see how far you can get. Not only can you reach much farther, but you stop when you reach the very edge, even if you try to move off the block. Stay crouched, look down at your feet, and turn around. By doing this, it looks like you're standing on empty space. You can see the edge of the block you're standing on. For some real fun, place a new block at the edge while crouching and walking backward. You can place a block, walk onto it, and then move to the very edge again.

This technique is the heart of building out. Ride the very edge, placing new blocks you can then use to reach even farther. In the case of a bridge, crouch-walk backward, placing new blocks as you go. You'll be across that chasm in no time! To build a ledge, crouch at the edge and walk side to side, laying new blocks to make the ledge wider. Then move out to the edge of the new blocks and go back the other way. In the case of your newly expanded house, get back on top of the wall and then crouch-walk your way toward the center, filling in the roof layer as you go.

This method is ideal for crossing lakes, Lava, and ravines, and for building sky bridges to anywhere you'd like to go.

YOU CAN DO ANYTHING WITH A LITTLE PRACTICE

Putting It All Together

There are times when you find a giant tree while exploring and think, "That would make a great treehouse!" Let's get some supplies and make it happen!

Treehouse Checklist

- **Really big tree:** Jungle trees are certainly tall enough, but you have to do some landscaping to clear out the leaves. Mega taiga spruces are ideal, as they're tall and thick, and the leaves are really high up. But any big tree will do!
- **Wood Planks:** You can easily find these in the nearby woods or bring them from another base camp.

- **Dirt blocks:** You can find these all around the tree.
- **Fences:** These are assembled from Sticks and serve as railings for your fort.
- **Ladders:** Once you've built the treehouse, you want an easy way to get up and down.

- **Trapdoor:** This keeps you from falling down through the Ladder hole!
- **Torches:** You need these to light everything!
- **Bed:** This comes in handy for sleeping when it gets dark. You'll be too high for most monsters, but an Arrow can still knock you off.

Build a Dirt pillar beside the tree, and stop at the tree's upper section. This doesn't have to be precise. Use the Wood Planks against the bark of the tree to create a small ledge. Walk onto it when the ledge is complete and crouch down. While crouching, walk around the tree in a spiral, building a ledge that completely circles the tree trunk. Continue circling until the ledge is several blocks wide. This will be your treehouse's floor, so make it as wide as you want. Once you're satisfied with the floor, set up the Bed and sleep if it's dark.

Now it's time for walls. Because monsters can't reach you, have some fun with this. Place Wood Fences all around the edges to act as railings, but leave the corners bare. These bare corners will become small pillars to support the roof. You may be under the leaves, but it's always nice to have something more solid overhead. Make Wood Plank pillars three or four blocks tall. When you're finished, crouch and build inward to start making a flat roof. Maybe later, you can convert it into storage space!

We're almost finished. Now it's time to make a Trapdoor and Ladder leading back to the ground. Go ahead and knock out one of the Wood Planks on the floor against the tree. Then place your Trapdoor in the open space. Open it and look down. It's a pretty big drop, but you can survive the fall if you're at full health. Place some Ladders against the tree and start working your way down to the ground. If you fall, no problem—that's what the Bed was for! Your spawn point is up in the tree, so if worse comes to worst, you start over and continue building down.

WHEN TO RISK IT ALL

It's best to start high-altitude construction projects when you've just lost a huge amount of experience, either to death or to some enchanting work. Don't risk a deadly fall when your character has 50 levels sitting there, ready to spend. It's better to try these large projects when you don't have much to lose!

Once you've made a Ladder, your fort is almost complete. Place Torches along the Fence posts for light, and add more by the Ladder to serve as markers. Knock down the remaining Dirt, since you don't need it anymore, or move it and make it even bigger to serve as a landmark. Maybe later, you can make a bridge over to the other trees and create a network of forts connected by bridges.

LANDSCAPING

Landscaping is the act of shaping the world around you. It ranges from tiny actions, like digging holes in the ground and clearing out trees, to something as grand as blowing up a mountain with TNT or reshaping an island in Creative Mode. If it changes the way the world looks, it's landscaping.

Groundskeeping

One of your earliest experiences with landscaping is clearing the area around your house. You can conduct all sorts of landscaping projects to make your region safer and more convenient.

Trees are useful, but having them close to the house is dangerous. The shade they provide allows Skeletons and Zombies to survive the sunlight, so they can attack you during the day. Clear the trees to make sure the monsters burn when the dawn comes.

Now that you've made the immediate area safer, it's time to flatten out some space to prepare for farms and animal pens. You might not do any farming or animal raising until much later, but flattening the area also makes it easier for you to get around and see incoming enemies. This is a great opportunity to evaluate the area and decide what to do with irregular holes and random cave entrances. You can seal cave entrances with Doors, widen the openings into proper mines, or remove the top layer of Dirt and rock to expose the area to sunlight for easier mining. If you have any small water holes nearby, flatten the area around them for later farming, or start planting crops right away around the edges.

Moving Mountains

You can clear the area around your house quickly, but some projects require more effort. Mountainous terrain, for instance, is annoying to navigate; it tends to be full of sudden drops, sheer cliffs, and lots of climbing. This can result in complex paths as you move from place to place. Winding through the landscape is a good way to get lost, so why not change it?

Tunnel through large obstacles to reduce travel time. This is useful in exploring, as it reduces the need for excessive landmarks. If you expect to return to a certain place, such as a Village, make a more permanent roadway. Trails of landmarks are great for exploring new territory, but sometimes you want something more permanent. A roadway lets you follow an obvious path instead of playing hide-and-seek with Signs.

With hand tools and time, you can make any tunnel you want. Pickaxes and Shovels are fine for most situations, but if you want to go through a really large obstacle, like a mountain, there are other options. Try blasting through heavy blocks with TNT—it lets you blow stuff up! Hissing like a Creeper is optional but highly recommended.

Getting Gunpowder can be dangerous, as it involves killing Creepers before they explode. Once you get a good Sword (Iron or Diamond), killing Creepers becomes much easier, and you get Gunpowder more frequently. If you have Gunpowder stockpiled in a Chest, why not put it to use?

Gunpowder forms an explosive block called TNT when mixed with Sand. You can place TNT like normal blocks, and then ignite it to produce violent explosions. Place a string of TNT blocks to make a chain reaction and blow large craters into the landscape, or place them one at a time to gradually blow through walls. No mountain can stand up to high explosives!

FORMING AND USING LANDMARKS

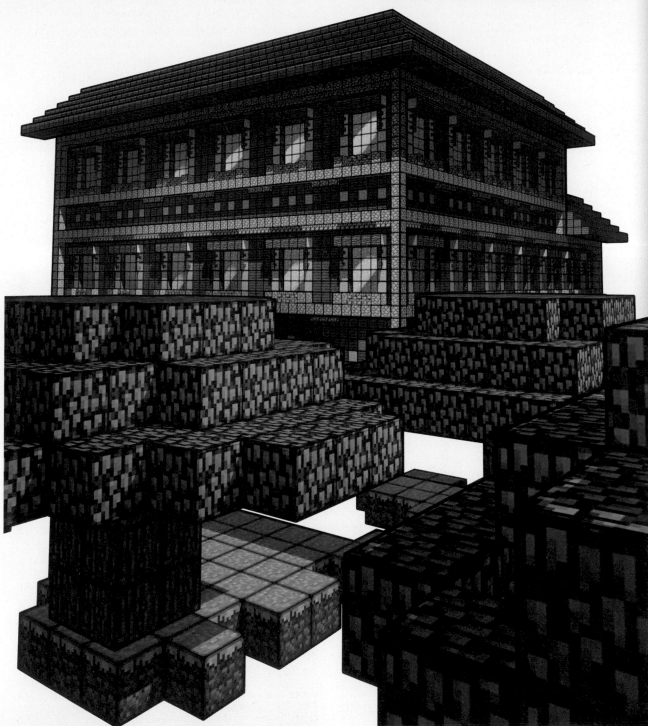

Let's explore the world! *Minecraft* worlds are big places, and eventually you'll venture out into one. The problem is that it's easy to get lost. How can you find your way back home? How do you ensure that you can return to the new places you find, or that someone else can follow your path?

Picture this: You've been walking around for ten minutes, filling your inventory with things like Sugar Cane, Clay that you found in rivers, patches of exposed Coal, and Iron, and you finally see a Village on the horizon just as it gets dark. You make your way over, but before you get inside, you hear the telltale hiss of a Creeper and the world explodes around you. Now you spawn back at home! How will you ever find your way back?

This is what landmarks are for. You can create distinctive features visible from far away when traveling or large-scale projects that are visible on a Map. That way, you can find your way around without getting lost, or lead other people to the incredible discoveries you've made.

Visual Landmarks

Visual landmarks are anything you can see while you're walking around. They can be quick projects, like a pillar of Dirt; large-scale ones, like giant sky arrows or writing on the side of a mountain; or anything in between. If you can see it from far away, you've made a visual landmark!

Pillars and Torches

Quick, place a Torch! Congratulations! You've made a landmark. Torches are visible from far away, they create pools of light, and they occur naturally in only a few places (Villages, Strongholds, and Abandoned Mineshafts). When you see a Torch, you know that a person placed it, or that you've come across something special! When you explore the Overworld, use Torches to leave a trail for yourself. Take a few stacks of Torches with you and regularly put one on the ground, on a tree, or on some other feature of the landscape. If you don't find anything interesting on your trip, turn around and recollect the Torches as you return, or leave them for later exploration.

If you find something you really want to come back to, dig Dirt blocks (or take some with you) and make a pillar. You don't have to go all the way up to the clouds, but you definitely want it higher than the trees, preferably 10-20 blocks above the highest one. Be careful, because you don't want to fall! You may be able to find your way back if you die, but it can be a long walk. Build the pillar two blocks wide as you go up, and then mine one of them downward, leaving a one-block-wide pillar to guide your future travels. Another method is to carry two Buckets of Water. With these, make a pool three blocks wide and filled at each end with Water from your Buckets. Refill the Buckets with the Water block in the middle of the stream, and you're left with a pool to jump into from the top of the Dirt pillar you're about to build.

Making a pillar is one of the first things you should do when you start a long-term base, so you can find your way back to it after hunting or gathering Wood.

Distinctive Landmarks

As time goes on, you collect more and more resources and you continue to explore. With more time and energy, you should create larger markers that are even more distinctive. Pillars and Torch trails are great when you're starting, but they can get confusing later on when you have multiple trails and many pillars marking different locations. It's time to make things more distinctive.

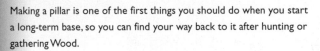

The Pillar of Fire

Lava is a great way to make a landmark visually stand out. Simply taking a **Bucket of Lava** to the top of a pillar and letting it flow down creates a distinctive, bright, and dangerous landmark. Be sure to wall off the base so Lava doesn't spill everywhere!

Regular wayposts with Signs attached are a simple and effective way to mark the world around you. Leave a message telling yourself where a trail of Torches leads and how long you have to travel to get there. This is an extremely useful way to remind yourself where all the neat things are. But why be satisfied with small landmarks? Take some time to carve an arrow into a nearby cliff!

Because you can leave blocks floating in midair, make a floating arrow pointing at your house! Convert some of the Redstone you've mined into blocks. Redstone is one of the easiest resources to get when you mine deep, so there should be plenty to spare. These bright red blocks show up extremely well, so they make excellent landmarks. Make at least ten Redstone blocks, preferably more, before you scout an entirely new region.

Cobblestone is abundant, so grab stacks of that as well. Bring Ladders, because some climbing is in your future. A Pickaxe and Shovel are essential too!

You've already made a Dirt pillar near your house as one of your first landmarks, so use the Ladders to ascend it. Once you get to the top, mine halfway down and make a small platform. This is where you'll start building the point of your arrow.

Crouch at the edge of the platform and place a Redstone block. This block will be the tip of the arrow pointing down. Now, place a Stone block beside the Redstone on either side. Then another Redstone block on top of each of the Stone squares. You can leave the Stone block, but your arrow will look pointier if you mine it out, so stand on the Redstone, stay crouched, and mine away. Leave it with three Redstone blocks making a glowing marker, or go as big as you want. Make a giant point if you're motivated!

Once you have a sufficiently pointy arrow, make a tail for it out of Stone by creating a pillar on top of the Redstone center block. Add Redstone blocks as you go up to make it even more distinctive.

Map Landmarks

Map landmarks are all about making places stand out visually when you look at them on a Map.

BE PREPARED

These epic-scale landmarks require extensive resources and time if you attempt them in Survival Mode. Even in Creative Mode, they can take hours, if not days, of work!

Maps show a top-down view of the world, so when you think about making a landmark big enough to be visible on a Map, you have to think in top-down terms. It helps to have a *very* clear idea before you start. It's even better to have a piece of paper with the pattern drawn on it. Go into these projects knowing they will take a *long* time to perfect.

Like all big projects in *Minecraft*, it really helps to have a friend! Get your buddies involved in the project and watch the hours melt away.

The Collection

You need two things to get started. The first are some Maps. Maps come in different scales, so having several of them lets you see how the project is progressing on each scale. On the lowest scale, a shape doesn't have to be thousands of blocks long to show up, but at the largest scale you really need to think *big*.

Next, you need lots and lots of colorful resources. Maps are all about showing off the land, and color plays a large role. So, if you're in a green field, think about collecting red Wool to make your marker pop out. If you're in a desert, think about something dark. Wool is easy to work with, because you can get multiple pieces from a Sheep using the Shears, and it can be dyed all sorts of colors.

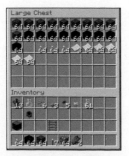

If you're playing in Survival Mode, start shearing any Sheep you find, breeding more using Wheat, and coming back to them again and again until you have a full Chest of Wool stacks.

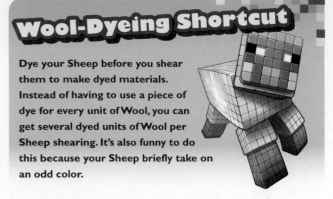

Wool-Dyeing Shortcut

Dye your Sheep before you shear them to make dyed materials. Instead of having to use a piece of dye for every unit of Wool, you can get several dyed units of Wool per Sheep shearing. It's also funny to do this because your Sheep briefly take on an odd color.

Next, you need to make dye, so you have to collect flowers and plant them to harvest for the dye materials. Lapis Lazuli is used to make Blue Dye, and you find it in abundance when you mine. Red Dye is easy due to all the flowers you can grow with Bone Meal. You could also start a Beetroot garden, and turn those crops into Red Dye.

Scale Progression

Find a flat area of land, or make one. Then start with a 30x30 square of red Wool and see how it shows up on a Map. Track your progress on the small-scale

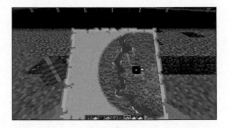

Map to see how it's coming along. If it looks pretty distinctive on the small scale, see how it shows up on larger scales. Be sure to sleep, and keep the area well-lit with Torches. The last thing you want is for a Creeper to undo tons of careful work.

Once you make a marker that shows up, the rest is all in how big you want to go!

BIOMES

What Are Biomes?

Biomes are often referred to as "ecosystems." They're large areas separated from each other by climate and geography. In *Minecraft*, just like the real world, each biome has its own set of geographical features, elevations of natural formations, plants and animals, temperatures, humidity ratings, weather, and sky and foliage colors.

The mixture of different biomes creates the world you explore in *Minecraft*. The specific set of biomes used to generate a world is called a "seed."

When you first create your *Minecraft* world, you have the option to use a randomly generated world (a random seed) or enter a known seed. Although you may be familiar with some features available in a known seed, your experience in the world will still be unique; the only difference is that you may have a little more knowledge ahead of time about nearby regions.

Looking Up Seeds

You can search online to find fun seeds that other people have discovered; you can also share exciting seeds of your own. Some worlds have especially awesome landmarks or rare Temples. Whatever you're looking for, feel free to search through other people's listings and try out their worlds.

Biome Categories

Regardless of how your world is created, you soon find yourself in one of several possible biomes. You can tell which biome you're in simply by looking around and examining the terrain's color, the number of mountains and hills, and the kinds of trees around you. The types of blocks immediately available to you also provide a good indication.

If you don't like the biome in your starting location, you have two options. First, you can restart and generate a different world. Each time you create a world, you start in a different location (you may not get a different biome; some biomes are more common than others). The second option is to pick a direction and run as fast and as far as you can. If you're still in a region you don't like by the time night falls, dig a hole three blocks deep, cap it off with a ceiling block, and wait inside for day to break. Either way, you'll eventually arrive at a biome with the conditions you prefer.

The biome types in *Minecraft* are divided by temperature. There are five categories: snowy, cold, medium, dry/warm, and neutral. The temperature ranges prevent biomes with large differences from being next to each other; for example, deserts aren't found next to Ice Plains.

Weather

A biome's temperature range also determines its weather. Depending on where you are, your biome may have snow, rain, both, or neither. In game terms, both snow and rain are considered the same weather effect, but whether you get snow or rain varies according to biome type. If a non-snowy biome touches a snowy biome, there can be both rain and snow. The required values for different weather conditions are <0.15 for snow, 0.15-0.95 for rain, and >1.0 for none.

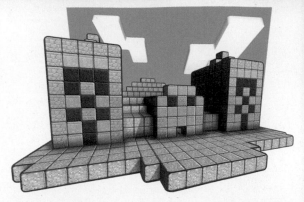

Elevation also plays a role in weather. An area with hills or mountains has a greater chance to have snow over rain. In the same way, a low, hot region of desert has no rain or snow at all.

Noteworthy weather can occur during the day or night. Usually, weather occurs every seven *Minecraft* days and continues for 15 minutes. If you don't like the weather, you can use a Bed to sleep through it during evenings or thunderstorms.

Both rain and snow have a chance to form thunderstorms. Thunderstorms are relatively rare occurrences; their dark conditions and potential for lightning make them more dangerous than other weather. Even if it's daytime during a thunderstorm, the low light causes monsters to spawn. There's also the potential for lightning to strike enemies. Creepers that are struck by lightning do a *huge* amount of damage, so be on the lookout at all times.

Possible Effects of Lightning

- Starts fires
- Turns Pigs into Zombie Pigmen
- Supercharges Creepers (watch out!)
- Damages players
- Turns Villagers into Witches (requires Version 1.8)
- Changes Horses into Skeleton Trap Horses

FREE IRRIGATION!

```
Storms bring water into a region, causing
crops to grow faster for a little while.
This offers the same effect as irrigating
your crops.
```

Biome Types

There are 61 total biomes. Some are quite similar to others, but each has a few distinct elements. Your current biome determines the availability of various blocks, plants, and creatures.

Snowy Biomes

Common Features	Snow at Any Elevation
Grass and Foliage	Blue/Green

BIOME	ID	FEATURES
Cold Beach	26	Desolate, cold beaches
Cold Taiga	30	More trees are here, making this an easier snowy biome to start
Cold Taiga (M)	158	Cold taiga with much taller mountains
Frozen River	11	Fairly clear area, few features, ice on all water
Ice Plains	12	Flat, snowy; has icy water, limited Wood
Ice Plains Spikes	140	Lovely fields of frozen spikes

Cold Biomes

Common Features	Snow at Higher Elevation, Rain at Lower Elevation
Grass and Foliage	Blue/Green

BIOME	ID	FEATURES
Extreme Hills	3	High peaks and low valleys
Extreme Hills (M)	131	Less plant growth, even higher mountains
Extreme Hills+	34	Adds some much-needed tree growth to the biome
Extreme Hills+ (M)	162	Again, adds more trees to the extreme hills (M) biome
Mega Spruce Taiga	160	Thick forests are here, limiting movement and visibility
Mega Taiga	32	Huge spruce trees dominate this area
Stone Beach	25	Raised beaches with stone drop-offs into the water
Taiga	5	Spruce trees, Wolves, and cold temperatures are key features here
Taiga (M)	133	Makes the taiga terrain more mountainous

Medium Biomes

Common Features	Snow Only at Extreme Elevations, Rain Anywhere Lower
Grass and Foliage	Green

BIOME	ID	FEATURES
Beach	16	Sandy lowlands that lead into the ocean
Birch Forest	27	A forest of birch trees
Birch Forest (M)	155	A forest of tall, impressive birch trees
Birch Forest Hills (M)	156	A forest of birch trees with large hills and taller trees
Flower Forest	132	A forest with slightly fewer trees and many more flowers
Forest	4	Simple biome with a strong mix of resources and few downsides; Wood and food are prevalent
Jungle	21	Dense wooded areas with heavy foliage; it's hard to move quickly through these areas, so they can be dangerous if you're caught by monsters
Jungle (M)	149	Adds mountainous terrain to the usual jungle biomes
Jungle Edge	23	Jungles thin out near their borders with other major biomes
Jungle Edge (M)	151	Greater elevation changes are present in this version
Mushroom Island	14	Has Mycelium instead of Dirt; Mushrooms are found in great quantities, and Mooshrooms are the only animals that appear in this area
Mushroom Island Shore	15	Provides a border between Mushroom Islands and the sea
Plains	1	Simple grasslands, not much Wood access; you can find Horses here
River	7	Clay blocks, fairly shallow water
Roofed Forest	29	Oak forest with a heavy canopy and little light
Roofed Forest (M)	157	Has cliffs and valleys to make the roofed forest even more daunting
Sunflower Plains	129	Similar to plains but with many more flowers in the area
Swampland	6	Movement is hampered by many pools of water; increased danger from unusual monster spawns (including Witches)

Dry/Warm Biomes

Common Features	No Rain or Snow
Grass and Foliage	Yellow/Brown

BIOME	ID	FEATURES
Desert	2	Sandy, dry area with Cacti
Desert (M)	130	There are occasional oases here
Mesa	37	Dry, Clay-filled hills
Mesa (Bryce)	165	A rare canyon biome
Plateau	36, 38, 39	Wide, open hills with livable areas up top
Plateau (M)	164, 166, 167	Very high plateaus
Savanna	35	Open grasslands with the potential for Horses
Savanna (M)	163	Mountainous grasslands

Neutral Biomes

Common Features	Mid-Range Temperature
Grass and Foliage	Varies

BIOME	ID	FEATURES
Deep Ocean	24	Especially deep water
Hills	17, 18, 19, 22, 28, 31, 33, 156, 161	These hill sections are often embedded in other biomes
Ocean	0	Large swaths of Water blocks

SPECIAL AREAS

Some interesting locations in *Minecraft* aren't common parts of their biomes. These places aren't 100% unique, but they're pretty close. You might go days or weeks without finding some of these, so they're awesome treats when you uncover them.

Abandoned Mineshafts

These pre-existing tunnels are found underground in the Overworld. They're useful because they often let you travel quickly through an area, finding spare railways, Coal, Iron, perhaps cobwebs, and such. Chests of both common and rare treasures are located in these shafts, so search them thoroughly. You might find Diamonds, special Seeds, Saddles, Horse Armor, or Enchanted Books.

While you search, remember to keep all Torches on one specific side of the shaft. This ensures that you know how to get back to the entrance when you decide to leave.

Monster Spawners in these shafts create Cave Spiders—they're poisonous, so be careful when you fight them. Keep your health high, and bring Milk if at all possible. It's nice to have as a backup after a close fight.

Dungeons

Huge cave complexes often have a small Cobblestone room with a Monster Spawner inside. These rooms are called Dungeons. They contain Chests of treasure, so they're excellent to find, and you can build deadly trap rooms to farm experience from the Monster Spawners if you have the inclination to do so.

Dungeons are found in the Overworld, and the best way to raise your chances of seeing them is to dig through areas until you find ravines or caverns. Follow these all the way to their ends, while looking for high concentrations of monsters; that's sometimes a tip-off that a Monster Spawner is there. If you dig in an area and hear monsters, always search for the cavern that houses the beasts, and you may find a Dungeon.

Dungeon Chests can hold Golden Apples, high-quality Horse Armor, Name Tags, Music Discs, Saddles, and other decent goodies. It's always good to loot these locations!

Nether Fortresses

These monster bastions are located in the Nether. They're made of Nether Bricks and are well-defended by Blazes, Wither Skeletons, Magma Cubes, and a Monster Spawner (which makes even more Blazes). You can't find Nether Wart anywhere else in *Minecraft*, so that alone is a good reason to search for a Nether Fortress. Nether Wart is required for any real brewing, so finding a source of this rare herb is amazingly good news.

If you find a Nether Fortress and don't get everything you want out of it, search directly north or south from there to find more Fortresses. They're always aligned in this way, so looking east or west will get you off-track. On the other hand, if you can't find *any* Fortresses, travel east or west in the hopes of finding your first one.

As with most special locations, Nether Fortresses have Chests of loot as well as rare resources. Diamonds, metal, Gold equipment, Saddles, Horse Armor, and Nether Wart are all possible rewards here.

Don't assume you've seen all of a Nether Fortress once you've explored the areas aboveground. These massive complexes can be buried in the ground, requiring some serious excavation to dig out.

Villages

Happy towns of peaceful Villagers exist in the Overworld. Search plains, desert, and savanna biomes to find them. Once you do, talk to the Villagers by approaching them and interacting with each person. They have different professions and items to trade. They request specific items and give you Emeralds as payment. These Emeralds can then be traded for items that the Villagers create.

Look for rare items in town. Chainmail armor, Bottles of Enchanting, and a few other fun toys are available this way.

If you cause too much trouble in a Village, the Iron Golems that defend it become aggressive toward your character.

THINGS THAT INFLUENCE YOUR POPULARITY IN A VILLAGE

Attacking a Villager	-1
Killing a Villager	-2
Attacking a Child	-3
Killing an Iron Golem	-5
Trading the Last Item on a Villager's List	+1

If you want to trade and walk safely around town, avoid hitting any Villagers, and run away from them if you get into any trouble. Don't fight your way out, and don't attack the Iron Golems even if they come after you.

Village Blacksmiths often have cool loot. Search their buildings for Chests, and trade with the Blacksmiths to see if they have anything fun to offer.

If you'd like to expand a Village, add Doors to its buildings. This causes even more Villagers to spawn. You're also free to add physical defenses so that fewer Zombies can reach and attack the Villagers. Zombies are a major threat to towns. Wall off remote areas to provide some defense. Zombies spawn within town limits, so there's only so much you can do, but building good walls is a start, and they make Villages look even more exciting.

Also, use Iron Golems for additional Village defenders. Either fight aggressively to protect townsfolk during the evening, or run away before sunset and keep your

distance from town to prevent it from being attacked. Zombies won't bother a Village unless you're nearby.

Strongholds

These large, dangerous complexes are major features in the Overworld. They can appear in any biome, and several of them are always closer to your starting point. They're a critical part of the game's progression, because you can only reach the End and face the Ender Dragon by finding a Stronghold and activating its Portal.

Use Eyes of Ender to locate Strongholds. These special items give you a direction to the nearest Stronghold. They're often deep underground, but they may bump into ravines or other special terrain features.

Once you find a Stronghold, be careful. Monster Eggs are common, so Silverfish are major threats. They attack in large groups if you trigger them, and Strongholds contain Monster Spawners that deploy even more Silverfish to hassle you.

Once you find the heart of the Stronghold, destroy its Monster Spawner and look for the End Portal. Activate these with more Eyes of Ender and explore the End.

Treasure Chests in Strongholds feature a huge range of rewards. Storage rooms have Chests with a chance to yield metal, food, and an Enchanted Book. Rooms with Slabs may have Ender Pearls, metal, food, Iron equipment, Golden Apples, Saddles, Enchanted Books, or Horse Armor. Library rooms can have Books, Paper, Maps, Compasses, or Enchanted Books.

Temples

Desert, ocean, and jungle biomes have the potential to host Temples. These neat land features are normally found at ground level and are quite fun to explore. They often hold considerable treasure, so everyone loves to look for them.

Don't relax while you wander through these structures. They frequently contain traps, and you don't want to get yourself killed and lose so much potential treasure in the process.

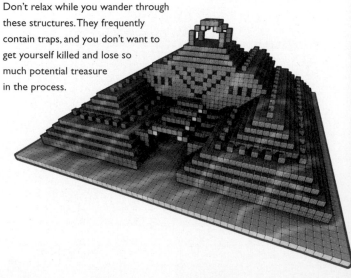

Explore carefully and look for traps before you trigger them. Be willing to dig around hallways and come in from the side or rear of each chamber to avoid trouble. Or disarm traps by finding their Tripwires/Pressure Plates; break those to disable the traps.

SECRETS REVEALED

Jungle Temples have a hidden Chest that is revealed if you find the proper settings for three Levers inside the Temple.

Desert Temples have a hidden room under the floor. That room is trapped to explode, so dig down to it carefully and avoid the Pressure Plate while you loot the place.

Witch Huts

Most often located in swamp or plains areas, Witch Huts are small residences that may have Witches in them—Witches don't spawn there forever, so any that have fallen out, left, or been killed won't reappear.

Woodland Mansions

Roofed forests sometimes spawn Woodland Mansions; these very large houses have rare monsters inside. They're staffed with Illagers (Villagers who aren't quite right). Expect to see Evokers and Vindicators, as well as Creepers and other naturally occurring enemies.

Bring heavy armor, extra Arrows, food, and Potions when you're exploring a Woodland Mansion. The fighting gets heavy.

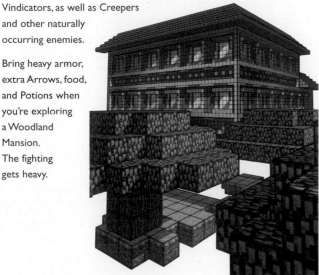

HOW TIME PASSES

It's smart to understand the day/night cycles in *Minecraft*, because getting caught out in the darkness is dangerous. Let's deal with time for a moment.

There are 20 minutes in each day/night cycle in *Minecraft*. You get ten minutes of sunshine and ten minutes of shadow (including dawn and dusk). Many of the dangerous creatures are limited to nighttime, so you're much, much safer playing outside during the day.

You can track the progress of the day by watching the sun—as long as you're outside! Watch as the sun travels through the sky, eventually setting and bringing on dusk. Before you have the resources to make a Clock, the sun is your best way to tell time.

That said, you can also use your own watch or clock in real life. Look at the time when dawn breaks and remember that the evening will come in ten minutes.

During the Day

Your first day begins at dawn. That's a good thing, because you have plenty to do in those short ten minutes. Make the most of them so Zombies don't eat your character when night falls.

Daylight prevents most monsters from spawning, helps crops to grow quickly, and is brighter than a Torch even when it's up close. In fact, it's so bright that some monsters aren't merely driven into hiding. Zombies and Skeletons are killed by direct sunlight. Endermen teleport to a safe, dark area. Spiders don't leave, but they become docile and don't attack until they are attacked or placed in shadow.

As the Moon Rises

Enjoy the pretty view while you can. Sunset is lovely, but danger grows with each passing second. When the light starts to dim, sprint back toward your home or dig an emergency shelter and lock yourself into a makeshift cave. The moon rises in the evening, and dusk lasts for a short time. Light levels diminish during the next minute and a half.

It's quite possible to stay outside all night, working as you wish. Fighting Creepers, Zombies, and Skeletons is dangerous work, but someone with a Sword, armor, and experience fighting these monsters should be okay. This doesn't mean that you should do it; using resources, risking your life, and killing enemies is fun but not always productive.

The best reason to stay outside and fight is if you're gathering specific resources: Bone, String, and Arrows from Skeletons; Gunpowder from Creepers; Ender Pearls from Endermen; and Carrots or Potatoes from Zombies. Once you get enough of these items, nighttime becomes even less appealing.

Telling Time

If you aren't using a real-world clock to tell time, make a Clock inside *Minecraft*. They are quite helpful when you're deciding whether to risk a long-range scouting expedition. They let you know how much daylight remains. They're even better underground, when you want to figure out whether it's a good time to return to the surface.

Getting Some Sleep

Night passes instantly if your character rests in a Bed. This does not advance time—at least, not exactly. Crops don't grow, your Furnaces won't cook any faster, and so forth. Beds simply advance your character to morning. Rain or snow that's falling can end thanks to "skipping ahead," but this is the only effect aside from getting you quickly through the night.

Beds save your position when you rest. If your character dies (anywhere, in any world), you return to the last place where your character slept. Always put your Bed somewhere safe, so you don't get attacked while you're trying to get your bearings. Keep a Bed inside your base, where you have resources to arm yourself. If you die, grab new tools, weapons, armor, food, and Torches, and then head out to retrieve any items that fell. You don't want to run back out there empty-handed!

Beds are handy to bring with you on long-distance exploration expeditions. If you want to see the Overworld, take a Bed in your inventory and use it as night falls. You get to sleep through the nighttime monster spawns and pick up your journey where you left off. If you die, you wake up where you last slept instead of back at home. It's a good way to save time and stay safe, while getting the most out of your exploration. It's also a potential lifesaver if you're the type who gets lost easily whenever you step outside your house.

 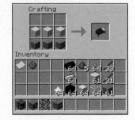

THE WAY MONSTERS ARE BORN

Minecraft wouldn't be complete without monsters! They provide an extra level of excitement and danger: a challenge or obstacle to overcome. We'll explain how monsters appear so you can protect your home from various bad guys.

Some Facts About Monsters

Most monsters start to notice your presence when you're roughly 16 blocks away. Monsters that immediately move to attack you are called hostile or aggressive. Some monsters can see you through rocks, and others can climb or fall to reach you.

Monsters are usually affected by the environment in the same ways you are. Thus, they take falling damage, can suffocate or drown underwater, and they can be set on fire. Additionally, and most importantly, monsters take damage from weapon attacks.

Monsters can also ride in Minecarts, and you can transport them around this way. Although monsters can't open Doors, they can break them down under the right conditions. If your difficulty level is set high enough, monsters attack and destroy Wood Doors.

When a monster is killed, it may drop an item. Some monsters can pick up blocks or equipment and use it against you, or simply carry things around. Other monsters wear armor or use creatures as mounts.

Born in the Darkness

Night is the time of monsters. As the sun sets, monsters appear. The sudden appearance of a monster into the world is called "spawning." Some monsters spawn more often than others—Zombies are the most common.

Light level is usually what determines monster spawning. The following table shows which monsters appear at a given illumination level:

LIGHT LEVEL	MONSTERS	ADDITIONAL DETAILS
7	Zombies, Skeletons, Wither Skeletons, Creepers, Witches, Endermen, Spiders, Spider Jockeys, Chicken Jockeys	Spiders are no longer hostile once the light level is 12 (they attack if you hit them, though).
8	Slimes	Only in Swamps. If below Layer 40 underground, Slimes spawn at any light level.
11	Silverfish, Blazes	—
Any	Zombie Pigmen, Ghasts, Magma Cubes, Endermites	Zombie Pigmen are found in the Nether but can appear in the Overworld under rare conditions. Rarely, Endermites are formed after an Enderman teleports.

When the sun rises, most of the monsters outside start to catch fire. Zombies and Skeletons, which are the most common monsters to spawn, can't deal with bright light and quickly become walking torches. If you attack them at close range while they're on fire, be careful; you can catch fire as well. However, if there's enough shade or a storm outside, monsters can survive the daytime. They might also wear protective armor (a helmet helps) to shield them from the sun's deadly rays.

Some monsters don't care about daylight; Witches, Creepers, and Spiders can all be found while the sun's out. Endermen often teleport away from the light to find more comfortable areas.

Monster Hideouts

Because monsters spawn anywhere the light isn't too bright, naturally occurring caves are monster playgrounds. Dark pits in the ground, large openings into mountains, or deep underground pockets make wonderful monster homes.

Light It or Wall It Off

If you're mining underground and break into a natural cave, it's a sure bet that monsters are in it somewhere. Go through the cave cautiously, and keep your ears open for the sounds of creatures. As you move through, put Torches on the walls at regular intervals. This keeps monsters from spawning after you leave. If you come to an area that you can't illuminate, or if you want to grab a lot of material at your own pace without monster interference, wall off a section. You can always come back and explore later; your safety is more precious than Gold.

Strongholds, Fortresses, Temples, Dungeons, and Abandoned Mineshafts are all places where monsters live. There are wonderful treasures to be found in these locations, but it's dangerous to go there unprepared.

Monster Spawners

Monster Spawners are bluish-black, cage-like blocks found in special locations: Fortresses, Dungeons, Abandoned Mineshafts, and Strongholds. Within the block, there are flames and a small, spinning monster soon to be spawned. Generally, Monster Spawners create only Zombies, Skeletons, Spiders, Blazes, and Silverfish, but they can make animals as well.

A Monster Spawner activates when you are 16 blocks away and immediately begins spawning a random monster within an 8x2x8 block area (eight blocks wide, two blocks high, and eight blocks long). As long as the light level is appropriate and any other conditions are met, monsters appear anywhere in this zone. They can even spawn midair.

You can stop Monster Spawners by surrounding their area with Torches (i.e., raising the light level) or attacking them with weapons. They drop 15-43 experience when you break them. Some people create traps of various types around Monster Spawners; when the monster appears, it finds itself falling into a large pit, for example. You can set up the traps to be instantly lethal as a means of gathering certain items. Or you can use this as a way to corral monsters if you want to slaughter them at your leisure. Any experience or items gained from the monster's destruction can then be gathered later.

Spawn Eggs

In Creative Mode, monsters come from eggs, called Spawn Eggs. Hostile monsters still appear during the evening in Creative Mode, but they almost never attack the player. But what if you want to decorate using monsters or have them wander around your house? Who wouldn't want a pet Creeper!

Select the Spawn Egg, put it on your hotbar, and use it; the creature immediately appears. Unlike Chicken Eggs, Spawn Eggs are not thrown; you have to be within range on an appropriate block. After that, the creature moves on its own. If you want, put Spawn Eggs in Dispensers; for example, you can surprise someone with an instantly appearing buddy!

Withers

You can summon a special boss monster, a Wither, in-game. You must be in the Overworld, and you cannot be in Creative Mode. To create a Wither in the crafting interface, put Soul Sand in a T shape, with the T's horizontal bar going across the middle section. Then add three Wither Skeleton Skulls on top. The Wither Skeleton Skulls must be added last. The sky immediately turns darker, and the Wither appears. As the Wither grows, it begins to flash blue. It doesn't move or attack at this point, and it can't take any damage. Don't stay close to it. Once the Wither reaches its full size, it explodes, blasting anything within range!

The Wither considers every living thing to be its enemy (especially you), and it attacks anything that isn't considered undead.

THREATS TO YOUR SURVIVAL

We've talked about health and mentioned that certain things can hurt your character: fire, falls, monsters, Poison, etc. Now it's time to discuss these specific dangers and how you can avoid, counter, or fall prey to them!

Your Health

Characters in *Minecraft* have ten Hearts' worth of health. Each Heart is split in half and is worth two points of damage, so it's possible to withstand up to 20 points of damage before dying.

Your health is restored naturally as long as you have nine points on your hunger meter. Keep yourself well-fed so you're always at nine or ten hunger. This way, you regenerate soon after you suffer any damage.

Restoring lost health drains your hunger meter quickly, so remember to eat soon after you heal from damage. You can use Potions and special foods, such as Golden Apples, to give your character extra health to help with dangerous battles.

Attack Damage

Armor reduces incoming attack damage.

Other players and monsters inflict damage to you if they attack with their bodies or weapons. Some of these foes have ranged weapons and can shoot you from far away. Others have to walk up to your character and attack directly to deal any damage.

Incoming attack damage is reduced if you're wearing armor. The stronger your armor, the greater the damage reduction. You're always better off wearing at least some protection when you fight. Avoid attack damage by dodging enemies or backing away from them. You can also keep a Shield equipped to block most attacks.

Starvation

Armor does not affect starvation damage.

If your hunger meter depletes entirely, starvation begins. Your character loses health somewhat quickly, and this continues until you're almost dead or you find something to eat. If you're playing on maximum difficulty, you can die directly from starvation.

The best way to avoid starvation is to keep your hunger meter high at all times. This isn't just good for regenerating health. Your hunger meter doesn't deplete unless your food saturation falls to zero; this is a hidden stat, so you can't tell exactly where it is. In a simple way, your saturation can be as high as your current hunger level. This means that recently eaten food "stays with" your character longer if you're already well-fed and high up on the hunger meter. When you're almost starving, it's easier to lose points on the hunger meter, even with relatively little exertion.

So, you're better off eating several pieces of food to fill your bar completely. Having one snack here and there isn't as effective, and it leaves you much more vulnerable to damage.

Some items trigger a Hunger effect that forces your hunger meter to fall even faster than usual. Rotten Flesh, Raw Chicken, and Pufferfish all have a chance to do this. Avoid eating these foods unless you're already about to starve. In that circumstance, eat as much Rotten Flesh as you need to

fill your hunger meter. The Hunger effect is not cumulative, so you pay the price only once instead of dealing with extra hunger for every piece you eat.

If you're forced to dine on foods that cause Poison or Hunger, drink Milk at the end of your foul feast. This cures your status effect and ensures that you hold on to as much health/food as possible.

Explosions

Armor reduces explosion damage.

TNT and Creepers have something in common: they love to explode. Explosive damage is high if your character stands too close to any detonation. Set off TNT carefully, and give Creepers a wide berth. In fact, it's usually better to shoot Creepers with Arrows or sprint away from them entirely until you're really good at killing them with hit-and-run melee attacks.

Explosions hurt everything in the area, so other monsters and even blocks take damage from these blasts. Use this as a way to break through tunnels quickly with TNT, or to kill groups of enemies by luring Creepers into their midst.

Falling

Armor does not reduce falling damage.

Falling downward more than three blocks damages your character. You take one point of damage for every block after the third. Landing in water negates this, so aim for a water landing anytime you jump off a high ledge.

Your character can also catch Ladders or Vines in mid-fall, and this instantly stops your descent without causing any damage. Gutsy players often use this to jump down mine tunnels without getting hurt—don't miss!

An armor enchantment called Feather Falling reduces damage from falling. Long falls can still kill you, but this enchantment gives you a larger survival window.

Fire

Armor does not reduce fire damage.

Your character catches fire if you touch Lava, get hit by a Ghast's fireball, or bump into anything that's already burning, such as Zombies, your house, and so forth. As a rule of thumb, don't touch anything that's aflame! Armor reduces damage from initial impacts against Lava or fireballs, but the burning damage itself is unmitigated, no matter what you're wearing.

If you're set ablaze, get into water as quickly as possible to save yourself from heavy fire damage. If no lakes or rivers are nearby, dump a Bucket of Water over yourself. Carry one of these and have it on your hotbar at all times. It's especially important when you mine near Lava. Dousing yourself extinguishes the fire and turns Lava into Obsidian, so it's one of the only ways to make it out of a Lava pool alive.

Drowning

Armor does not reduce drowning damage.

A meter of air bubbles appears when you dive into water. If this fully depletes, your character begins to take drowning damage. This does not bring immediate death, but you won't last too long. Find your way to the surface before this happens.

A neat trick here is to place certain items against a surface when you're desperate for air. Things like Torches create an air pocket for a short time. The water soon puts them out, but your character breathes comfortably for the moment before this happens. Ladders, Signs, Trapdoors, Doors, Fences, and Sugar Cane can create permanent air bubbles underwater. Use any of these items to save yourself from drowning.

Suffocation

Armor does not reduce suffocation damage.

Characters or monsters that are covered in Sand or Gravel start to take this type of damage because they cannot breathe. It even hurts tougher monsters, like Iron Golems, so that's interesting.

You can't do anything about this damage directly. The only escape is to free yourself. Use a Shovel to dig out of Sand and Gravel, or a Pickaxe if you've accidentally run into a harder block. Break free, and the damage stops.

Poison

Armor does not reduce Poison damage.

Poison hits your character if you eat the wrong item, get bitten by a Cave Spider, or drink the wrong Potion. Poison inflicts damage over time, and you can't reduce it with armor. However, you can negate the Poison by drinking Milk. Carry around a Bucket of Milk if you're worried about Poison damage. A good time to do this is when you explore an Abandoned Mineshaft, because those places often host plenty of Cave Spiders.

The Wither Effect

Armor does not reduce Wither Effect damage.

Wither Skeletons place a minor Poison-like effect on their targets. If a Wither Skeleton strikes you, expect to suffer additional damage over time. Armor doesn't help, so back off, keep your health and hunger meters as high as possible, and try not to take additional hits until you're back in good shape.

Lightning

Armor reduces lightning damage.

Lightning inflicts five damage points to your character if you're ever unlucky enough for it to strike you. This happens only outside, during thunderstorms. To stay safe, don't play outside during thunderstorms!

Falling Into the Abyss

Armor does not reduce damage from the void.

If you find a way to get below the bedrock, your character falls into the void. This abyss of darkness offers no salvation. Unless you can teleport back to safety with an Ender Pearl, your character will die.

Status Effects

Look on the side of your screen if anything strange happens to your character. Some items and monsters are able to put status effects on you. These are temporary changes to how your character survives. Some of them are good (food and Potions can often help you). But negative status effects make it harder to get by. Learn what all of these effects do so that you can counter and bad ones and seek out the good ones.

EFFECT NAME	ABILITY	CAUSED BY
Absorption	Adds special health that cannot be regenerated	Golden Apple, Enchanted Golden Apple
Fire Resistance	Negates damage from fire, Lava, and Blaze attacks	Enchanted Golden Apple, Potion of Fire Resistance
Glowing	Causes something to glow, even if it's hidden by a wall	Spectral Arrow
Haste	Improves attack speed (+10%/level) and block destruction (+20%/level)	Beacon
Hunger	You lose points off of your food meter very quickly	Eating Rotten Flesh, Raw Chicken, or Pufferfish
Invisibility	You can't be seen unless you're very close to a target	Potion of Invisibility
Leaping	Improves jumping height and reduces falling damage	Beacon, Potion of Leaping
Levitation	The target rises upward without being in control of the movement	Shulker attacks
Luck	Improves loot quality when fishing or when going into containers that have a special loot table	Potion of Luck
Mining Fatigue	Slows attack speed and block destruction	Getting close to an Elder Guardian
Nausea	Distorts the screen	Eating a Pufferfish (tetrodotoxin is not yummy)
Night Vision	Greatly improves vision in dark areas (and underwater)	Potion of Night Vision
Poison	Does damage over time	Eating a Spider Eye, being hit by a Cave Spider, Poisonous Potatoes, Pufferfish, Potion of Poison
Regeneration	Regenerate health every 2.5 seconds	Golden Apple, Enchanted Golden Apple, and Potion of Regeneration
Resistance	Reduces damage taken	Beacon, Enchanted Golden Apple
Slowness	Decreases movement speed by 15% per level	Potion of Slowness
Speed	Increases movement speed by 20% per level	Beacon, Potion of Swiftness
Strength	Improves melee attack damage (+3/level)	Beacon, Potion of Strength
Water Breathing	Allows you to swim underwater without drowning (and improves sight underwater)	Potion of Water Breathing
Weakness	Reduces your melee damage dealt	Potion of Weakness
Wither	Does damage over time	Being struck by the Wither or by Wither Skeletons

THE INTRICACIES OF COMBAT

Minecraft doesn't have an overwhelming combat system. You won't need to spend dozens of hours getting used to it to be able to fight and survive. It's simple enough that you can quickly learn how to dispatch most enemies in the game. However, there are a few systems that offer advantages to those who delve a bit deeper. Let's talk about these.

Attack Strength

Tools and weapons each have maximum damage that they can inflict with a single swing. You only deal that much if you wait for a cooldown to finish after making each attack. That means you have to be patient with your swings, make each one count, avoid missing, and wait for the cooldown icon that appears so that you know when your weapon is ready to go.

ITEM DAMAGE TABLE

ITEM NAME	ATTACK SPEED	DAMAGE PER SWING	MAXIMUM DAMAGE PER SECOND
Hoe, Wood	1	1	1
Hoe, Stone	2	1	2
Hoe, Iron	3	1	3
Hoe, Gold	1	1	1
Hoe, Diamond	4	1	4
Shovel, Wood	1	2.5	2.5
Shovel, Stone	1	3.5	3.5
Shovel, Iron	1	4.5	4.5
Shovel, Gold	1	2.5	2.5
Shovel, Diamond	1	5.5	5.5
Pickaxe, Wood	1.2	2	2.4
Pickaxe, Stone	1.2	3	3.6
Pickaxe, Iron	1.2	4	4.8

ITEM NAME	ATTACK SPEED	DAMAGE PER SWING	MAXIMUM DAMAGE PER SECOND
Pickaxe, Gold	1.2	2	2.4
Pickaxe, Diamond	1.2	5	6
Axe, Wood	0.8	7	5.6
Axe, Stone	0.8	9	7.2
Axe, Iron	0.9	9	8.1
Axe, Gold	1	7	7
Axe, Diamond	1	9	9
Sword, Wood	1.6	4	6.4
Sword, Stone	1.6	5	8
Sword, Iron	1.6	6	9.6
Sword, Gold	1.6	4	6.4
Sword, Diamond	1.6	7	11.2

Hoes are worthless for their damage output. They only have validity when you want to attack something quickly. They're the fastest potential weapons, but that isn't usually much of an advantage unless you're harassing someone or attacking a creature with very low health and you only care about finishing it off. Even then, Swords are usually far superior.

Pickaxes and Shovels also have low damage output. That's fine; they were never intended for fighting prolonged battles, and you only use them when something suddenly jumps you.

Axes and Swords are where you get to have your real fun. It used to be true that Axes were almost invalid. They did lower damage per swing than Swords, and they weren't any faster to swing. There was no real reason to use one in battle. However, ever since Update 1.9, Axes have had more of a place in a fight. The high damage per hit of an Axe makes them your best weapon for sudden attacks and ambushes. If you're lurking around a corner or have to charge a ranged enemy, you want to deliver maximum damage per hit. Axes do just that. Early in the game, a Stone Axe can do almost twice the damage of an equivalent Sword (per swing). That's quite nice.

Swords, though lower in their damage per hit, make up for it in spades with damage over time. These weapons can be used quickly to slap targets around. If you're good at timing your attacks, you can do more damage per second with a Sword, but this requires that you swing at just the right time and stick close to your victim.

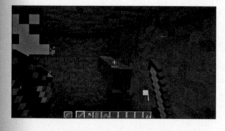

It's good to have a quality Sword and Axe so that you have flexibility in your fighting. Use Axes to break enemy Shields, to ambush targets for high initial damage, and for hit-and-run battles where you attack once, back off, and come forward again when you're fully charged.

Use your Sword when you're confident in a kill and can safely stay on the target, using fast swings for maximum damage output. Swords don't take as much durability damage in combat, so they're a superior choice most of the time. It's just that the game now has moments where Axes share the spotlight!

How Good Are Shields?

Shields are crafted from Iron and Wood. They go into your offhand and serve as protection against enemy attacks. They're one of the best items for dual-wielding when you go into battle (a Bow being another).

Use your right-click to raise a Shield and protect yourself when enemies are firing at your character (or swinging at you in melee).

While blocking like this, you move as if you were sneaking, and you cannot attack. This is purely a defensive option.

If you block a missile attack, it has a chance to ricochet and strike another target nearby. This sometimes helps when you're fighting a mix of melee and missile troops. Shields are nice to have when you're facing other players and Skeletons.

Shields are at their worst when you're fighting someone who has an Axe ready to go. Each Axe blow that lands has a chance to disable the Shield for five seconds. That leaves the defender vulnerable. If it happens to you, back off as quickly as you can to get your bearings, and swing your primary weapon to ward off your attacker.

Shields are repaired with Wood, but you need to do this at an Anvil.

Ranged Combat

Bows give you a major advantage against targets that don't have any ability to fire back. Use ranged attacks to harass or kill these enemies while backing away from them to ensure that you have tons of firing time.

Regular Arrows are fine, but they don't have any special properties beyond the ability to do decent damage. Spectral Arrows help you mark and go after targets in the dark (or when they hide behind objects). This imparts the Glowing status effect, so that the victim is easy to track for ten seconds. This is helpful in player-versus-player combat, when your opponent is most likely to hide, ambush, and be hard to figure out.

Tipped Arrows let you transfer the effects of a Lingering Potion onto your Arrows. They only do one-eighth of the effect per Arrow, but each recipe creates eight altered Arrows, so you aren't wasting any power.

POSSIBLE TIPPED ARROWS

- Arrow of Regeneration
- Arrow of Swiftness
- Arrow of Fire Resistance
- Arrow of Healing
- Arrow of Night Vision
- Arrow of Strength
- Arrow of Leaping
- Arrow of Invisibility
- Arrow of Poison
- Arrow of Weakness
- Arrow of Slowness
- Arrow of Harming
- Arrow of Water Breathing
- Arrow of Luck

Some of these Arrows are intuitive. Harming and Poison are both good effects to add to your Arrows, especially when fighting against powerful targets (whether humans or

monsters). But the other special types of Tipped Arrows open the door for a number of odder and more interesting encounters.

Think about Arrows of Healing against undead monsters! Healing does damage to undead creatures, so that's a fun little trick.

For group situations, you can buff your friends at long range using the more positive Arrows. Use a weaker Bow without enchantments. This ensures that you do very light damage with the Arrow itself (especially if your friends are armored). They'll primarily get the effect of the buff (Regeneration, Swiftness, Healing, etc.).

In custom areas, you can set up fake traps that are meant to scare people, but that actually help them.

Special Attacks

Swords and Axes have special attack properties that make them more versatile in combat. The Sweep Attack that you get with Swords doesn't do much direct damage, but it creates a wide swath in front of the player that knocks targets away. This is a powerful defensive option to get a horde of targets off of you. It's used automatically as long as you're striking a monster, aren't running, and have your swing time charged all the way up.

The sweep knocks enemies back while dealing normal damage to the primary targets and a bit of damage to the secondary ones. After the sweep, use the time you've earned yourself to back up and look for a chokepoint so that the group of enemies can't swarm you again as easily.

Axes are better for smashing individuals (especially players). Instead of knocking a group away from you, the Crushing Blow can disable Shields for five seconds. The base chance for success is 25%, but this is improved by 5% per level of Efficiency enchantment on the weapon. Also, you get +75% more bonus points if you're sprinting when you unleash the attack, making this pretty much a guarantee.

This is why it's nice to keep an Axe around for dealing with tanky enemies that are Shield-blocking all the time. Sprint up to them, nail them with your Axe, and take your free shots afterward.

Axes are better when you're culling herds of animals for meat. You don't want to accidentally cut down more animals or scare the ones close to your target. It's safer to bring an Axe and only hurt the animals you need to kill.

Dual-Wielding

Items in your main hand are shown in your hotbar. They're highlighted with a white box. Your offhand items are displayed in a box off to the side of the hotbar (on its left). You can quickly swap hands by pressing the "Swap Item in Hands" button. By default, this is the "F" on your keyboard, but you can change that in the Controls Menu.

Right-clicking normally activates your offhand item as long as your main-hand item doesn't have an ability triggered by its right-click. Though having items in each hand makes you quite formidable, you can't use them simultaneously. Thus, you cannot block with a Shield while swinging your Sword. The system is there to give you more options, but it has limitations to prevent people from being too powerful.

Weapons normally can't be used from the offhand. You only get to use the alt-click actions for the things in your offhand. Thus, you can place objects like blocks, Torches, etc. You can use specific tools. And there are a few minor weapon exceptions. You generally want to have a prominent tool or weapon in your main hand and then something supportive in your offhand. A Sword and a Shield. A Pickaxe and a Torch. These are traditional choices.

Once you know the basic rules, as we've discussed here, it's useful to go into the details because there are many interesting exceptions.

OFFHAND TOOL EXCEPTIONS

- Buckets
- Ender Pearls
- Fishing Rods
- Flint and Steel
- Hoes
- Leads
- Shears
- Shovels

OFFHAND WEAPON EXCEPTIONS

- Bows can be fired from either hand
- Chicken Eggs and Snowballs can be thrown
- Lingering and Splash Potions are also throwable
- Shields can block in the offhand

Ideal Dual-Wielding Combinations

MAIN HAND	OFFHAND	FUNCTION
Any Weapon	Map	Having a Map in your offhand puts a minimap onto the screen, making it possible to explore much more easily while still defending yourself against sudden attackers.
Any Weapon	Clock	If you like to keep an eye on the time, this makes it much easier.
Any Weapon	Compass	Race back toward home as night falls without losing track of where you're going.
Bow	Specific Arrows	If you have several types of Arrows, this lets you control which specific ones are selected when you fire your Bow.
Hoe	Seeds	Farm at maximum speed by tilling and planting without having to shift anything on your hotbar. Simply hold down your right mouse button to do both!
Ladder	Block	It's much faster to build upward with this configuration; you're able to place blocks with your right-click and hold the button down to also place the Ladder. You can effectively build and climb the new block at almost full speed.
Melee Weapon	Food	Before you have access to Potions, this is a good way to keep yourself topped off on grub so that you heal after extended combat.
Melee Weapon	Ender Pearl	Allows for massive mobility during combat; it's easier to escape mobs or confuse human opponents.
Melee Weapon	Shield	A traditional blend of offense and defense. This is best when facing ranged attackers, because you can defend yourself during the approach and then massacre the ranged targets once you reach them.
Melee Weapon	Bow	Heavily offensive. You get to shoot at range and still have a melee weapon ready in case anyone closes the gap.
Melee Weapon	Potion	Though expensive, this combination is wonderful in a wide range of conditions. Select Potions to restore your health if you're worried about survival. Try offensive Splash Potions if you want to end fights quickly. Attack, throw as your weapon cools down, and repeat.
Melee Weapon	Milk	Use this to counter enemies that inflict negative status effects on you frequently (Witches, other players, etc.).
Pickaxe	Bucket of Water	If you're tunneling near Lava, every second can count. Have water at the ready so that you can douse the Lava and save yourself from a fiery death.
Pickaxe	Block	This helps for blocking Lava or stopping sudden monsters that pop up as you break into new caverns. Put down a few blocks to obstruct your tunnels and buy time to flee or prepare your weaponry.
Pickaxe or Shovel	Torch	An absolute must for digging and tunneling. It's fast for placing Torches to keep your mining safe.

DEATH AND REBIRTH

Despite your best plans and intentions, you will get killed at some point in *Minecraft*. A lucky Creeper, a fall into Lava, or some other curse will befall you. When that happens, the game is not necessarily over. Let's see what happens.

Hardcore Mode

If you're playing *Minecraft* in Hardcore Mode, well, then technically the game *is* over. You get only one life in Hardcore Mode, so death is the end of all things. You have to play conservatively to survive on this setting. When your character does die, it's time to start over with a new game. You can respawn in Spectator Mode to watch what's going on. This is sometimes done to see who will win a battle between multiple surviving players. But once you're done watching, it's time to move on.

If you're really naughty, it's possible to create a copy of your save file and then restore that when your character dies. We don't mind telling you this is possible, but we won't mention exactly how to do it. It's your responsibility if you choose to skirt the rules!

Death Penalties
The Cost of Dying

- Huge loss of experience
- Potential loss of equipment and resources that you were carrying
- Time spent getting back to where you were

For any other mode, death is not the end. Your character drops everything he or she is carrying when something reduces his or her health to zero. Unless you're on a block that destroys objects, your inventory is still available to be retrieved for several minutes.

The clock has started! (Or not—we'll talk about this in a moment.)

Your character is reborn with full health and a full hunger meter at the last place you slept. Hurry toward your Chests of goodies and grab at least a full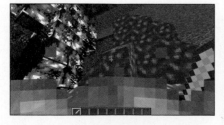

set of basic tools, a Sword, any armor you still have, and a mix of food and Torches. Backtrack to the place where you died, keeping in mind the threat that took you down. If it's night outside and that's where you died, quickly sleep on your Bed to start the next day. This doesn't count against your timer; your loot is still out there.

If you make it back to your items in time, you get to keep them, along with *some* of the experience your character had at the time of death. It isn't a great amount, but you won't have to start from scratch without any levels. Yay?

Lava deaths are the worst, because your items fall into the Lava when you die, and they're burned to cinders. There won't be anything left when you return, unless a few pieces flew up and out, and then landed safely on a nearby shore. It's worth checking, but don't get your hopes too high. Lava is evil, and that's why you need a Bucket of Water wherever you go.

Explosive deaths can be nasty, too. Depending on the circumstances, some of your items might be destroyed by subsequent explosions or fires.

If you don't make it back to the place where you died within five minutes, everything goes away. Take a deep breath, remember that you can always mine more treasure, and get back to doing what you like— that's *Minecraft*.

But Wait! There's Still a Chance

There is a slight catch here, in your favor. You have to get close to the area where you died for the timer to really begin ticking down. That five minutes doesn't start until you're in the same region (called "chunks") as your body.

Characters that die far away from home aren't always doomed. Get prepared before you enter the region that holds your body, and then beeline toward your corpse. There's still some hope.

We still recommend trying to get to your body as soon as possible. It's easy to forget where you were, and the longer you wait, the more likely it is that you take a wrong turn and lose time trying to find the location.

TRAPS AND DEFENSES

There are many ways to rig traps around your home and mines. These work to kill monsters and possibly harm or kill other players who come into your territory without permission (on servers where PvP is allowed).

There are so many ideas for cool traps that we can't cover more than a sampling of them, but we want to get you started with a few general concepts.

Pressure Plates

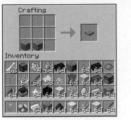

Pressure Plates are critical in many traps. These items activate a charge whenever anything steps on them. A block of TNT nearby turns this into an explosive mine. But that's pretty easy to spot. Almost anyone gets suspicious once they see TNT lying around. As an alternative, you can put the TNT below a Pressure Plate to add a layer of trickery. Consider making a Door into your house that you don't use. Put a Pressure Plate on the inside and have Gravel or Sand and TNT below that. Anyone who enters that way will have a bad experience. Just don't put anything valuable in that room, and make sure it's easy to rebuild the area and the trap. This is better for a funny joke than for a serious defense.

Pistons

Pistons move blocks and make it possible to set up slightly more elaborate traps. Use Pistons for making mechanical doorways or to block passages. A Pressure Plate with Redstone channels and Pistons on the other side of a wall lets you open or close passages.

Combine this with secondary traps to make your Dungeons even deadlier. Have someone step onto a Pressure Plate, use the Pistons to block the character into a small space, and then let another Piston push aside the Stones holding back the Lava directly above them. Bye-bye!

Iron Doors

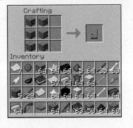

Iron Doors are excellent to pair with traps, because these items can't be opened manually. They must be activated with a Button, Pressure Plate, Lever, etc. Because of this, you should make it easy for other players to get into your target area; leave a Pressure Plate for them to walk over so that the Door opens. Once they're in, the Door closes automatically, and the trap has been sprung. They can't turn around and leave without rushing to use their Pickaxe, and hopefully your TNT, Lava, or other deadly surprise is already on its way.

To make an Iron Door, use the standard Door recipe, but substitute Iron Ingots for Wood Planks.

Pits

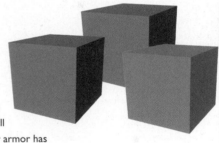

Most characters won't survive a fall 23 blocks down; they'll take full damage and die even if they have full health. Unless their armor has Feather Falling, it's Game Over.

Thus, many traps use long falls as a way to kill monsters and players. You can lure people onto blocks and tempt them to mine away, but this doesn't work very often. Few experienced players will mine directly downward, even if a sign says "FREE LOOT INSIDE!" So, make things more interesting. Build a bridge that leads toward your base/safe area, and hide the drop with Pistons. Use a Pressure Plate to trigger a wall that pushes people into the deadly pit while they're crossing the bridge. This still isn't very subtle, but it sometimes works!

Many common pit traps have a top layer with a Pressure Plate, a piece of TNT underneath, and then a fall below that. This is too much work to use against monsters, but it's reliable against human intruders.

Trapped Chests

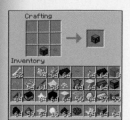

Trapped Chests have the normal function and use of standard Chests. Double them up for extra storage, and place what you want inside. However, these Chests have a red tinge around their locks and set off a Redstone signal when they're opened. Use this to activate TNT, Lava traps, pits, etc.

Water Suffocation Traps

Water is used to kill monsters and to funnel loot around your base. A waterway that flows down through a tunnel can be passed under a low ceiling, so that the clearance is only a single block. This traps characters and other tall monsters so that they start to suffocate. This eventually kills the enemy in question and allows their loot to drop into the water. The current carries the loot to a place deeper inside your base, where you can safely collect it. Make multiple waterways converge in one area for maximum efficiency!

Monster Holding Areas

Build a large room near your main base. Leave it lit while you're constructing it, but destroy any Torches when you finish the entire task. Inside, create a long strip of water that flows down toward a single block. Make several of these strips converge at the same block for extra efficiency. For the final block, use a Sticky Piston and connect that to a Lever that's somewhere safe and convenient. Or use an open Trapdoor so that monsters wander onto it and then fall. Dig a pit that's 22 blocks deep under the Sticky Piston/Trapdoor.

Use this to capture monsters that get trapped by the water currents. Use the Lever to open the pit, or simply wait if you're using the Trapdoor method. Build a secondary tunnel inside your base leading to the monster holding area below.

All of your foes are badly injured by the fall and die from a single hit from any decent weapon. You still get their loot and their experience.

If you don't care about the experience, make the pit a little deeper to inflict fatal injuries. This costs you certain types of loot as well, but it's safer if you aren't into fighting.

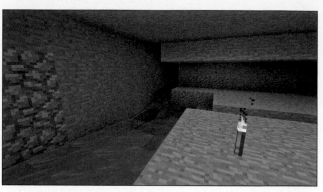

Soul Sand and Ice

You gather Soul Sand in the Nether, and it slows anything that tries to walk over it. Place Ice underneath Soul Sand for an even more potent slowing effect. This is a double whammy if you create a room with any other traps, because victims can't run away.

Monster Spawners

When you find Monster Spawners, don't just destroy them without thinking. These items are extremely useful for creating high-quality monster farms. You can use the techniques we've described in and around Monster Spawners to ensure that you gather and/or kill all of the creatures they summon.

The biggest downside of making a good monster farm with Monster Spawners is that you have to stay fairly close by to get the most out of them. Monsters don't spawn unless you're within range.

Thus, this works really well if you stay in a particular area to mine. Otherwise, go ahead and destroy the Monster Spawner, or wall it off for now and leave a Sign to remind yourself where it is.

MODERN CONVENIENCES

Some machines and items are quite useful for your character; they make your time in *Minecraft* easier to manage. Let's see what we can build!

Cobblestone Generator

Cobblestone isn't hard to get, but there's something nifty about making an infinite source of it. Having a Cobblestone generator in your base provides a limitless supply of the rock that you can harvest at will.

To create one of these generators, hollow out a decent room. Make a long trench surrounded by Stone; avoid placing anything that might catch on fire nearby. Bring two Buckets here, one with Water and one with Lava. Dump out each one at opposite ends of the trench, and watch the two fluids meet. Wherever they touch, Cobblestone forms. Break it, collect it, and repeat the process.

Water turns the Lava block into Obsidian if they ever touch, so avoid letting the water flow that far.

To make the generator more effective, use a Piston at the major point of contact between the two flows to push completed Cobblestone out of the way. This allows more Cobblestone to be created even when you're not there to mine everything. Use Clock Circuits to make sure the system triggers at a smooth, even pace.

Clock Circuits are very nice! These are made in a variety of ways. Clock Circuits are effectively a group of devices to ensure that your system toggles on and off on its own. You can have these set to different lengths of time, depending on the setup you install.

A common setup for a Clock Circuit is to use Repeaters. Place two Repeaters and connect them with a loop of Redstone Dust. Add a Lever to control the initial energy of the circuit. Also add a Redstone Torch onto a powered block next to this circuit. The Torch starts off generating power, but turns off around one second later because it was placed onto a powered block. Your circuit now has power and is timed with a one-second pulse. Destroy the powered block and the Redstone Torch if you like (to use elsewhere), because the circuit is going to continue circulating its own power unless something damages it.

Garbage Pits

Several types of features make good garbage bins. Dig a small pit and fill it with Lava for dangerous but effective disposal of items that you're sick of keeping around. Take that, stacks of Dirt! Cacti accomplish the same task without the danger of burning down your house, so there's that!

If you want something less effective but more aesthetically pleasing, a small fountain works well enough. Throw extra items in there and leave them for several minutes. They'll disappear on their own as long as you don't jump into the fountain to collect them.

Ender Chests

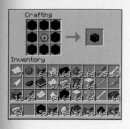

Once you kill enough Endermen, you start to get a supply of Ender Pearls. Craft these with Blaze Rods to make Eyes of Ender. Combine Eyes of Ender with Obsidian to make Ender Chests. These special containers are linked, so any Ender Chest you make contains the items you placed in any of your other Ender Chests. If you have Ender Chests, you can effectively store items anywhere in the game and collect them anywhere else.

This is incredibly nice when you work in the Nether and the End. Place your treasure in the Ender Chest, and it'll be available back in your safe house even if you get killed!

Pressure Plate Doors

Tired of opening Doors for yourself like a sucker? Place Pressure Plates in front of your Doors (on the inside of the house only). This lets you run out without stopping to mess with anything. Don't try this outside your home, because monsters can find their way in.

Maps and Compasses

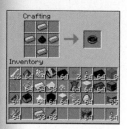

As we've mentioned before, you may face walls of Cobblestone at any time. Although all Cobblestones maintain the same orientation no matter how they're placed, it takes a moment of looking to figure this out. A better way to reference your orientation is to craft a Compass.

Compasses make navigation easier, so craft one as soon as you can, and pay attention to your movements. The more you do this, the more your sense of direction will improve.

If you still have trouble finding your way around, make Maps. Then expand on your Maps to make them cover more territory; do this by crafting the existing Map with even more Paper.

Carry your Map in your inventory so you can switch to it and figure out where you're going. This, combined with a Compass, makes exploration safer and easier.

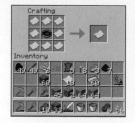

Surface features like biome colors, Lava, water, and elevation are all reflected in the Maps you make. Anything below the surface isn't shown, so you only get a position relative to your topside base when you're down in the tunnels.

THINKING OUTSIDE THE BLOCKS

This section is designed to give you some ideas for decorating your living space in your *Minecraft* world. Many recipes for functional items are already in the game, but what about fun, decorative items?

Like anything else in *Minecraft*, what you create is limited only by your imagination. Here, you'll find a few ideas to help you get started. With the right materials, you can make everything from a nice kitchen to a bathroom (complete with running water), or even a realistic forge.

Common Materials

Creating furniture doesn't require complicated materials. Mostly, you need simple blocks (of anything) and the means to make Signs, Levers, Trapdoors, Tripwires, and Pistons. Some recipes call for something specific: a block of Wool in a certain color, or a chunk of Netherrack, or a Dispenser. The real challenge is using ordinary things in unusual ways. For example, Trapdoors can be used in more ways than just outside, over pits; instead, try one on a wall next to a window as a shutter.

Ideas by Room

Living Room

Sofas

One of the simplest ways to make a sofa is to place two or more Slabs together to form the seat. Place two Signs on the far ends of the Slabs to create the sofa's arms.

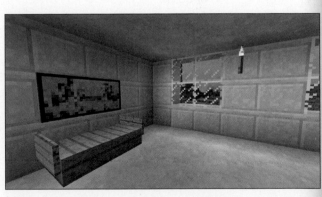

This type of sofa looks like a bench if you use Wood Slabs. If you like, you can use a wide Picture as the sofa's back.

You can make another common sofa using sets of Stairs. Put two Stair pieces beside each other and cap off the ends with Signs. Because Stairs can be made with Wood, Stone, Bricks, Nether Brick, Sandstone, and Quartz, you can choose from a wide range of sofa colors.

If you want a thicker sofa, create two Slabs as the seat and then surround the Slabs with blocks as the arms and back. You can make some very nice sofas this way using blocks of colored Wool.

Chairs

You can make a chair the same way as a sofa, except that the "seat" is only one square wide. So, use one Slab or one Stair piece instead of two, as described for the sofas.

Dining Room

Tables

You can make a small table using a Fence Post and a Pressure Plate. All you have to do is place the Fence Post on the ground (it looks nice near a wall), and then put a Pressure Plate on top of the post as the table's surface.

You can make larger tables using Pistons, provided you don't completely dig out an underground basement for your house. Dig two blocks down and place a Redstone Torch at the bottom to power the Piston. Then put the Piston on top of the Torch, which causes the Piston to extend. Because you can put any number of Pistons next to each other with this method, you can make your table as wide or long as you like.

Kitchen

Sink

You can construct an easy sink using one Cauldron and one Tripwire Hook. The Cauldron forms most of the sink, and a Tripwire Hook against the wall above the Cauldron makes a faucet. If you want your sink to be filled with water, pour a Bucket of Water into the Cauldron.

Cabinets

To make cabinets, put any number of blocks against a wall. Iron blocks look nice for this, because they really stand out against Wood or Stone walls. Make cabinet doors by placing Trapdoors on the cabinets' front sides, facing you. If you use Bookshelves instead of blocks, it gives the illusion of having food or dinnerware within the cabinet.

Bathroom

Toilets

Toilets are slightly more complicated than some other pieces of furniture. Most toilets are made in rooms with Slab floors, so they don't seem quite as large or unsightly. You need two spaces to make a nice toilet. The first space is filled by a Cauldron (you can fill it with water by using a Bucket). Behind the Cauldron, stack two large blocks. Put a Button on one side of the upper block as a flusher.

A Trapdoor over the Cauldron as a lid completes the toilet.

Showers and Bathtubs

Pick a corner and create the shower's base with Slabs. Then place a Piston in the ceiling or wall and a water source behind it. Fill in the space marked out by the Slabs with Glass blocks or Glass Panes. A Lever linked with the Piston lets you turn the water on or off.

Bedroom

Dressers

Make a nice dresser by stacking two large Chests on top of each other. Another dresser uses four Stair pieces, two Trapdoors, and two Doors. Place two Stairs facing each other, so they form a "V." Stack two more Stairs directly on top of the first set, forming a hole in the center topped by another open "V." The Trapdoors then go on top of the dresser. Set the two Doors against the front of the Stairs, making a fully opening dresser.

Beds

Minecraft already has a recipe for a functional Bed, but you can do more with it to make it *yours*. To make a four-poster Bed, craft two Beds with the standard recipe. Make a headboard and footboard with a layer of blocks at the top and bottom. If you wish, you can use Wool blocks (dyed or natural) to complement the crafted Beds' red color; Glowstone blocks also create a nice effect. If you don't like the look of full blocks around the Bed, try Slabs (but leave full blocks on the corners). By stacking Fences on top of the corner blocks, you can make the bedposts.

To create a canopy over a four-poster Bed, outline the area with either Fences or Gates to make a lattice. Using more Fences, connect the ceiling lattice to the bedframe. You can then fill in the rest of the area within the ceiling space with additional blocks of your choice.

Other

Fireplaces

Who doesn't love fire? Fireplaces are easy to build and are very dramatic. First, you need a place where you can dig down at least two squares. Put a block of Netherrack in the hole at the bottom. If you want a larger fire in your fireplace, make the "pit" larger.

Next, construct the fireplace's chimney with blocks of material, the most obvious being Stone or Brick. If you want your fireplace to narrow into a chimney, use Stairs to slim the larger section into a smaller column. Light the Netherrack using Flint and Tinder, and the fire will burn continuously. For decoration, add a Glass Pane or Iron Bar frontpiece.

Note that fireplaces contain actual fire. If you don't surround your fireplace with a 3x3x9 area of nonflammable materials, adjacent objects run the risk of catching fire. You can accidentally set fire to your home or furniture if you don't make nearby walls, floors, and furniture out of Stone or Brick.

REDSTONE

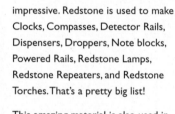

You can mine Redstone deep underground in the Overworld. Once you start mining down there, Redstone collects quickly. Each vein yields a fair number of pieces, and it's hard to miss these veins even when you're running through a cavern, because they're bright red. Always keep an Iron Pickaxe handy. Lesser materials fail to break Redstone properly. Iron tools are required for quite a few of the special metals and ores, so an Iron Pickaxe isn't a particular burden here.

You can craft blocks of Redstone to make pretty crimson decor around your house, but its real uses are much more impressive. Redstone is used to make Clocks, Compasses, Detector Rails, Dispensers, Droppers, Note blocks, Powered Rails, Redstone Lamps, Redstone Repeaters, and Redstone Torches. That's a pretty big list!

This amazing material is also used in brewing to make Potions last longer. If that's not enough for you, you can also place Redstone on the ground as a red trail of dust. Redstone Dust lets you channel power from one area to another, allowing for the construction of complex machines.

Transmission of Redstone Power

Trails of Redstone Dust send power up to 15 blocks from their source. Power is generated by a number of objects. Pressure Plates, Redstone Torches, Levers, and Buttons are just a few examples of items that trigger some type of power. Placing Redstone Dust on a block next to these items lets their power transmit to somewhere else.

Create a trail of dust that goes where you need it to go, and make sure you don't shift the height of your trail more than one block at a time. Redstone Dust stops sending power if its elevation changes more abruptly than that. It also fails if you shift the trail up or down one block and don't leave either air or Glass in between. Trying to send the trail up and under another heavy block doesn't work.

When power is continuous along a line of dust, the material turns bright red instead of dark red. This lets you see how well power is flowing along your lines. If the energy isn't going far enough, add additional sources of energy, such as a Redstone Torch.

Redstone Machinery

Now things get a bit more complex. You know that Redstone can carry energy around, but what does that actually do? A good question! The energy from these signals lets you operate a range of mechanisms in the game, providing automation for farms, traps, transportation, and more. It's hard to get a handle on all of this when you first start *Minecraft*. In fact, this presents a steeper skill/learning curve than almost anything else in the game. Don't try to master this right away. Take your time, dabble in Redstone, and figure it out as you go.

When you're starting out, don't be afraid to look at other people's machines for inspiration. See how they did what they did. Most people need to see a few machines set up in the game before they start to understand Redstone's use and potential.

Having said that, let's move forward. We'll keep this as simple as possible. Let's start by breaking down the major parts of a potential machine.

Pieces of a Machine

- **Power:** some device needs to provide power for your machine
- **Transmission:** the power needs to be sent from its source to somewhere else of your choosing
- **Mechanism:** this device needs to receive power and use it to accomplish your goal

Items that Produce Power

Power is produced by a wide range of items.

ITEM	HOW TO ACTIVATE IT	POWER PRODUCED
Button	Interact with it or use a Bow to shoot it.	Activate nearby dust/components for 1.5 seconds when touched, or one minute if shot by a Bow.
Daylight Sensor	Turns on during the day and off at night; the opposite is true if used belowground.	Adds more power as the day/night progresses.
Detector Rail	Adds power when a Minecart is detected nearby.	Powers itself and adjacent blocks.
Lever	Produces power when turned on.	Power remains on as long as the Lever is not turned off.
Pressure Plate	Provides power when touched; Wood Pressure Plates can be shot with Arrows to produce power.	Powers the block underneath it; any trails/components next to either the plate or the block below are activated.
Redstone Block	Always on.	Strong power for all nearby components.
Redstone Torch	Provides continuous power unless it receives power from another source—this turns it off.	Powers adjacent blocks but not the block to which it is attached.
Trapped Chest	Provides power when someone opens the Chest.	The Trapped Chest and the block underneath it power adjacent dust/mechanisms.
Tripwire Hook	Turns on if the wires are damaged or crossed.	The hook and the block it's placed on produce power.
Weighted Pressure Plate	Adds increasing power based on how many objects are on top of it.	The plate and the block it's placed on produce power.

How to Transmit Power

Power sources add energy to adjacent blocks, which is sometimes all you need. Add a mechanism next to a power source, and you're good to go. However, power transmission is wonderful if you need to make something happen several blocks (or more) away from the power source. The following three items let you send power this way.

Redstone Dust

This is the most basic way to send a Redstone signal along a short length of blocks. The power goes as far as the strength of the original signal. This means that a strong power source can send power 15 blocks away; a source with less power can transmit power only a portion of that distance. For example, a Daylight Sensor will send its signal farther as the day goes on and the sun rises higher in the sky.

Create a simple test to observe this. Make a Daylight Sensor with a trail of Redstone Dust that leads 15 blocks away from it. Watch the line of dust turn bright red across a greater distance as the day progresses— pretty neat!

Redstone Repeater

Sometimes, you may want to send a signal along a greater distance than 15 blocks. Redstone Repeaters let you strengthen a signal in a single direction. Place your line of Redstone Dust so that it leads up to the rear of the Redstone Repeater and then continues out its front side.

This strengthens your signal and allows it to reach greater distances. If you want, add more Repeaters so the signal continues toward any destination. There's a short delay in this process, but that's good too. Redstone Repeaters are often used as a way to slow down a signal so that it doesn't get to its final mechanism too quickly.

Redstone Comparator

Comparators are the most complex way of transmitting power. Like Repeaters, they have a front and a back, but they don't reinforce the signal. Instead, they have two modes: Comparison Mode and Subtraction Mode.

Comparators send their signals from back to front, and they output a signal that's equal in strength to the signal they receive. Thus, a trail of activated Redstone Dust that would normally travel five more blocks can enter the back of this device and exit the front to power five more blocks of dust. You might be thinking, "That doesn't seem to do anything important at all." Well, not yet.

The Comparator comes into play when there are signals coming into the back *and* the side of the device. This changes its output. In Comparison Mode, the signal is shut down if the value of the side signal is stronger than the one entering the rear. Thus, Comparison Mode gives you a way to shut down machines based on a separate circuit.

Subtraction Mode *reduces* the signal strength of the main line by the strength of the signal entering the side of the comparator.

Mechanisms

At the end of your signal, place a mechanism of some sort to use the power you're sending. Mechanisms can accomplish a wide range of tasks.

MECHANISM	EFFECT
Activator Rail	Triggers Minecarts that pass over it, detonating TNT, executing Command blocks, or silencing Hoppers.
Command Block	Power causes the block to execute its command a single time.
Dispenser	Shoots one item from a random slot.
Door	Toggles between open and closed.
Dropper	Drops one item from a random slot in its inventory.
Fence Gate	Toggles between open and closed.
Hopper	Power stops Hoppers from pulling items into themselves.
Note Block	Creates sound.
Piston	Pushes the block in front of the Piston (and up to 12 total blocks beyond that).
Powered Rail	Speeds Minecarts.
Rail	Toggles junctions.
Redstone Lamp	Creates powerful light.
TNT	Begins the detonation sequence for the block of TNT.
Trapdoor	Toggles the position of the Trapdoor.

What to Make

Even though we just explained Redstone functionality, this barely scratches the surface. None of this information really means anything until you start to build your own devices.

Following are some simple ideas to get you started with Redstone.

Heavy Doors

Iron Doors keep out monsters on any difficulty, no matter how many of them there are. They don't even try to pound their way through. Use six Iron Ingots to craft a Door, and use power to open and close it. On the inside of your house, a Pressure Plate in front of the Door works perfectly for easy escape. On the outside, you don't want that because monsters might walk right in.

Instead, use a Button outside your Door. Neither of these items leaves the power on continuously, so your Door closes as soon as you move away or wait too long.

Fast Minecarts

Place Powered Rails over long stretches so your Minecarts can travel across great distances. You can climb large inclines as well, making it easier to travel up and down from your mines without wasting time.

Easy Pits

Dig a pit near the front of your house and place a Trapdoor over it. On the inside of the house, place a Lever on a block that's adjacent to the Trapdoor. When you use the Lever as a power source, the block it's attached to gains power. This, in turn, transmits to the Trapdoor and activates it. You can now drop creatures into a pit from the safety of your home. If anyone you don't like comes up to your house, drop them into the pit. A deadly fall should do the trick nicely, but Lava and other fun toys work just as well.

Night-Lights

Redstone Lamps, Redstone Torches, and Daylight Sensors let you craft lighting that turns on only when the light level falls to a certain point. Put the Redstone Lamps and the Redstone Torches next to each other, so they're turned on by default. Then place a line of Redstone Dust that leads to the blocks underneath the Redstone Torches. Connect this to your Daylight Sensors. When there's enough light during the day, they'll provide power to the dust and turn off the Redstone Torches. As night falls, they'll lose power and the Redstone Torches will begin powering the Redstone Lamps again. This is an example of an inverter (i.e., using Redstone Torches to turn *off* a signal rather than turn it on).

The same technique lets you close Doors and Fence Gates in the evening, to prevent monsters from coming into your areas.

ENCHANTMENT AND USING EXPERIENCE

Minecraft isn't a run-of-the-mill RPG or game where levels give you more health, damage, and other basic stats. You're a farmer, a miner, and a survivor. These stats aren't really going to change for you.

Instead, you use levels to enchant your weapons, armor, and tools, to make them better at performing various tasks. We'll discuss gaining and using experience, and what you can get with the enchanting system.

Gaining Experience

Almost every activity in *Minecraft* gets you experience. This comes in the form of glowing orbs that appear when you do something important: kill monsters, breed animals, mine special items, smelt ores, etc. Collect these orbs by walking close to them; they'll try to reach you on their own if you go anywhere near them!

Activities That Generate Experience

- Animal breeding
- Bottles of Enchanting
- Cooking food and other various items in a Furnace
- Destroying Monster Spawners
- Fishing
- Killing monsters or having them die within several seconds of being damaged by your character
- Mining ore or smelting it
- Killing regular farm animals is worth experience too, but not much

Levels Require Different Amounts of Experience

Getting from Level 1 to 2 takes much less experience than going from Level 39 to 40. As you progress higher and higher in level, the amount of experience you need to go higher increases. You don't want to stockpile levels beyond whatever point you currently need. In general, Level 30 (for Enchanting Table work) or Level 39 (for Anvil work) is the highest you ever need to go. Pushing for levels beyond this yields diminishing returns. You're much better off spending your levels to enchant something and then progressing in levels again.

LEVEL(S)	EXPERIENCE REQUIRED	TOTAL EXPERIENCE REQUIRED
1	7	7
2	9	16
3	11	27
4	13	40
5	15	55
6	17	72
7	19	91
8	21	112
9	23	135
10	25	160
11	27	187
12	29	216
13	31	247
14	33	280
15	35	315
16	37	352
17	42	394
18	47	441
19	52	493
20	57	550
21	62	612
22	67	679
23	72	751
24	77	828
25	82	910
26	87	997
27	92	1089
28	97	1186
29	102	1288
30	107	1395
31	112	1507
32	121	1628
33	130	1758
34	139	1897
35	148	2045
36	157	2202
37	166	2368
38	175	2543
39	184	2727
40	193	2920

Losing Experience

Death causes your character to lose a huge amount of experience. *Some* of your experience falls to the ground, and you can retrieve it if you make your way back to your corpse in time, but the rest is gone forever. Wear armor and stay away from deadly drops, Lava, and unwinnable fights to avoid death's experience penalty. Furthermore, spend your experience to invest in enchanted items and Books, so your experience isn't sitting around, doing nothing.

Making an Enchanting Table

When you're ready to spend some experience levels, make an Enchanting Table. You need Diamonds, Obsidian, and a Book to do this. Make a Diamond Pick to mine the Obsidian, gather more Diamonds as needed, and use Leather and Paper to make your Book.

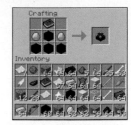

When you're done, you have an Enchanting Table ready to go, but it can't handle major enchantments. Basic Enchanting Tables only add low-cost enchantments to items. These are still nice, but the really incredible stuff requires more effort.

We Need More Power

To give your Enchanting Table more options, place Bookshelves around it. It takes 15 Bookshelves to fully power an Enchanting Table. Arrange these Bookshelves two blocks away from the table either in a "U" shape around the table or wedged into a nearby corner.

Bookshelves only count if they're two spaces away—they can't be adjacent to the Enchanting Table. Stack the shelves two high but not three high. Diagonal spaces count just fine. Given these double stacks, you can have 18 Bookshelves in your "U," which is more than you need.

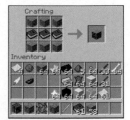

You need a huge amount of Leather and Paper to craft all of those Bookshelves. We suggest you create a large animal pen, lure at least two Cows there, and start breeding them as soon as possible. Visit the pen every five minutes to feed the Cows more Wheat. Don't kill any of the Cows in your pen until you have roughly eight adults.

Once you hit that mark, perform some minor culling after each breeding session. After a major breeding session, slaughter two Cows, and keep the count between six and eight adults every time you go out after that. The pen starts to fill quickly, and you get quite a haul of Leather.

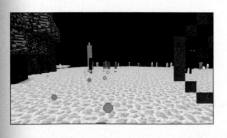

As you can see, the amount needed for a single level rises substantially over time. In earlier versions of the game, there were specific levels where things got much harder, but that isn't as much the case now. Though the quantities needed to level up rise, they never go up by an alarming amount.

For many people, the ideal will be to get up to Level 33, enchant their favorite item, and level up to 33 again. This way, you always have access to the most powerful enchantments in case you need to enchant something else rather suddenly. However, it is slightly more efficient to ping-pong between 27 and 30, if you're not worried about enchanting something at any given moment.

Grow Sugar Cane along local waterways and harvest it each time you go out. This stuff grows like weeds, so getting piles of it for Paper isn't a big deal. If it isn't going quickly enough, reinvest some of the harvested Sugar Cane into additional stalks to increase your yield.

The Finishing Touch

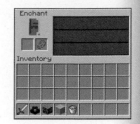

Now that you have 15 Bookshelves near your Enchanting Table, you can use high-level enchantments. Interact with the Enchanting Table to open the interface for enchanting items. Place a weapon, tool, or piece of armor in the slot on the left. You need to add Lapis Lazuli as well, but this material is easy to harvest while you're out looking for Diamonds and other precious underground materials.

The strange lettering on the right is associated with the cost of your possible enchantments. The higher the cost (in levels), the better your potential enchantment will be. Items that are enchanted directly like this can end up with multiple effects, so you might get something really awesome out of this.

Items have three possible tiers of enchantments. Each tier costs 1 Lapis and 1 character level (so enchanting can cost you up to 3 levels per item). You're guaranteed at least one effect, which is listed in the description of the item when you hover over it in the enchantment interface. You may also get other effects, but this is determined randomly after you decide what level of enchantment to give the item.

Also, there are minimum total character levels required for each tier. Even though a full enchantment only costs 3 character levels, you need to be character Level 30 to unlock the ability to spend that much at once.

Select the cost you're willing to pay, click on that bar, and enjoy your enchanted item. Anything you enchant gets a pretty glow to show that it's magical. This makes it easier to sort enchanted items in your inventory, so you don't lose them, put them in a Chest to be forgotten, or make some other mistake.

Other Means of Enchanting

There are several other ways to enchant your equipment. Let's go over those.

Priests

Villages often have Priests. These special Villagers can add specific enchantments to your items. They'll show the enchantment in the trading interface, so you don't have to guess what you'll get. Add the item you want enchanted, pay some Emeralds, and that's that. This is a somewhat costly process in terms of resources, but you don't need to spend a single level. That's neat!

Enchanted Books

Craft Books and then enchant them at your Enchanting Table. You can stack multiple enchantments on a single Book and then transfer all of them onto another item when you have a combination that you like. You do this by working with an Anvil and using the Enchanted Book and the item you're trying to enchant. This costs additional levels.

Book enchanting is a costly process. You're likely to spend many more levels investing in the final item than you would by going to the Enchanting Table with the same item. However, Enchanted Books are useful. They're the best way to infuse an item with a specific combination of powerful enchantments. Otherwise, you're playing a game of chance each time you spend your levels. You might end up with a fairly weak enchantment and produce a Diamond Sword that doesn't do anything you care about. That's a bummer.

Anvils

Anvils let you combine items, including their enchantments. The primary item is saved, and the secondary item is destroyed, all of its pertinent enchantments transferred to the primary item. Enchantments that aren't allowed to affect a specific item are not transferred, so they're simply lost. Thus, you can't put armor enchantments on a Bow, even if you combine a Bow with an Enchanted Book that has multiple armor enchantments.

Anvils can also combine two regular items, as long as they're of the same type. Two Diamond Picks with the same enchantments could be used in the Anvil together. The second would be destroyed to repair the primary one.

Types of Enchantments

ENCHANTMENT TYPE	MAXIMUM RANK	EQUIPMENT TYPE	DESCRIPTION
Aqua Affinity	I	Helm	Increases underwater mining rate dramatically
Bane of Arthropods	V	Sword	Increases damage to Spiders, Cave Spiders, Silverfish, and Endermites by 2.5 per rank
Blast Protection	IV	Any Armor	Reduces explosive damage and reduces knockback
Depth Strider	III	Boots	Reduces water's slowing effect by one-third per level
Efficiency	V	Tools	Increases mining/harvesting speed by 30% per rank
Feather Falling	IV	Boots	Reduces damage from falling and Ender Pearls
Fire Aspect	II	Sword	Adds three rounds of burn damage (or seven at Rank II)
Fire Protection	IV	Any Armor	Reduces fire damage and decreases burning duration
Flame	I	Bow	Sets your Arrows on fire, adding three rounds of burning to targets hit
Fortune	III	Tools	Multiplies the number of drops from Coal, Diamonds, Emeralds, Nether Quartz, and Lapis Lazuli
Frost Walker	II	Boots	Freezes water as you walk over it, allowing for faster travel over rivers, ocean blocks, etc.
Infinity	I	Bow	You don't need more than one Arrow to fire your Bow forever
Knockback	II	Sword	Increases knockback against your targets
Looting	III	Sword	Slain monsters drop more regular loot and have a higher chance to drop their rare treasures
Luck of the Sea	III	Fishing Rod	Reduces the chance of getting poor results from fishing and raises the chance of getting higher-quality items
Lure	III	Fishing Rod	Greatly improves the speed at which you fish
Mending	I	Any	Uses collected experience to repair the enchanted item
Power	V	Bow	Increases Arrow damage by 25% (+25% more per rank)
Projectile Protection	IV	Any Armor	Reduces incoming damage from Arrows, Blazes, and Ghasts
Protection	IV	Any Armor	Reduces many types of damage taken
Punch	II	Bow	Increases knockback by Arrows
Respiration	III	Helm	Lets you stay underwater for 15 seconds more per rank, improves vision underwater, and slows suffocation
Sharpness	V	Sword	Increases damage by 1.25 per rank
Silk Touch	I	Tools	Allows you to harvest resources directly to get cobwebs, ore blocks, Ice, etc. (one of the most desirable enchantments)
Smite	V	Sword or Axe	Adds 2.5 damage per rank against undead monsters
Thorns	III	Any Armor	Adds a chance to wound attackers for 1-4 damage
Unbreaking	III	Any	Increases durability of the item

BREWING

Brewing is a fun way to make Potions. Potions help you endure tough fights, survive in dangerous areas, and damage some of your enemies. You can't brew early in the game because you need a number of tricky ingredients to get anywhere with this art. We'll tell you what to do!

Collect Ingredients to Make a Brewing Stand

The first step is to gather the primary ingredients you need. Nether Wart and Blaze Rods are two of the toughest (and most important) things on the list, so let's focus on these.

Both materials are found in the Nether. Make a Nether Portal and bring ample supplies through to the other side. Seek out a Nether Fortress, and then scour the place for Chests and for stairways with Soul Sand nearby. These are the only two places in the game where Nether Wart is available. Not all of the Chests have Nether Wart, and not all Nether Fortresses have the Stair gardens. Finding these items is luck of the draw.

Blazes, on the other hand, are found frequently in Nether Fortresses. Fight them with ranged attacks, or retreat to draw them forward. Kill as many as you can to get Blaze Rods.

Once you have a few of these goodies, make a Nether Wart garden. You don't want to search Nether Fortresses every time you need more Nether Wart, so don't do any brewing just yet. Wait until you have an adequate Nether Wart garden.

Sadly, you can't use Bone Meal to speed up your garden; getting a large garden going is a fairly time-intensive process, but it's well worth your investment.

Break all of your initial Nether Wart into Seeds, and plant all of them. Do the same thing with the yields from your initial planting, and continue to increase the garden from there, taking only one or two Nether Wart at first to play with, and then more as your garden reaches a substantial size.

Now, craft a Brewing Stand, a Cauldron, and some Glass Bottles. Fill your Cauldron with water. This is useful for filling Water Bottles, and they look cool in your brewing area anyway. Having an infinite water source nearby isn't a bad thing, either.

Place all of your crafted items in one room with a Chest or two, and grab your Nether Wart. With these and a number of other odds and ends, you're ready to start brewing.

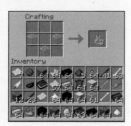

Blaze Powder acts as a fuel source for your brewing work. Every piece of this powder lets you brew 20 ingredients' worth of Potions, so it lasts fairly well!

Types of Potions

Potions come in two stages. You make the first stage by interacting with the Brewing Stand and adding a Water Bottle with some ingredients. After adding your ingredients, wait for the brewing to finish, and collect your finished Potion.

There are five basic Potions, as follows:

BASE POTIONS

POTION NAME	INGREDIENTS	EFFECT
Awkward Potion	Water Bottle + Nether Wart	Builds into much more powerful Potions
Mundane Potion (Extended)	Water Bottle + Redstone	Used to make a Potion of Weakness (Extended)
Mundane Potion	Water Bottle + one of the following: Blaze Powder, Ghast Tear, Glistering Melon, Magma Cream, Spider Eye, Sugar	Used to make a Potion of Weakness
Potion of Weakness	Water Bottle + Fermented Spider Eye	Reduces melee attacks by 0.5 damage
Thick Potion	Water Bottle + Glowstone Dust	Used to make a Potion of Weakness

So far, it doesn't look like brewing is very useful. You can make a Potion that reduces your own melee damage—yay? But trust us, this gets much better.

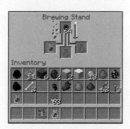

After you have a primary Potion, use the Brewing Stand again. This time, you add one of the primary Potions instead of a Water Bottle. Now you start having fun!

SECONDARY POTIONS

POTION NAME	INGREDIENTS	EFFECT
Potion of Fire Resistance	Awkward Potion + Magma Cream	Three minutes of fire immunity
Potion of Healing	Awkward Potion + Glistering Melon	Restores 4 damage
Potion of Leaping	Awkward Potion + Rabbit's Foot	Boosts jumping height and reduces falling damage for three minutes
Potion of Night Vision	Awkward Potion + Golden Carrot	Lets you see as if the area is perfectly lit for three minutes
Potion of Poison	Awkward Potion + Spider Eye	Poisons a target for 1 damage every 1.5 seconds (for 45 seconds)

POTION NAME	INGREDIENTS	EFFECT
Potion of Regeneration	Awkward Potion + Ghast Tear	Restores 2 damage every 2.4 seconds (for 45 seconds)
Potion of Strength	Awkward Potion + Blaze Powder	Adds 130% to your melee damage for three minutes
Potion of Swiftness	Awkward Potion + Sugar	Increases speed and jumping distance by 20% for three minutes
Potion of Water Breathing	Awkward Potion + Pufferfish	You don't need to breathe underwater for three minutes
Potion of Weakness (Extended)	Awkward Potion + Fermented Spider Eye	Reduces melee damage by 0.5 for four minutes

Now you start to see a lot of possibilities. Potions of Healing let you restore health instantly, unlike food. Fire Resistance is useful when you fight Blazes and Ghasts in the Nether. Regeneration is critical to your survival in boss fights, against Withers or the Ender Dragon.

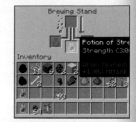

Nether Wart and a few key ingredients allow you to make extremely useful Potions, and you can brew even more powerful versions if you're willing to spend a bit more time and effort. Read on!

TERTIARY POTIONS

POTION NAME	INGREDIENTS	EFFECT
Potion of Fire Resistance (Extended)	Potion of Fire Resistance + Redstone	Eight minutes of fire immunity
Potion of Harming	Potion of Healing or Poison + Fermented Spider Eye	Inflicts 6 damage
Potion of Harming II	Potion of Healing II or Poison II + Fermented Spider Eye or Glowstone Dust	Inflicts 12 damage
Potion of Healing II	Potion of Healing + Glowstone Dust	Restores 8 damage
Potion of Invisibility	Potion of Night Vision + Fermented Spider Eye	Turns you invisible (but not your weapon or armor) for three minutes
Potion of Invisibility (Extended)	Potion of Night Vision (Extended) + Fermented Spider Eye	Turns you invisible (but not your weapon or armor) for eight minutes
Potion of Leaping (Extended)	Potion of Leaping + Redstone	Lets you jump higher for eight minutes
Potion of Leaping II	Potion of Leaping + Glowstone Dust	You can jump even higher
Potion of Night Vision (Extended)	Potion of Night Vision + Redstone	Lets you see as if the area is perfectly lit for eight minutes
Potion of Poison (Extended)	Potion of Poison + Redstone	Poisons a target for 1 damage every two seconds (for two minutes)
Potion of Poison II	Potion of Poison + Glowstone Dust	Poisons a target for 1 damage every second (for 22 seconds)
Potion of Regeneration (Extended)	Potion of Regeneration + Redstone	Restores 2 damage every 2.4 seconds (for two minutes)
Potion of Regeneration II	Potion of Regeneration + Glowstone Dust	Restores 2 damage every 1.2 seconds (for 16 seconds)
Potion of Slowness	Potion of Fire Resistance or Swiftness + Fermented Spider Eye	Slows movement for 1.5 minutes
Potion of Slowness (Extended)	Potion of Fire Resistance (Extended) or Swiftness (Extended) + Redstone or Fermented Spider Eye	Slows movement for three minutes
Potion of Strength (Extended)	Potion of Strength + Redstone	Adds 130% to your melee damage for eight minutes
Potion of Strength II	Potion of Strength + Glowstone Dust	Adds 260% to your melee damage for 1.5 minutes
Potion of Swiftness (Extended)	Potion of Swiftness + Redstone	Increases speed and jumping distance by 20% for eight minutes
Potion of Swiftness II	Potion of Swiftness + Glowstone Dust	Increases speed and jumping distance by 40% for 1.5 minutes
Potion of Water Breathing (Extended)	Potion of Water Breathing + Redstone	You don't need to breathe underwater for eight minutes

There are a few simple ways to remember how the Potion system works. Everything starts with Nether Wart. Your initial Potion should almost always be

made by adding Nether Wart to a Water Bottle. Done.

For Tier 2 Potions, use your Awkward Potion from the first stage and add an ingredient to get whatever base effect you need. Look at our Secondary Potion table to figure out what you need/want.

To make Potions last longer, add Redstone to a Secondary Potion.

To make Potions stronger, add Glowstone Dust to a Secondary Potion.

To make Potions work when thrown, use Gunpowder.

Gunpowder turns normal Potions into Splash Potions. This makes Potions of Weakness and Potions of Poison useful against specific enemies. Potions of Poison II really add damage over time.

If you want a Potion to have effects that target an area and last longer, try to craft Lingering Potions. Start with a Splash Potion of the type you want, and then brew it with Dragon's Breath to create a Lingering version of the effect. When thrown, this spreads out on the ground and delivers its effects over time against anything that stands in the affected spot.

POISON DOESN'T ALWAYS WORK

Don't try to poison Spiders, Cave Spiders, or the Ender Dragon. They don't take any damage from Poison.

Skeletons, Wither Skeletons, Withers, Zombies, and Zombie Pigmen are immune to Poison and don't take damage from Potions of Harm, either. In fact, they heal from them instead! However, they take damage from Splash Potions of Healing.

Witches take reduced Poison damage, so it's not worth your time to use Poison against them.

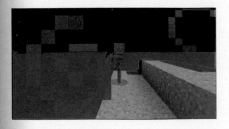

People often brew Splash Potions of Healing so they can heal themselves as quickly as possible. Tossing the Potion into the ground at your feet gives you health much faster than just about any other option. It's *way* faster than food and considerably faster than drinking a Potion of Healing in a normal way.

TRAVELING THE WORLD

There are several ways to get around the world, and it's always nice to have options. Most of the methods we describe here cost more in terms of either crafted resources or food, but they're worthwhile when you can get where you're going faster and without any hassles.

Walking, Sprinting, and Jumping

Walking is the most basic travel method, but it's slow. Monsters easily catch up with you, and that means you end up fighting more often and taking damage.

Sprinting is faster by a fair margin—it's almost one-third faster. Although you need to eat more often, it's useful to sprint once your character has a decent supply of food. Jumping and sprinting together makes your character move even faster, though the hunger increase is more substantial.

For the best possible walking and sprinting speed, use Potions of Speed.

Mounts

Horses are the best mounts for speedy travel. They vary in terms of maximum speed, but even the slow ones are pretty darn good. The best Horses are amazing and should be bred with other speedy Horses so you have a stable of racers. They're perfect for long-distance travel aboveground.

Boats

Don't swim across large stretches of water. It's painfully slow. Construct a Boat and bring enough spare Wood to make more Boats in case your first one gets destroyed; this happens easily if you bump into anything heavy. To provide a nice impact cushion for your Boat, plunk down a piece of Soul Sand in front of it.

Boats are decently quick once they get going.

Railways

Railways are very fast. Put down a long stretch of regular Rails, and drop one Powered Rail with a Redstone Torch every 32 blocks. Your Minecarts rush across distance quite well in this manner, whether you're aboveground or down in the depths.

Descending tracks have even less trouble maintaining speed, but flat railways are the easiest to create.

Ender Pearls

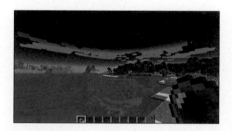

Throw Ender Pearls to teleport your character. This is a resource-intensive travel method, so it's best reserved for when you're in a tough spot and need to escape. Use these items to get away from battle, cross ravines, or reach really tricky spots in a cavern.

Be warned! Ender Pearls deal damage to your character when you teleport. They're not for the faint of heart. Plus, they have a slight chance to spawn a monster when you throw them (the tiny but malicious Endermites).

The Nether Shortcut

The Nether and the Overworld are connected. A Portal you place in one of these worlds always corresponds to a sister Portal in the other. The interesting thing about this is that the locations are related in relative direction—this requires an explanation.

If you make two Portals near your base, there will be two Nether Portals created in the Nether. If your Portals in the Overworld are directly north/south of each other, then their Nether counterparts will also be directly north/south of each other.

However, the *number of blocks between* the Portals in each world is not the same. One block of distance in the Nether equals eight blocks in the Overworld. If you want to create bases far away from home in the Overworld, take a short trip inside the Nether and make a new Portal somewhere else. You pop out fairly far away in the Overworld and can explore someplace completely new!

TRADING

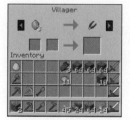

In "Special Areas," we talked about Villages where your character can meet people and trade with them by using Emeralds (or giving them items that they request to earn their Emeralds). The more you trade with these individuals, the more they'll be willing to buy and sell with you. Do your best to sell as much as possible, and only buy items that are extremely useful (because everything is quite overpriced).

Armorer

TIER	ITEM (BUYS)	QUANTITY	PRICE	ITEM (SELLS)	QUANTITY	PRICE
1	Coal	16-24	1	Iron Helmet	1	4-6
2	Iron Ingot	7-9	1	Iron Chestplate	1	10-14
3	Diamond	3-4	1	Enchanted Diamond Chestplate	1	16-19
4	—	—	—	Chainmail Boots	1	5-7
4	—	—	—	Chainmail Leggings	1	9-11
4	—	—	—	Chainmail Helmet	1	5-7
4	—	—	—	Chainmail Chestplate	1	11-15

Butcher

TIER	BUYS ITEM	QUANTITY	PRICE	SELLS ITEM	QUANTITY	PRICE
1	Raw Porkchop	14-18	1	—	—	—
1	Raw Chicken	14-18	1	—	—	—
2	Coal	16-24	1	Cooked Porkchop	5-7	1
2	—	—	—	Cooked Chicken	6-8	1

Cartographer

TIER	BUYS ITEM	QUANTITY	PRICE	SELLS ITEM	QUANTITY	PRICE
1	Paper	24-36	1	—	—	—
2	Compass	1	1	—	—	—
3	—	—	—	Empty Map	1	7-11
4	—	—	—	Ocean Explorer Map	1	12-20
4	—	—	—	Woodland Explorer Map	1	16-28

Cleric

TIER	BUYS ITEM	QUANTITY	PRICE	SELLS ITEM	QUANTITY	PRICE
1	Rotten Flesh	36-40	1	—	—	—
1	Gold Ingot	8-10	1	—	—	—
2	—	—	—	Redstone Dust	1-4	1
2	—	—	—	Lapis Lazuli	1-2	1
3	—	—	—	Ender Peal	1	4-7
3	—	—	—	Glowstone	1-3	1
4	—	—	—	Bottle o' Enchanting	1	3-11

Farmer

TIER	BUYS ITEM	QUANTITY	PRICE	SELLS ITEM	QUANTITY	PRICE
1	Wheat	18-22	1	Bread	2-4	1
1	Potato	15-19	1	—	—	—
1	Carrot	15-19	1	—	—	—
2	Pumpkin	8-13	1	Pumpkin Pie	2-3	1
3	Melon	7-12	1	Apple	5	1
4	—	—	—	Cookie	6	1
4	—	—	—	Cake	1	1

Fisherman

TIER	BUYS ITEM	QUANTITY	PRICE	SELLS ITEM	QUANTITY	PRICE
1	String	15-20	1	Cooked Fish	6	1/6
1	Coal	16-24	1	—	—	—
2	—	—	—	Enchanted Fishing Rod	1	7-8

Fletcher

TIER	BUYS ITEM	QUANTITY	PRICE	SELLS ITEM	QUANTITY	PRICE
1	String	15-20	1	Arrow	8-12	1
2	—	—	—	Bow	1	2-3
2	—	—	—	Flint	6-10	10 Gravel/1 Emerald

Leatherworker

TIER	BUYS ITEM	QUANTITY	PRICE	SELLS ITEM	QUANTITY	PRICE
1	Leather	9-12	1	Leather Pants	1	2-4
2	—	—	—	Enchanted Leather Tunic	1	7-12
3	—	—	—	Saddle	1	8-10

Librarian

TIER	BUYS ITEM	QUANTITY	PRICE	SELLS ITEM	QUANTITY	PRICE
1	Paper	24-36	1	Enchanted Book	1	5-64
2	Book	8-10	1	Compass	1	10-12
2	—	—	—	Bookshelf	1	3-4
3	Written Book	2	1	Clock	1	10-12
3	—	—	—	Glass	3-5	1
4	—	—	—	Enchanted Book	1	5-64
5	—	—	—	Enchanted Book	1	5-64
6	—	—	—	Name Tag	1	20-22

Shepherd

TIER	BUYS ITEM	QUANTITY	PRICE	SELLS ITEM	QUANTITY	PRICE
1	White Wool	16-22	1	Shears	1	3-4
2	—	—	—	Colored Wool	1	1-2

Toolsmith

TIER	BUYS ITEM	QUANTITY	PRICE	SELLS ITEM	QUANTITY	PRICE
1	Coal	16-24	1	Enchanted Iron Shovel	1	5-7
2	Iron Ingot	7-9	1	Enchanted Iron Pickaxe	1	9-11
3	Diamond	3-4	1	Enchanted Diamond Pickaxe	1	12-15

Weaponsmith

TIER	BUYS ITEM	QUANTITY	PRICE	SELLS ITEM	QUANTITY	PRICE
1	Coal	16-24	1	Iron Axe	1	6-8
2	Iron Ingot	7-9	1	Enchanted Iron Sword	1	9-10
3	Diamond	3-4	1	Enchanted Diamond Sword	1	12-15
3	—	—	—	Enchanted Diamond Axe	1	9-12

THE NETHER

The Nether is a world of Redstone, fire, and strange beasts. It's possible to enter this dimension after gathering several special materials from the Overworld. After you make a Nether Portal, it's possible to travel back and forth between these dimensions at will.

Monsters from the Nether

- Blazes
- Ghasts
- Magma Cubes
- Wither Skeletons
- Zombie Pigmen

Resources in the Nether

- Glowstone
- Nether Quartz
- Nether Wart
- Netherrack
- Soul Sand

Creating a Nether Portal

To access the Nether, you need to construct a Nether Portal. To do this, your character must have access to a source of fire (Flint and Steel), Diamonds (for a Diamond Pick), and Obsidian. Once you have access to all of these materials, mine 14 blocks of Obsidian and bring them to your base. Construct a Nether Portal by placing four blocks of Obsidian in a line on the ground. Build the two ends into pillars of Obsidian that are five blocks high, and then fill in the gap on top with two connecting blocks. Light the inner hollow space of this Obsidian frame—use your Flint and Steel to do this.

Now that the Nether Portal is active, you can jump into it and wait for the teleportation spell to zip you between worlds. Don't jump out from the Portal on the other side until you make sure you won't fall into Lava or suffer any other ill effects.

What to Bring into the Nether

The Nether is one of the most dangerous places in *Minecraft*. Light is dim, Lava is plentiful and flows faster than usual, and monsters are deadlier than in the Overworld. It's easy to die, so take only what you need to survive. Don't bring items you can't afford to lose.

Diamond tools are not required in the Nether. You don't need to cut through any hard materials, so Iron Pickaxes are sufficient. Bring those, some Swords, a Bow, Arrows, Wood and Cobblestone (neither of which is found naturally in the Nether), food, Torches, Flint and Steel, and anything else that might seem useful. The weapons are necessary to fight the Nether's monsters, and some items are standard equipment for any mining or exploration trip. Bring Flint and Steel on any Nether trip; if your Nether Portal gets snuffed out over there (for example, by getting hit by a Ghast's fireball), you have to relight it.

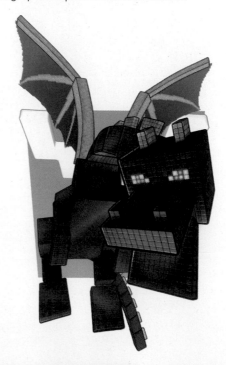

When you arrive, make a central base as close to your Portal as possible. Wall it off with Cobblestone from back home. Cobblestone doesn't burn; Netherrack, the natural stone of this area, does! Any long-term structure you build in the Nether should be made from heavier, non-flammable materials.

Your base needs to have a Crafting Table, Furnace, Chests, and preferably an Ender Chest once you can craft those. Put your best loot into the Chests each time you take a break to ensure you don't lose anything if your character falls or tunnels into Lava. In the Nether, this is not a rare occurrence.

New Rules Compared to the Overworld

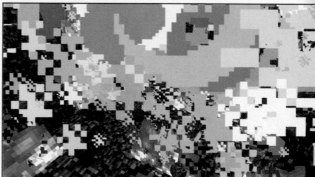

You can't use water in the Nether. It boils away instantly, so that's pretty useless.

Beds aren't great to bring, either, unless you plan to use them as makeshift TNT. When you try to sleep in a Bed, the whole thing explodes. It's better to avoid the situation entirely unless you're interested in blowing things up with a piece of bedroom furniture.

What to Do in the Nether

Besides fun and exploration, you can accomplish several goals when you get to the Nether. Harvest Netherrack, Nether Quartz, Soul Sand, and Glowstone as soon as possible. These are fairly common materials, and you can't find them anywhere back home. Collect an ample supply of each.

Netherrack is the least useful. It burns forever, so you can make cool fire pits and fireplaces with it, but that's about it. The stone is way too ugly to be useful for nice bases or homes.

Nether Quartz is lovely. The blocks you make with it are really cool-looking, though it takes a good while to farm enough Nether Quartz to make large buildings. We recommend making a wizard's tower out of Nether Quartz. So cool!

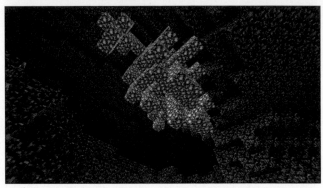

Glowstone is a bright material used to create blocks that are better than Torches; they work underwater and shine quite clearly even from long distances. Glowstone breaks into chunks when you mine it, so a Pickaxe with Silk Touch is useful, though not required.

Soul Sand is hard to walk on. It's fun for making traps, slowing other players and monsters, and for a few specific tasks, like summoning the Wither. Look for Soul Sand when you travel, and get at least a partial stack of it.

Locating and Assaulting Nether Fortresses

Nether Fortresses contain even more valuable materials than the Nether itself. Blaze Rods and Nether Wart are both amazingly useful, and you won't find either of these without going to a Nether Fortress.

Search for Nether Fortresses by walking east or west from your starting point. Nether Fortresses are aligned north to south and are built along lines that run the entire length of the Nether. Once you bump into a Nether Fortress, you're set! Additional forts are located north *and* south from there, so exploration isn't as challenging.

Additionally, Nether Fortresses are large enough that you won't usually wander past them. They're made of compressed Netherrack, called Nether Brick. Their Fences, Stairs, and sundry monsters make them major landmarks.

Fight carefully through Nether Fortresses to snag Nether Wart from small growing areas near some of the Stairs, and collect material from slain enemies. Wither Skeletons drop Wither Skeleton Skulls if you're especially lucky. You need three of them to summon a special boss monster, and it takes a long time to gather them.

Grinding

Getting three skulls from Wither Skeletons takes more time than almost any other gathering task in *Minecraft*. It's tough, so do everything you can to improve your chances of finding these rare items.

Use enchanted Swords to deal maximum damage versus undead. It's even better if these weapons have Looting III on them. It doesn't quite double the rate of skull drops, but it's still a 60% improvement! Not bad.

If too few Wither Skeletons appear in your current Nether Fortress, don't be afraid to search for a new one. Thanks to differences in their layouts, some forts spawn more Wither Skeletons than others.

Ranged weapons are a must in these forts. Blazes have ranged attacks, and Wither Skeletons can too if they pick up a Bow. Also, some regular Skeletons spawn in Nether Fortresses, so be on the lookout for them.

You'll find Magma Cubes near the base of these areas, and they too drop useful items. Fight them at range to avoid damage, or go in for melee attacks if you're well-armored and feeling lucky.

Not all Nether Fortresses have gardens of Nether Wart, but even the ones that don't often contain Chests of loot. These can yield Diamonds, pieces of metal, Gold equipment, more Nether Wart (yay!), Saddles, and Horse Armor. Because of this, you can collect your first Nether Wart and start a garden of your own by searching carefully for Chests and growing areas along the steps.

Destroying a Wither

Once you hunt enough Wither Skeletons to get the three Wither Skeleton Skulls you need, bring them back to the Overworld with a supply of Soul Sand.

Choose a spot for battle in advance. Don't do this near your base, because the Wither's explosive attacks will wreck the whole area. Underground areas are a bit easier, because you won't have to navigate massive Dirt chasms and such while racing back toward the Wither.

Use a Potion of Night Vision before the battle. Torches don't survive the Wither's explosions, and you won't want to fight in pitch-darkness.

Also, bring the following useful items: a Diamond Sword (with Smite), Splash Potions of Healing, Strength Potions, an enchanted Bow (with Power), Diamond armor (Protection IV is almost a must), and an Enchanted Golden Apple.

To summon your Wither, build a small altar of Soul Sand—one block on the bottom, three horizontal blocks stacked above it. Then place the three skulls on top of the altar. This brings the Wither into being. Run! Immediately!

The Wither charges to full health and detonates the area around the altar when it reaches full power. You don't want to be around for this blast.

After you hear the strange explosion, return for battle. Use your Bow to reduce the Wither to half health. This isn't too hard, because the Wither's ranged attacks take a moment to reach you, so ranged combat gives you an advantage. Dodge the explosive skulls the Wither sends your way, and fire back as often as you can.

Drink potions to restore health if you get behind, and then use your Enchanted Golden Apple and Strength Potions when it's time to go for melee attacks. Withers become immune to ranged damage at half health, so you have to finish them with your blade.

Once you're buffed with the Enchanted Golden Apple's and Strength Potions' positive effects, charge toward the Wither and go for broke. Attack aggressively and kill it while the Apple's regenerative effects are still working.

The Nether Star that drops is required to make Beacons, and these offer really neat bonuses for your character and any friends. Plus, you can get multiple achievements by going to the Nether, farming materials, summoning a Wither, and killing it. It's all worthwhile!

Light a Beacon

Once you have a Nether Star, return to your base and craft a huge pyramid of blocks. The largest effective pyramid has to contain 164 blocks of Iron, Gold, or Diamond. Each block costs nine Ingots of the material in question, so it's quite a daunting amount of resources to gather.

You can always construct your pyramid in tiers. The first level only needs to have the Beacon on top and then nine blocks in a square beneath it.

That's 81 Ingots of material, so it isn't too bad. Once you have that, save up more resources until you can craft the second stage. Go on from there so you don't have to wait until you have the entire thing ready before you get the perks of an active Beacon.

You can cluster multiple Beacons together by placing them on a large pyramid. In the end, this saves on space and materials by quite a large margin. A 2x2 top with four Beacons, with a 4x4 tier beneath it, is much more useful than a single large pyramid with one Beacon.

What Do Beacons Do?

Completed Beacons light the sky and look wonderful, but that's the least of their effects. Once they're constructed, you turn on Beacons by adding a single piece of Iron, Gold, Emerald, or Diamond. This activates a buff that influences your character and any friends within a certain range.

RANGE OF EACH PYRAMID

Tier I	20 Blocks
Tier II	30 Blocks
Tier III	40 Blocks
Tier IV	50 Blocks

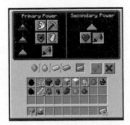

A Beacon's range reaches horizontally by the number of blocks listed in the preceding table. However, the Beacon's powers reach upward (vertically) by 250 blocks. This is why many players construct Beacons near the bottom of the Overworld. Note that your Beacon has to have open access to the sky to work properly, so you have to dig a hole down toward the bedrock to let the Beacon shine free.

Normally, Beacons give you one power each. As you make larger pyramids, you get more choices for powers, but you don't get any secondary powers until Tier IV. These maximum-sized pyramids let you make strong primary powers or get a free secondary Regeneration effect.

Some of the primary effects are locked until you make a certain pyramid size. The initial choices are Speed and Haste. Resistance and Jump Boost require a Tier II pyramid. Strength requires a Tier III pyramid.

POSITIVE EFFECTS FROM EACH BEACON (CHOOSE ONE)

Haste	Faster mining
Jump Boost	Higher and longer jumps
Resistance	Improved armor rating
Speed	Faster walking and sprinting
Strength	Increased melee damage

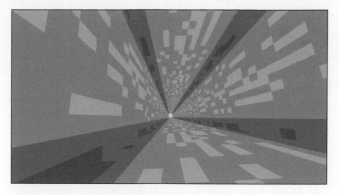

For the best effect, craft four Beacons and use the wider pyramids to get almost all of these buffs. A Tier II pyramid built in this fashion needs to have "only" 52 blocks but gets you four primary powers. That's less than one-third the cost of a single-Beacon Tier IV pyramid.

If you ever get enough material together for a four-Beacon Tier IV pyramid, life is great. The increased range really helps, and your total number of effects makes it a joy to mine, work, or farm near the pyramid.

THE END

The End is another special dimension in *Minecraft*. You cannot get there at first, but Endermen help you reach it eventually.

Endermen and Eyes of Ender

Endermen are rare monsters, but you find them here and there throughout the Overworld. Large, dark areas that are at least three blocks high have a chance to spawn Endermen at any time.

Fight these enemies by attacking their feet. This prevents them from teleporting. Don't use ranged attacks, and don't look them in the eyes, because that makes them aggressive before you're ready to fight.

Kill enough Endermen, and you start to accrue Ender Pearls. These items are useful for instant teleportation. Throw them at your target, and bam!—you're there. This causes damage to your character, but it's still fun.

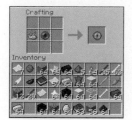

That said, you're best off saving most of your Ender Pearls; they're crafted into Eyes of Ender. These items help you find Strongholds and then activate Portals located only within those Strongholds.

Craft more than 12 Eyes of Ender when you want to reach the End. Use the Eyes to locate the nearest Stronghold, attack that base, and look for the room with the End Portal. This is where Silverfish spawn. Track them back to that room, destroy their Monster Spawner, and then fill in the 12 slots around the End Portal with your Eyes of Ender. Doing so opens the way—you can now get to the End.

Note that you can't get back, so don't step through the Portal until you stash your best items at home.

Going to the End

End Portals stay activated once you've found them and used your Eyes of Ender. That's good news, because your trip to the End won't always go well. We recommend not taking all of your good equipment for your first trip there. You should get your bearings, make sure your spawn location is "safe," and try to build a starting base with your first life there.

The game's final boss is here; it's called the Ender Dragon. This thing is so powerful that it breaks most blocks by flying through them. Obsidian and the End Stone that dominate this dimension are both exceptions. Bring enough Obsidian to quickly create a small room beside the Portal where you spawn (not *on* it). Form this room and drop an Ender Chest there, if you have one. This lets you harvest End Stone and transport it back to the Overworld even before you're able to kill the Ender Dragon. We'll discuss strategies for fighting this boss in a moment.

Dragon's Breath

Dragon's Breath is a shimmering material left behind after the Ender

Dragon breathes at you. Look on the ground for it! If you see any, rush over and use Glass Bottles to harvest as much of the Dragon's Breath as you can. It's a

primary ingredient for making Lingering Potions (these turn your Splash Potions into area-of-effect items that last over time).

The Outer Islands

There are outer islands in the End. You can't get to these islands by flying or throwing Ender Pearls. The distance to reach them is way

too far for that. Instead, you reach the islands by taking an End Gateway. These spawn near the central Portal every time you kill an Ender Dragon. This

is one of the reasons it's sometimes worth respawning the boss so that you can fight it again. Given enough time and effort, you can cause up to 20 of these Gateways to appear, each leading to different areas on the periphery of the End.

To go through a Gateway, throw an Ender Pearl into it. There isn't enough room for you to get in between the blocks on your own, and this method is a quick way to go through.

End Cities

The outer islands can be explored after you've defeated the Ender Dragon, when it's relatively safe. A prominent feature on the islands is the End City. Look for

these structures and explore them carefully when you discover one of them. They're filled with Chests of loot, which makes them quite valuable. However, they're guarded. Expect to encounter Shulkers, disguised as Purpur blocks.

Chorus Plants

The outer islands have Chorus Plants and Chorus Flowers. These are like Cacti in the regular Overworld. Destroy the bottom of the plant to bring down

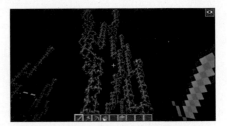

the entire formation. The Chorus Flowers can be replanted onto End Stone to make them grow.

After you've gathered End Stone and Chorus Flowers, you can make your own farms of these plant formations without too much trouble. Manual harvest of them is easy via chopping down the bottom block of the tree, but more advanced farming methods work better. Water pools can be made to help drag the falling plants to the center of an area for easy harvesting. You can put a Hopper and Chest below or gather on your own.

Chorus Fruit restores four points of hunger when eaten and has a chance to teleport the user a short distance away.

Smelting Chorus Fruit turns it into Popped Chorus Fruit. Though now inedible, these items are used to create Purpur blocks and End Rods.

End Ships and Elytra

Some End Cities have a pier that spawns an End Ship beside it. These too have great loot, including a few things you aren't going to see often on their own. End

Ships have more Shulkers to contend with, but they're also filled with Potions, a Brewing Stand, an Item Frame of Elytra, and a Dragon Head. This is must-have material, so hunt aggressively each time you encounter an End City.

Elytra are Chest items that grant gliding powers to your character. When you're falling, tap the Jump button to start a glide. Your Elytra lose durability when in use, but these items can be repaired by merging two together or using Leather and an Anvil to reforge them (this being a much less-costly method in the long run).

Gliding is really, really fun. There's something magical about leaping off of mountains and towers and soaring over the land. Keep your view slightly above the horizon to glide for as long as possible, or dive down to gain speed (but at the cost of your total glide time *and* distance covered).

If you try to raise your angle of flight too high, you can effectively stall out. This is dangerous, because you can take falling damage while using the Elytra if you hit the ground while going too fast. Be careful!

Start off with gentle flights to test the mechanics of the wings, and then get bolder as you become comfortable with the way everything works.

Fighting Ender Dragons

Once you're comfortable going to the End and getting your bearings, start arming yourself for the final engagement. You want a Bow with the best Power enchantment you can get. A few stacks of Arrows won't hurt, though you likely won't need all of them unless things go very badly.

A good Sword helps, too. The Ender Dragon is too mobile to kill with a Sword, but Endermen also inhabit the End, and they're an additional threat. Swords should have either Fire Aspect or the highest possible damage output.

Diamond armor with Protection IV is your smartest bet for safety. Your helm can be either a Pumpkin or a Diamond Helm. The latter is better for survival. Pumpkins are better for avoiding extra fights with Endermen, because they don't attack when you look at them. This is a matter of personal preference.

Potions of Healing and Regeneration are both useful during the battle. Golden Apples or Enchanted Golden Apples are great, too.

Ender Pearls are helpful as well. They let you teleport from smaller islands over to the main island, possibly saving you if you're knocked over the edge during the boss fight.

Keep a Bucket of Water handy so that you can cushion your fall if you're knocked high into the air. Deploy the water directly under your character right before you land. This saves you from massive damage when things go badly!

Slaying the Dragon

A series of Ender Crystals keeps the Ender Dragon alive and healthy. Each crystal is placed on top of an Obsidian pillar, like the ones on which you arrive. Destroying these is a critical part of the boss fight. If you don't break the crystals, the Ender Dragon can stay at or near full health indefinitely, despite your best efforts.

Watch for the healing beams that emanate from the Ender Crystals. Their energy flows toward the Dragon. Trace it back to figure out where the crystals are, and use your Bow to shoot at them until they explode.

A couple of the crystals are usually protected by Iron Bars. They can't be shot as easily as the others. You have to either pull the Dragon away

from them so that it doesn't get much healing, or you have to quickly build your way up to the protected crystals so that they can be destroyed directly. It's challenging, but may need to be done if the crystals are well-placed and providing substantial healing.

When you're done destroying as many crystals as you can, turn the Bow on him! Head shots are the way to go if you want to win this fight anytime soon; they inflict quadruple damage. The best way to achieve these hits is to wait for the Ender Dragon to come after your character. Nail it in the head with a fully charged attack. Get another shot in immediately afterward, and then watch the Dragon fly away. Chase it and wait for the boss to turn and come after you again. Repeat your attacks and wait for the kill!

A risky trick is to dig a small hole, place a Bed into it when the Dragon is ready to charge you, and set the Bed off just before the Dragon attacks. You need to have a safe spot to jump when this happens, so the technique requires practice, setup time, and precision. It isn't a technique for first-time Dragon killers, but it shaves tons of time off of the battle once you know how to do it reliably.

Another tactics is to craft Ender Crystals (with Glass, Eyes of Ender, and Ghast Tears). Place these is spots where the Dragon is likely to charge, and then detonate the crystals as the Dragon passes. They do very high damage.

The Aftermath

The Ender Dragon drops so much experience that even a character with no experience will gain dozens of levels almost immediately. It's better to bring a few friends to spread around the experience, or bring in materials for enchanting work so you can enchant multiple items and still max out your experience.

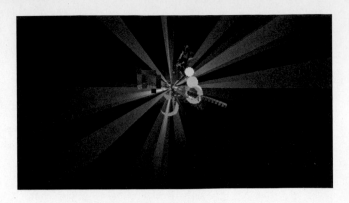

The Ender Dragon also drops a Dragon Egg. This doesn't have a use (yet). However, you can collect it. Clicking on the Dragon Egg causes it to teleport. Do this one time to get the Egg away from the End Portal, which appears to take you home. You don't want the Egg to fall into the End Portal and break.

After the Dragon Egg teleports, track it down. It sometimes appears below the ground. Tunnel until you find it, and then get two blocks beneath it. Destroy the End Stone there, place a Torch, and then destroy the block above to drop the Dragon Egg onto the Torch. This turns the Egg into a resource and allows you to collect it.

You've now completed the End. Come back here to farm Endermen or End Stone, and use your new End Portal to return home at any time.

If you craft Ender Crystals and place one on each side of the Exit Portal, you can respawn the Ender Dragon. This is done to practice killing it, to harvest Dragon's Breath (in Glass Bottles), or for pure fun.

ADVANCEMENTS

Advancements are mini-goals to let you know you're on the right track in *Minecraft*. These rewards are available in the PC and console versions of the game. They help guide you toward the various activities within the game, especially when you're a new player and don't know what to do. By the time you figure out how to get most of these, you'll be an expert at *Minecraft*!

ADVANCEMENT LIST

ADVANCEMENT	REQUIREMENTS AND TIPS
A Balanced Diet	Eat every type of food.
A Furious Cocktail	Have every type of Potion effect applied to your character at the same time.
A Seedy Place	Plant Beetroots, Melons, Nether Wart, Pumpkins, or Wheat.
A Terrible Fortress	Enter a Nether Fortress.
Acquire Hardware	Get an Iron Ingot.
Adventure	Kill or be killed by any creature.
Adventuring Time	Visit every type of standard biome.
Beaconator	Make a Tier IV pyramid for a Beacon and stand within its area of effect.
Best Friends Forever	Tame a Horse, Llama, Ocelot, Parrot, or Wolf.
Bring Home the Beacon	Make any size of pyramid for a Beacon and stand within its area of effect.
Cover Me with Diamonds	Craft or find your first piece of Diamond armor.
Diamonds!	Get a Diamond in your inventory.
Enchanter	Enchant an item at the Enchanting Table.
Eye Spy	Enter a Stronghold.
Free the End	Kill an Ender Dragon.
Getting an Upgrade	Get a Stone Pickaxe.
Great View From Up Here	Move at least 50 vertical blocks while the Levitation effect is applied to your character.
Hired Help	Summon an Iron Golem.
Hot Stuff	Fill a Bucket with Lava.
How Did We Get Here?	Have every effect from Potions and general status ailments influence you at the same time.
Ice Bucket Challenge	Get your first block of Obsidian.
Into Fire	Get a Blaze Rod from the Nether.
Isn't It Iron Pick	Get your first Iron Pick.
Local Brewery	Get your first item from a Brewing Stand.
Minecraft	Make your first Crafting Table and add it to your inventory.
Monster Hunter	Kill any aggressive monster.
Monsters Hunted	Hunt every type of monster in the game.
Nether	Enter the Nether.

ADVANCEMENT	REQUIREMENTS AND TIPS
Not Today, Thank You	Deflect a projectile with a Shield.
Postmortal	Use a Totem of Undying to cheat death.
Remote Getaway	Walk into the End Gateway or throw an Ender Pearl through it.
Return to Sender	Kill a Ghast by reflecting its fireball back into itself.
Serious Dedication	Use a Diamond Hoe until it completely breaks from loss of durability.
Sky's the Limit	Get a set of Elytra.
Sniper Duel	Kill a Skeleton from over 50 blocks away.
Spooky Scary Skeleton	Get your first Wither Skeleton Skull.
Stone Age	Acquire your first Cobblestones.
Subspace Bubble	Use the Nether to go between two Overworld Portals that are at least 7000 blocks apart.
Suit Up	Get your first piece of Iron armor.
Sweet Dreams	Lie down in a Bed.
Take Aim	Hit any living target with a shot from your Bow.
The City at the End of the Game	Enter an End City.
The End...Again	Use Ender Crystals to resummon an Ender Dragon.
The End?	Enter the End.
The Next Generation	Get a Dragon Egg.
The Parrots and the Bats	Breed two animals together.
Two by Two	Breed Chickens, Cows, Horses, Llamas, Mooshrooms, Ocelots, Pigs, Rabbits, Sheep, and Wolves.
Uneasy Alliance	Bring a Ghast back into the Overworld and kill it there.
We Need to Go Deeper	Enter the Nether.
What a Deal!	Complete a trade with any Villager.
Withering Heights	Be within 100 blocks of a Wither when it's summoned.
You Need a Mint	Use a Glass Bottle to collect Dragon's Breath from the Ender Dragon.
Zombie Doctor	Throw a Splash Potion of Weakness at a Zombie Villager, then give it a Golden Apple (face it, equip the Golden Apple, and use the Apple).

Tools, Resources, and Consumables

This chapter shows you all of the items in *Minecraft*. The following index includes everything in one place. After the index, we break all of the information into more detailed entries.

INDEX

NAME	CATEGORY	PAGE NUMBER
Coal Ore	Blocks and Structures	103
Cobblestone	Blocks and Structures	104
Cobweb	Blocks and Structures	104
Cocoa	Blocks and Structures	104
Command Block	Blocks and Structures	104
Compass	Tools	166
Concrete	Blocks and Structures	104
Cooked Chicken	Food and Food Ingredients	156
Cooked Porkchop	Food and Food Ingredients	156
Cooked Salmon	Food and Food Ingredients	156
Cookie	Food and Food Ingredients	156
Crafting Table	Crafting	130
Cyan Dye	Crafting	130
Dandelion	Blocks and Structures	105
Dandelion Yellow	Crafting	130
Daylight Sensor	Crafting	131
Dead Bush	Blocks and Structures	105
Detector Rail	Crafting	131
Diamond	Common Items	119
Diamond Ore	Blocks and Structures	105
Diorite	Crafting	131
Dirt	Blocks and Structures	105
Dispenser	Crafting	132
Door	Crafting	132
Dragon Egg	Blocks and Structures	105
Dropper	Crafting	132
Dyed Wool	Crafting	133
Egg	Food and Food Ingredients	157
Elytra	Weapons and Armor	170
Emerald Ore	Blocks and Structures	106
Empty Map	Tools	166
Enchanted Book	Crafting	133
Enchanted Golden Apple	Food and Food Ingredients	157
Enchantment Table	Crafting	133
End Crystal	Blocks and Structures	106
End Portal Block	Blocks and Structures	106
End Rod	Blocks and Structures	106
End Stone	Blocks and Structures	106
Ender Chest	Crafting	133
Ender Pearl	Common Items	120
Explorer Map	Common Items	120
Eye of Ender	Crafting	134
Farmland	Blocks and Structures	107
Feather	Common Items	120
Fence	Crafting	134
Fence Gate	Crafting	134
Fermented Spider Eye	Crafting	135
Fire	Blocks and Structures	107
Fire Charge	Tools	166
Fireworks	Common Items	120
Fishing Rod	Tools	167
Flint	Common Items	120
Flint and Steel	Tools	167
Flower Pot	Crafting	135
Furnace	Crafting	135
Ghast Tear	Common Items	120
Glass Bottle	Crafting	135
Glass Pane	Crafting	136
Glistering Melon	Crafting	136

NAME	CATEGORY	PAGE NUMBER
Glowstone	Crafting	136
Glowstone Dust	Common Items	121
Gold Block	Food and Food Ingredients	157
Gold Ingot	Crafting	136
Gold Nugget	Crafting	137
Gold Ore	Blocks and Structures	107
Golden Apple	Food and Food Ingredients	157
Golden Carrot	Food and Food Ingredients	158
Granite	Crafting	137
Grass	Blocks and Structures	107
Gravel	Blocks and Structures	107
Gray Dye	Crafting	137
Gunpowder	Common Items	121
Hardened Clay	Blocks and Structures	108
Hay Bale	Crafting	137
Helmet	Weapons and Armor	170
Hoe	Tools	167
Hopper	Crafting	138
Horse Armor	Common Items	121
Huge Mushroom	Blocks and Structures	108
Ice	Blocks and Structures	108
Ink Sac	Common Items	121
Iron Bars	Crafting	138
Iron Ingot	Common Items	121
Iron Ore	Blocks and Structures	108
Item Frame	Crafting	138
Jack-o'-Lantern	Crafting	138
Jukebox	Crafting	139
Ladder	Crafting	139
Lapis Lazuli Ore	Blocks and Structures	108
Large Fern	Blocks and Structures	109
Lava	Blocks and Structures	109
Lead	Crafting	139
Leather	Common Items	122
Leaves	Blocks and Structures	109
Leggings	Weapons and Armor	171
Lever	Crafting	139
Light Blue Dye	Crafting	140
Light Gray Dye	Crafting	140
Lilac	Blocks and Structures	109
Lily Pad	Blocks and Structures	110
Lime Dye	Crafting	140
Magenta Dye	Crafting	141
Magma Block	Blocks and Structures	110
Magma Cream	Crafting	141
Melon	Food and Food Ingredients	158
Melon Block	Crafting	141
Milk	Food and Food Ingredients	158
Minecart	Crafting	141
Monster Egg	Blocks and Structures	110
Monster Spawner	Blocks and Structures	110
Moss Stone	Blocks and Structures	110
Mundane Potion	Potions	162
Mundane Potion (X)	Potions	162
Mushroom Stew	Food and Food Ingredients	158
Music Disc	Common Items	122
Mycelium	Blocks and Structures	111
Name Tag	Common Items	122
Nether Brick	Blocks and Structures	111

TOOLS, RESOURCES, AND CONSUMABLES

BLOCKS AND STRUCTURES

This section covers the objects that make up the majority of the world in *Minecraft*. Most of the blocks here are either for ground cover—such as Dirt, Stone, bedrock, and Netherrack—or structures that appear on top of those blocks (including various flowers and decorations).

Air

LOCATION	GATHERED WITH	USES
Empty space throughout all worlds	—	—

You cannot mine or collect air. It's all around, making up the *Minecraft* world's empty space, but it has a major use for your character.

When you remove an object from an area, air is left behind. This is true even when surrounded by water or Lava, though these substances quickly flow into the empty space unless there's something to stop them.

Allium

LOCATION	GATHERED WITH	USES
Flower Forest	Anything	Magenta Dye

Allium is a pink flower found in Flower Forest areas. You can harvest it with your bare hands and use it to create Magenta Dye. One piece of Allium creates two pieces of Magenta Dye.

Azure Bluet

LOCATION	GATHERED WITH	USES
Plains, Sunflower Plains, Flower Forests	Anything	Light Gray Dye

Azure Bluet is a light-colored flower found in multiple biomes. Each piece that you harvest can be replanted for decoration or used to make Light Gray Dye in a 1:1 ratio.

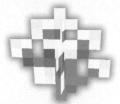

Banner

LOCATION	GATHERED WITH	USES
Crafted	Anything	Awesome decorations

Banners are crafted so that you can decorate regions with many different styles. You can place Banners on the ground, onto walls, put them in Item Frames, and arrange them in different orientations. Creatures can move through Banners as if they weren't there, so don't count on these are barriers against enemy movement.

The initial Wool color determines the base color of the Banner you're making. Once completed, you can then decorate the Banner by crafting it with a huge array of materials. This can be a costly process, if the ingredients are hard to come by. To compensate for that, it's possible to copy Banner patterns. This way you can make multiple awesome-looking Banners and only need to spend the Wool and Sticks for each new Banner while retaining your symbol. Do this by crafting, using your completed Banner and a plain Banner of the same color.

RECIPE

INGREDIENTS	CRAFTING RECIPE	RESULT
Wool (6), Stick		Banner

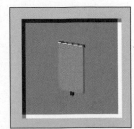

RECIPE

INGREDIENTS	CRAFTING RECIPE	RESULT
Banner (2)		Both Banners must have the same base color, and one Banner must be free of patterns; it will receive the final pattern of the other Banner

Stripe Patterns

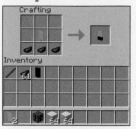
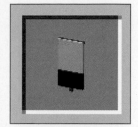

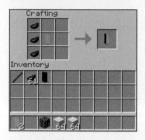

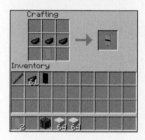
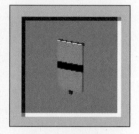

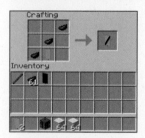

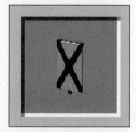

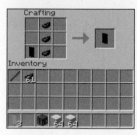

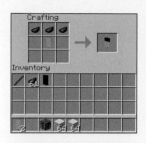

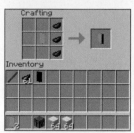
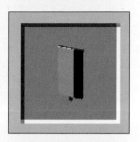

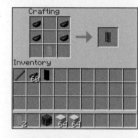
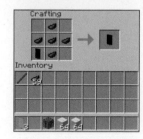

Half-Tone

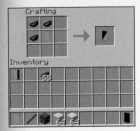 

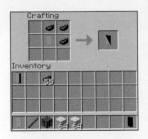 

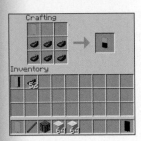 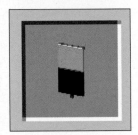

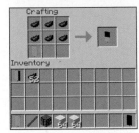 

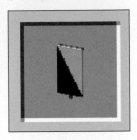 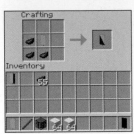

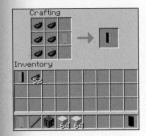 

 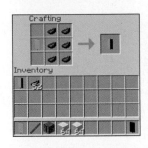

Shapes

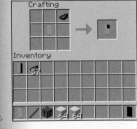 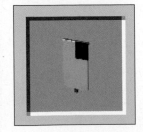

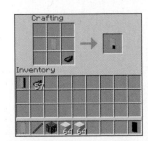 

TOOLS, RESOURCES, AND CONSUMABLES

Shapes (Continued)

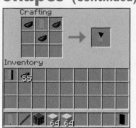 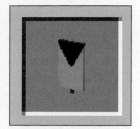

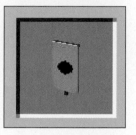 

 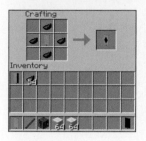

Borders

 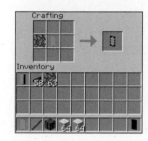

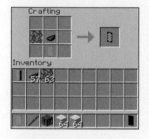 

Backgrounds

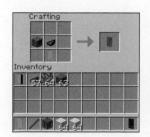 

Gradients

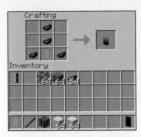 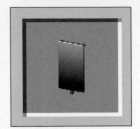

Symbols

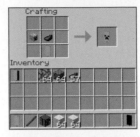 

 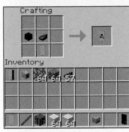

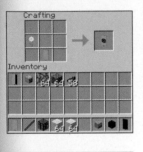 

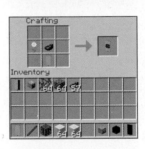 

Bedrock

LOCATION	GATHERED WITH	USES
Bottom of all worlds, at the top of the Nether	—	—

Bedrock normally prevents players from getting outside the borders of the world. You find it commonly near the bottom of the Overworld (until eventually it covers everything). It's also at the bottom and top of the Nether. Normal mining and explosions do not damage bedrock. Only special cheat codes or specific circumstances can be used to damage even a single piece of the rock.

When you see bedrock, that's your hint that it's time to mine outward instead of downward!

TOOLS, RESOURCES, AND CONSUMABLES

Blue Orchid

LOCATION	GATHERED WITH	USES
Swamps	Anything	Light Blue Dye

Blue Orchids are found in swamp biomes and make Light Blue Dye in a 1:1 ratio. They're quite pretty, so gather them for Flower Pots if you like their color.

Bone Block

LOCATION	GATHERED WITH	USES
Deserts, swamplands	Pickaxe	Decoration, source of Bone Meal

Bone blocks generate near the surface in deserts and swamplands. Use a Pickaxe to mine them, and use these blocks either for decoration, or to break into Bone Meal with simple crafting.

Cactus

LOCATION	GATHERED WITH	USES
Deserts, mesas	Axe	Refined into Cactus Green (a dye), garbage pits

Cacti are spiky plants that you usually find in the desert. They hurt any player or monster that tries to bump into them, so be careful when you walk near a patch of these things. Use an Axe to chop a few down if you'd like to harvest them. If you dig out the block beneath a Cactus, that also causes the plant to drop.

A fun trick is to make a garbage pit with Cacti inside. These plants destroy almost anything that comes into contact with them. You can dig out a modest pit with room for Cacti on each side, and then throw anything you're done with into the pit.

Note that Cacti grow on Sand, so harvest some of that while you're in the area. Bring the plants home and create your own patch as decoration, or to injure monsters that come close to your home.

Chorus Flower

LOCATION	GATHERED WITH	USES
The End	Anything	Growing Chorus Plants

Harvest Chorus Plants from the base of the growing vegetation. They drop everything onto the ground. Use the Chorus Flowers to grow new plants, and the Chorus Fruit as food.

Chorus Plant

LOCATION	GATHERED WITH	USES
The End	Anything	Decoration

The main body of a Chorus Plant is decorative in nature. It can grow quite large as long as there's enough room. Remember to harvest End Stone if you're going to make a garden of Chorus Plants.

Coal Ore

LOCATION	GATHERED WITH	USES
In areas of Stone blocks	Pickaxes	Burning in a Furnace

Coal Ore is a fairly common sight in large, stony areas. Dig through the Stone until you see flecks of dark material in the walls, and focus on harvesting those as often as possible. This nets a fair amount of experience for your character, and it gives you free fuel for your Furnaces! Coal is a long-lasting material for burning, so you can smelt ore, cook food, and keep your home looking nice and cozy for days on end.

Cobblestone

LOCATION	GATHERED WITH	USES
Seen in special areas (such as Strongholds and Dungeons)	Pickaxes	Construction material, used for making Stone tools, Furnaces, Dispensers, and many other items

Cobblestone is one of the most common crafting ingredients in the game. You get it by cutting into Stone with a Pickaxe; simply beating on Stone with your bare hands will not work. Make a Wood Pickaxe, break a few Stones, and then go back to make a Stone Pickaxe for yourself. Now you're ready to harvest Cobblestone in large quantities.

You can make buildings, tools, and decorative items all with the same Cobblestone. It's great stuff, and you can always get more without investing much time. Dig down into the soil, and there's likely to be more Stone waiting to be found.

Because Cobblestone always orients itself in the same direction after you place it, these blocks offer a way to see which direction you're heading. Look closely at the top of a Cobblestone block. In the block's upper left, when you're facing north, there's a small "L" on the stones. Use this as a way to tell where you're going if you can't see the sun or moon and don't have a Map or Compass.

Cobweb

LOCATION	GATHERED WITH	USES
Mineshafts	Shears that have Silk Touch	Slows movement (when walking or falling)

Cobwebs are naturally found in Abandoned Mineshafts. They slow down anything that tries to move through them, so put them in areas with your traps to make them even more effective.

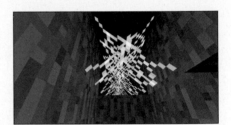

You cannot harvest cobwebs with normal equipment because they're fragile. You need a set of Shears enchanted with Silk Touch to gather cobwebs without breaking them. Afterward, you're free to hang these Halloween decorations wherever you like. Place them near a Tripwire with a nasty trap or two.

Cocoa

LOCATION	GATHERED WITH	USES
Grow on jungle trees	Anything	Making Cookies and Brown Dye

Cocoa grows on jungle trees, so it's exclusive to specific biomes. Once you find the trees, harvest some Cocoa Beans to bring home and plant on the trunk of a jungle tree to start your own Cocoa farm. You need only a single block of a jungle tree to work with, so grow such a tree and cut it down except for its trunk.

Then plant your Cocoa Beans, and wait for their third growth stage to harvest them. Break them open, collect your Beans, and you're ready to replant and repeat the process. You can use Cocoa Beans to make Cookies (a low-quality food item) or a dark Brown Dye.

Command Block

LOCATION	GATHERED WITH	USES
Special	—	Specific commands when activated by a Redstone current

You can put Command blocks into custom Maps by using the following text entry:

```
command /give <player name> minecraft: command_block <desired quantity>
```

Command blocks are complex items that most players don't mess around with. However, if you're making a world for Adventure Mode, these handy tools let you create teleporters, traps, and direct control of the game world.

Concrete

LOCATION	GATHERED WITH	USES
Crafted item	Pickaxe	Decoration, construction

Concrete is made in a multi-step process. The end result is a block that's a little harder than Cobblestone, though it doesn't have very much resistance to explosions, so it's not always ideal for an exterior location where Creepers are a legitimate threat.

CONCRETE POWDER RECIPE

INGREDIENTS	CRAFTING RECIPE	RESULT
Dye, Sand (x4), Gravel (x4)		Construction item

To make Concrete, you have to start with Concrete Powder. Craft that by combining four Gravel, four Sand, and a dye to make whatever color of Concrete Powder you desire. Then drop this powder into water to let it solidify into Concrete. Or have a proper source of water pour over the Concrete Powder; this hardens it into its final state.

Dandelion

LOCATION	GATHERED WITH	USES
Common grassy flower	Anything	Decoration, making Dandelion Yellow Dye

Dandelions are easy to find because they grow in many biomes: plains, forests, and others as well. You won't have trouble getting your hands on these. A single flower can be turned into dye whenever you like, or you can plant them on your own in grass, tilled Dirt, or regular Dirt.

That's about all there is to Dandelions. They're pretty much weeds.

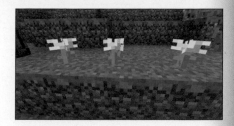

Dead Bush

LOCATION	GATHERED WITH	USES
Hot/arid areas of the Overworld	Shears	Decoration only

Dead Bushes are available in warmer areas and cannot be gathered without using Shears. They're drab in color and aren't used in any crafting recipes. If you want to make a place look inhospitable, they're somewhat useful for that.

Diamond Ore

LOCATION	GATHERED WITH	USES
Deep inside the Overworld	Iron or Diamond Pickaxes	High-quality tools

Diamond blocks are found in the Overworld's lowest levels. If you press F3 to look at your character's position, you can see your "Y" value. This tells you how close you are to the bottom of the world. Diamond is found between 0-15 in the "Y" values. This means you have to dig far down into the earth to collect it, and it's rare even at those depths.

Also, bring at least an Iron Pickaxe when you hunt for Diamonds. It's impossible to mine these blocks when you have inferior equipment. If you find Iron Ore on the way down, you can always make a Workbench, a Furnace, refine the Iron, and craft an Iron Pickaxe right there.

The tools you make with Diamonds are the best in the game. Always focus your best enchantments on them, because these items last for a very long time. They're amazing!

Dirt

LOCATION	GATHERED WITH	USES
The Overworld	Shovels	Construction, farming

Dirt is one of the easiest things to gather in *Minecraft*. Use it to make sod buildings, obstacles, or to lay the foundation for some Farmland (many crops grow on Dirt). Grass blocks become Dirt when you dig them up, and Dirt that you place in direct sunlight often shifts to a Grass block eventually.

Shovels let you dig into Dirt effectively, but any object can be used to harvest Dirt, including your bare hands. To turn regular Dirt into tilled Farmland, use a Hoe.

Dragon Egg

LOCATION	GATHERED WITH	USES
The End	Special technique	None yet

Dragon Eggs fall when you slay the Ender Dragon. You cannot walk up and harvest a Dragon Egg normally; it'll teleport away from your character and could even end up being irretrievable. Instead, you need to dig underneath the Dragon Egg two blocks down. Place a Torch down there, and then break the block between the Dragon Egg and the Torch. Collect the Egg after it "breaks" on the Torch. Use this same technique to quickly harvest Gravel or Sand by dropping their blocks onto a Torch. It's a neat trick.

Emerald Ore

LOCATION	GATHERED WITH	USES
Extreme Hills biomes, well below the surface	Iron or Diamond Pickaxes	Trading with Villagers

Emerald Ore is brutal to find. Don't even look for it outside of Extreme Hills; you must locate one of these biomes and then create a mine that leads below a "Y" value of 30. Emeralds are down there, but not very many of them. They're spread out and don't occur in veins, so finding them requires patience.

If at all possible, bring a Pickaxe with Fortune anytime you hunt for Emeralds. These enchantments make your time so much more productive because you get many extra Emeralds (2x-4x, depending on how good your enchantment is and how lucky you are).

End Crystal

LOCATION	GATHERED WITH	USES
The End	Crafted	Summoning a new Ender Dragon

Use this recipe to craft Ender Crystals. Place one of them on each side of the Exit Portal that leads out of the End. Doing this resummons the Ender Dragon, allowing you to defeat the boss as many times as you like.

End Portal Block

LOCATION	GATHERED WITH	USES
Strongholds	—	Creating a Portal into the End

Each Overworld has several Strongholds hidden within a certain area, not too far from where the first player begins his or her journey. End Portal blocks (also called End Portal Frames in some versions of the game) are inside these Strongholds.

Insert Eyes of Ender into these blocks to complete a Portal. Every End Portal block must be charged by Eyes of Ender before the Portal begins to function. When it does, you can travel into the End and face the threat of the Ender Dragon!

End Rod

LOCATION	GATHERED WITH	USES
End Cities	Pickaxe	Decoration

End Rods let you light up an area. They have the same illumination as Torches.

End Stone

LOCATION	GATHERED WITH	USES
The End	Pickaxe	Construction material

End Stone is a block type that dominates the End. It's resistant to damage and explosions, so it's a decent building material if you manage to harvest enough of it. The only problem is that you can't easily pop back and forth to the End until you slay the Ender Dragon. That said, there is a way to gather this stone even if you haven't killed the Dragon yet. To do this, place an Ender Chest in the End, harvest the stones, and put your loot in the Chest. This way, when you die in the End and respawn in the Overworld, your stones will be waiting in any Ender Chests you place there!

Farmland

LOCATION	GATHERED WITH	USES
Villages	Shovels	Growing crops

Farmland is created when you use a Hoe on Dirt or Grass blocks. This nice, tilled soil lets you grow a variety of items, with Wheat being the most common. Plant Seeds in your Farmland and give them time to grow to create a renewable source of food.

Proper growth requires light (from any source), a Water block that is at most four blocks away, and time. We discuss farming in detail at several points in this book, because it's a great way to keep your characters fed!

Fire

LOCATION	GATHERED WITH	USES
The Nether	—	Destruction, decoration

You can find fire on its own in the Nether, but it can be triggered in other areas with the use of Lava, Flint and Steel, lightning strikes, and from various enemy attacks. Whenever fire touches vulnerable wooden objects, it spreads, igniting them as well. This can destroy wooded areas and buildings and put characters at risk.

To fight fires, either attack the flames directly by hitting the object that's on fire, put blocks on top of the fire, or douse the area with water. Whatever you do, work quickly! A small fire can quickly become one that's too large to handle.

Gold Ore

LOCATION	GATHERED WITH	USES
Deep inside the Overworld	Iron or Diamond Pickaxes	Creating Gold Ingots that are used for Gold tools, Clocks, armor, and a few special items

You can find Gold between the bedrock and "Y" values up to 30 in the Overworld. It's a bright yellow ore that is easy to spot once you uncover it. Make sure you use an Iron or Diamond Pickaxe, and then harvest it like you would any other type of ore.

Once refined into Gold Ingots, you can do many things with this metal. Gold tools, weapons, and armor are pretty but not terribly effective. It's best to save most of your Gold for Clocks, Golden Apples, and Redstone construction (because certain powered items require Gold).

Grass

LOCATION	GATHERED WITH	USES
Dirt areas that are exposed to decent levels of light	Shovels	Construction, farming (same as Dirt)

Grass blocks are found wherever Dirt is given good light and time to grow. Grass itself grows on top of Grass blocks; flowers and shrubs can also grow this way. Dig into Grass blocks to collect Dirt, or cut through the grass above with any object to grab Seeds. The best way to get material for a Wheat farm is to rip up huge swaths of grass until you have enough Seeds to start your farm. If the grass is thick enough, you can get dozens of Seeds in a minute or two of running around. That's enough to kick-start a farming project.

Gravel

LOCATION	GATHERED WITH	USES
The Overworld	Shovels	Gathering Flint

Gravel appears in areas with Dirt and Stone. It has a more rugged surface, so you can tell with a glance what is Stone and what is Gravel. When blocks underneath Gravel are destroyed, the Gravel blocks above fall into place as if affected by gravity. This is true for Sand as well. Make sure to avoid standing underneath Gravel when you mine, because your character takes damage if you're struck by falling Gravel.

A quick way to harvest this material is to dig down two blocks under the stack of Gravel. Put a Torch underneath the Gravel stack before you destroy the block of Stone or Dirt that holds the Gravel in place. This causes the entire stack of Gravel to fall onto the Torch, destroying the blocks and turning them into a resource that's easy to gather. Quick mining without damaging your tools. That's pretty nifty, eh?

Hardened Clay

LOCATION	GATHERED WITH	USES
Mesas, deserts, river areas	Pickaxe	Construction material

Clay is a natural block in the Overworld. You can find heavy concentrations of it in certain biomes, such as rivers and mesas. Collect these blocks as if you're mining Stone. Bring them back to your house to use as a construction material with even more decorative options.

You can make Hardened Clay by cooking Clay in your Furnace. Hardened Clay can then be stained with any dyeing agent to give it a more desirable color.

Huge Mushroom

LOCATION	GATHERED WITH	USES
Mushroom Islands, Roofed Forests	Axe	Gathering Mushrooms, shade farming

Mushrooms grow in low or no-light areas. Huge Mushrooms are really cool-looking and grow naturally in somewhat uncommon biomes. If you want to reproduce these interesting features, use Bone Meal to grow regular Mushrooms into their giant cousins.

Because Mushrooms prefer areas with low light, they're great for making underground farms.

Ice

LOCATION	GATHERED WITH	USES
Cold areas	Any tool with Silk Touch	Decoration, transportation

Ice forms in cold regions of the Overworld. One often sees it on the surface of water, but it can also be on open ground. You can smash Ice with a Pickaxe (or any other object if you're willing to spend more time).

Movement on Ice is fast and slippery. This makes it possible to cross distances quickly and jump a bit farther as well.

Placing smaller blocks on top of Ice is interesting. For example, a Stone Slab on top of Ice retains the slippery characteristic that is common on Ice. If you run water over Ice, this property works as well, so water transportation over Ice is faster than it otherwise should be. Some players use this as a way to rapidly funnel objects that fall into water to a central area.

Iron Ore

LOCATION	GATHERED WITH	USES
Underground, in the Overworld	Pickaxe	Powerful tools

Iron Ore is a modestly common mineral that appears throughout the world. It can appear at practically any elevation, as long as there are Stone and Dirt blocks present. Look for a brownish, rusty tinge to a Stone block. That's what Iron Ore looks like.

After you mine Iron Ore, you have to smelt it in a Furnace before it turns into Iron Ingots; these are what you need for your recipes. Toss all of your Iron Ore into the Furnace and wait for it to cook completely. Remove the Iron Ingots and try making a variety of tools with it, including improved basic tools (Pickaxes being the best choice), Shears, Buckets, and more.

Smelted metals give you experience after you remove them from a Furnace. It's not a huge bonus, but it's still nice.

Lapis Lazuli Ore

LOCATION	GATHERED WITH	USES
Deep under the Overworld	Pickaxe	Decorative elements

Lapis Lazuli is a blue mineral found in very deep tunnels under the ground. Your "Y" location value should be near 15 to find Lapis Lazuli. It's easy to mine with any decent Pickaxe, and it doesn't take long to gather. Veins of this mineral often yield a large amount of the blocks, so you come back with a good haul if you find even one or two veins.

Large Fern

LOCATION	GATHERED WITH	USES
Grass blocks	Shears or any tools	Decoration

Ferns grow in jungles, taigas, and mega taigas. They appear on Grass blocks, much like regular grass, Dead Bushes, and tallgrass. You can find smaller and larger Ferns, but the main difference between them is that you get two Ferns if you cut them down with Shears.

Ferns can be broken with any tool to get Seeds, or cut down with Shears to harvest for decoration. If you want to make an area look nice with Ferns, build Flower Pots and plant Ferns in them around your property.

Ferns are usually spaced out a bit, so they're not necessarily a great source of Seeds. Thick areas of grass are superior, because you can harvest it much faster.

Lava

LOCATION	GATHERED WITH	USES
The Overworld, the Nether	Bucket	Light, Furnace fuel, garbage disposal

One frequently finds Lava in the deep recesses of the Overworld, and it's even more common in the Nether, where it's practically the world's lifeblood. You can sometimes find Lava near or on the Overworld's surface if you're lucky. Or unlucky, as the case may be.

Lava is quite dangerous. It sets flammable things on fire if they come into contact with it or stay too long beside it. Anything that catches fire takes damage over time—armor can't save you from this. If you're on fire, jump into water or pour out water from a Bucket to save yourself. It's possible to survive Lava without water, but you must have a great deal of health before you're set aflame.

Lava makes a telltale bubbling noise when you're nearby. Always use caution when you hear this noise so you don't wander over an edge and fall in. It's difficult to swim out of Lava once you're in it.

Pour water over Lava to create Obsidian blocks, a type of dark, hard rock that can be used for special construction. If Lava is poured over water instead, you end up with Cobblestone.

Leaves

LOCATION	GATHERED WITH	USES
On trees	Shears	Decoration

Trees automatically spawn leaves around themselves. These blocks prevent easy movement, so they're sometimes quite annoying. Destroy them with any tool that you have, or use your bare hands if you like. Shears gather leaves instead of destroying them, but at least they're quick about finishing the task.

Breaking leaves provides a chance to drop items, including Saplings of the tree that spawned the leaves. You might also get an Apple here and there, but this isn't a reliable way to get much food.

If you destroy every Wood block on a tree, the leaves nearby begin to disappear, dropping Saplings or Apples as if they're destroyed by hand. If you want to clear leaves and have some time, simply kill the tree and walk away. The leaves go away on their own, and you don't have to bother with anything.

Lilac

LOCATION	GATHERED WITH	USES
Forest and Flower Forest biomes	Anything	Magenta Dye

Lilacs are harvested from certain forests, and you can easily turn them into Magenta Dye. If you cut them with Shears, you can plant them as decoration around your house. They have a pleasing color, so you might as well grab a few if you find a place where they grow.

Lily Pad

LOCATION	GATHERED WITH	USES
Grows on Water blocks in swampy areas	Anything	Decoration, bridges

Lily Pads grow on top of water in swamps, and you also occasionally find them when you fish. These items are decorative, but they have minor functionality as well. It's possible to walk on top of Lily Pads, so they're sometimes used as bridges when people don't feel like bringing blocks of heavier material all the way out to a waterway.

Magma Block

LOCATION	GATHERED WITH	USES
The Nether	Pickaxe	Light, traps, decoration

Magma blocks are naturally found at the lower levels of the Nether. They're somewhat bright, keeping the area around them decently lit. Anything that stands on top of them takes damage over time. In addition, lighting a Magma block on fire sets it on fire indefinitely. This lets you create traps to damage or ward off monsters if you bring these blocks back to the Overworld.

RECIPE

INGREDIENTS	CRAFTING RECIPE	RESULT
Magma Cream (x4)		Dangerous trap block

If you have extra Magma Cream, you can craft Magma blocks.

Monster Egg

LOCATION	GATHERED WITH	USES
Deep in the Overworld	Anything	Spawning Silverfish

Stone isn't always what it appears to be. Certain blocks of Cobblestone, regular Stone, and Stone Bricks are actually Monster Eggs. They break to reveal Silverfish, nasty little beasts that call their friends to swarm you.

One most often finds Silverfish in Strongholds and underneath Extreme Hills biomes. It takes a bit more time to break a Monster Egg compared to a normal block of the same type, so it's possible to realize that you're dealing with one before you unleash the beast. When this happens, it's best to back off and mine elsewhere.

Monster Spawner

LOCATION	GATHERED WITH	USES
Special areas	Pickaxe	Creating monsters!

Monster Spawners are found in rare areas: Dungeons, Abandoned Mineshafts, Strongholds, and Nether Fortresses. These blocks create a specific type of monster; you can tell which by looking inside the Spawner's cage.

Conditions must be right for a Monster Spawner to create one of its creatures. If you illuminate an area around a Monster Spawner, it cannot generate any creature that wouldn't normally appear in bright areas. This provides a way to deactivate Monster Spawners without breaking them. Make the conditions poor for the monsters, and then you have the option of setting up a kill room. Monster Spawners with deadly traps are a great way to generate free experience for your character!

Moss Stone

LOCATION	GATHERED WITH	USES
Dungeons, Jungle Temples, mega taiga biomes	Pickaxe	Decoration, construction

Moss Stones are blocks of Stone that have Vines growing on top of them. They're pretty cool-looking and let you spice up your home base. Gather these with any normal Pickaxe, or make your own by crafting Cobblestone and Vines together.

RECIPE

INGREDIENTS	CRAFTING RECIPE	RESULT
Cobblestone, Vines		Moss Stone

Mycelium

LOCATION	GATHERED WITH	USES
Mushroom Islands	Shovel	Mushroom farming

Mycelium is a special type of Dirt block. You find it all around Mushroom Islands, and it allows Mushrooms to grow well even in direct light. If you want to spread Mycelium, cut grass off of the Dirt blocks around Mycelium to give it space to grow!

Nether Brick

LOCATION	GATHERED WITH	USES
Nether Fortresses	Pickaxe	Construction

Nether Bricks are the general foundation of Nether Fortresses, a special set of areas in the Nether. These dangerous locations feature powerful monsters but the potential for a few rare prizes as well.

Smelt Netherrack to make smaller Nether Bricks. These are crafted in quantities of four to make blocks of Nether Brick. It's non-flammable, but otherwise has no special properties. If you're building a defensive area in the Nether and don't have Cobblestone to use, this is a fair alternative.

RECIPE

INGREDIENTS	CRAFTING RECIPE		RESULT
Nether Brick (4)		→	Nether Brick block

Nether Quartz Ore

LOCATION	GATHERED WITH	USES
The Nether	Pickaxe	Special tools

Nether Quartz Ore is found commonly in the Nether; it's a pale vein of minerals seen inside of the Netherrack. It looks alarmingly like marbled flesh. Mine Nether Quartz Ore and then smelt it to get Nether Quartz. That material is used for several decorative elements, as well as for Redstone Comparators and Daylight Sensors. Neat stuff!

Nether Wart

LOCATION	GATHERED WITH	USES
The Nether, in Nether Fortresses	Anything	Brewing

Nether Wart is an herb that appears naturally only in the Nether. It grows on top of Soul Sand, so you must have both Nether Wart and Soul Sand anywhere you want to have a Nether Wart garden.

You can't do any substantial brewing work without Nether Wart. It's a core ingredient that leads to almost all good things. So, brewing isn't particularly fun or viable until you gather these herbs.

To get them, go into the Nether and search for Nether Fortresses. They contain gardens of Nether Wart along certain staircases, and you sometimes find Nether Wart inside Chests in these Fortresses as well.

Nether Wart Block

LOCATION	GATHERED WITH	USES
Crafted	Anything	Decoration

Nine Nether Wart can be turned into a red Nether Wart block. These blocks have no value and can't be broken down into Nether Wart, so this is purely a decorative element of the game.

RECIPE

INGREDIENTS	CRAFTING RECIPE		RESULT
Nether Wart (x9)		→	Decorative block

Netherrack

LOCATION	GATHERED WITH	USES
The Nether	Pickaxe	Construction, decorative fireplaces

This type of stone is found in the Nether, and it's that area's most common resource. It's easy to mine Netherrack, but it doesn't have many uses. It isn't a pretty stone to work with, and it can be a hazard because any fire that gets onto Netherrack burns *forever*.

However, this does point to one neat use of Netherrack. A fireplace is great if you put a piece of Netherrack underneath its viewing area. Light the Netherrack with Flint and Steel, and encase the fire in some type of nicer Stone fireplace, so your house doesn't burn down. That's pretty cool.

If you wish, you can also turn Netherrack into Nether Bricks by smelting it. Nether Bricks aren't flammable, so they're more useful and look a little nicer.

Observer

LOCATION	GATHERED WITH	USES
Crafted item	Pickaxe	Conditional power generation

Observer blocks have an active face that detects any change in the space in front of them. If something is detected, a strong pulse of power is generated that can power Redstone Dust or machinery adjacent to the Observer.

RECIPE

INGREDIENTS	CRAFTING RECIPE	RESULT
Cobblestone (x6), Redstone (x2), Nether Quartz		Conditional power generation

Obsidian

LOCATION	GATHERED WITH	USES
Anywhere	Diamond Pickaxe	Construction, Enchanting Tables, Portal to the Nether, specialty items

Obsidian is formed when Lava and water crash together. This can occur naturally (especially in impressive underground caves) or is encouraged by dumping a water-filled Bucket on top of a Lava pool. The end result is a dense black stone impervious to everything but a Diamond Pickaxe, and even that takes a bit to penetrate the material.

Obsidian has a number of specialty uses in addition to being an impressive construction material. First, you need it to construct Enchanting Tables (which, in turn, can provide enchantments to help you mine Obsidian). It's also required in constructing Nether Portals, the only means of traveling to the Nether. It can be used to make Ender Chests, which allow you to access anything stored in them, across any location. Finally, Obsidian is used to make Beacon blocks, which create skyward light beams and provide status effects to nearby players.

Oxeye Daisy

LOCATION	GATHERED WITH	USES
The Overworld	Anything	Decoration, making Light Gray Dye

Oxeye Daisies are white flowers with yellow centers. They grow on grassy or Dirt areas in plains and Flower Forests. They can be used to make Light Gray Dye, but mostly they're simply pretty to look at and add some color to your garden or environment.

Packed Ice

LOCATION	GATHERED WITH	USES
Ice Plains Spikes biome in the Overworld	Pickaxe with Silk Touch	Decoration, construction

Packed Ice is found only in the rare Ice Plains Spikes biome, and it can be harvested only by using the Silk Touch enchantment. Packed Ice blocks are darker, not transparent, and can't melt. If you (or a monster) walk on them, you can slide, which makes Packed Ice walkways slightly faster. Most often, Packed Ice is used to create decorative Ice Spikes, similar to the area where it's naturally found.

Peony

LOCATION	GATHERED WITH	USES
The Overworld	Anything	Decoration, making Pink Dye

Peonies are pink flowers that grow on grass or Dirt in forests or Flower Forests. They're very pretty plants and can spruce up your home garden, or they can be used to make Pink Dye.

Popped Chorus Fruit

LOCATION	GATHERED WITH	USES
Crafted	Cooked in Furnace	Crafting ingredient

Cook Chorus Fruits in your Furnace to turn them into Popped Chorus Fruit. This renders the fruit inedible, but it can then be turned into End Rods or Purpur blocks.

Poppy

LOCATION	GATHERED WITH	USES
The Overworld	Anything	Decoration, making Rose Red Dye

Bright red Poppies are among the most common flowers in the Overworld, found pretty much everywhere except swamps. They make any location more festive and add drama to any dense forest. You can pick Poppies and plant them all around your house and grounds. They can also be crushed down and used in Rose Red Dye.

Prismarine

LOCATION	GATHERED WITH	USES
Crafted item	Crafted	Decoration

Blocks of Prismarine are used to decorate people's homes and tunnels. Their various forms are made with Prismarine Shards and Ink Sacs (in the case of Dark Prismarine).

Prismarine is a rare type of stone that you won't find except around Ocean Temples. Make sure to harvest this if you ever see it, because the stones are useful for colored accents and have their own animation changes over time. Seriously awesome stuff.

RECIPE

INGREDIENTS	CRAFTING RECIPE	RESULT
Prismarine Shard (4)		Prismarine block
Prismarine Shard (9)		Prismarine Brick
Prismarine Shard (8), Ink Sac		Dark Prismarine

Purpur Block

LOCATION	GATHERED WITH	USES
End Cities	Pickaxe	Decoration

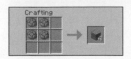

Search End Cities for these purple blocks, and gather them once you've cleared the areas of any Shulkers that are hiding nearby.

Purpur Pillar

LOCATION	GATHERED WITH	USES
End Cities	Pickaxe	Decoration

Purpur Pillars are very nice-looking, and they're easy to put together.

Purpur Slab

LOCATION	GATHERED WITH	USES
End Cities	Pickaxe	Decoration

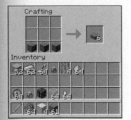

Purpur Slabs make nice pathways because their color really stands out in most areas.

Purpur Stairs

LOCATION	GATHERED WITH	USES
End Cities	Pickaxe	Decoration

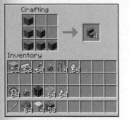

This recipe lets you turn Purpur blocks into Stairs. It's similar to existing Stair recipes, so you won't have any trouble getting used to them.

Red Nether Brick

LOCATION	GATHERED WITH	USES
Crafted	Pickaxe	Decoration

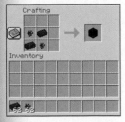

Nether Wart and Nether Bricks can be turned into Red Nether Bricks to give you more decorative choices. These costly blocks are brighter than their normal Nether Brick cousins, but are functionally quite similar.

CRAFTING RECIPE

INGREDIENTS	CRAFTING RECIPE	RESULT
Nether Wart (x2), Nether Brick (2)		Decorative block

Redstone Ore

LOCATION	GATHERED WITH	USES
Underground, deep in the Overworld	Iron Pickaxe or better	Redstone Circuits, blocks of Redstone, brewing, creating bright lights, Clocks, Compasses, specialty items

You can find Redstone Ore in the bottom 16 levels of the Overworld. You have to dig deep, but once you get there, it isn't too tough to find. Make sure you have at least an Iron Pickaxe with you, because nothing else will release the glowing red ore.

The glow of Redstone is linked to its most wonderful property: it can transmit and conduct energy. Redstone Ore itself produces light and bright red particles when anything nearby touches it, making it useful as a monster alert system.

Redstone Ore (Continued)

You can use the Redstone you gain when you split Redstone Ore apart even more creatively. Redstone Torches form a power source, and Redstone Dust (also called Redstone Wire) can be sprinkled along a path to transmit that power. Thus, you can use Redstone to make any number of electromechanical creations that can move or shift whenever you want. This includes working Dispensers, Repeaters, Pistons, Droppers, and much more. Any working mine needs a long Minecart Rail system marked with Redstone Torches and strengthened by Redstone-linked Powered Rails.

You can also use Redstone to make your daily *Minecraft* life a bit more regular; it's a necessary ingredient in both Clocks and Compasses. Clocks help you to plan out your day, and a Compass is a vital piece of equipment for any explorer—it can be a lifesaver.

Finally, Redstone is a component employed in brewing. It's used to make Mundane Potions (the base for many other Potions), and it can be used to strengthen other Potions or revert them to a lower tier.

Redstone Dust (Redstone Wire)

LOCATION	GATHERED WITH	USES
Anywhere	Anything	Redstone Circuits

The moment you plunk down a piece of Redstone in the world, it crumbles into Redstone Dust. The pieces of dust make a line capable of transmitting Redstone power from one location to another, which leads to another name for this material: Redstone Wire. Any energy flowing through the line makes it glow bright red.

The essence of Redstone Dust is that it allows you to create working, moving, and shiftable mechanical creations. It's a vital component of Redstone-based Circuits. The Redstone Dust links a power source, such as a Redstone Torch, a Lever, or Button, to a transmitter component, such as a Door, a Repeater, a Piston, or an Activator Rail to start a Minecart. This allows you to transmit energy to create a desired effect. For example, you can make a Door on the far side of your house open by pressing a Button. Or you could climb into a Minecart and ride down into the underground depths. Many types of things are possible with Redstone-powered materials, and you're limited only by your quantity of Redstone Dust and your imagination.

For more information on Redstone, check out the "Redstone" section in **Chapter 6**.

Rose Bush

LOCATION	GATHERED WITH	USES
The Overworld	Anything	Decoration, making Rose Red Dye

These are shy plants, found only in forests and Flower Forests. However, if you stumble upon them, Rose Bushes are renowned for their beauty. They make a gorgeous addition to any garden, and they can be used to make Rose Red Dye.

Sand

LOCATION	GATHERED WITH	USES
The Overworld, along coasts and in deserts and some mesas (as Red Sand)	Shovel	Construction, Sandstone blocks, Glass, TNT, farming

Some people may discount Sand as an unimpressive material, but they'd be wrong! While Sand may not seem exciting, it definitely has its uses. Sand can be stacked on its own, as in a seawall against the ocean, or compressed into Sandstone and used to construct anything else. It's also a necessary ingredient for Glass; all you have to do is melt it in a Furnace.

Sand is a wonderful base on which to grow Cacti and Sugar Cane, so it's a nice addition to your farm. Most areas have at least some Sand nearby, so it usually isn't difficult to acquire.

Finally, add some Sand to your Gunpowder to make an explosive creation! TNT can be used to blow up mountains, expand your mines, and generally stir up some fun. You owe it to yourself to at least try to blow something up.

Slime Block

LOCATION	GATHERED WITH	USES
Crafted item	Anything	Transportation

Slime blocks look almost like living Slime monsters, which makes sense; they're made from Slimeballs. Slime blocks have a few unique properties. They can make anything bounce that lands on them—including you! If you want a trampoline, you can make a pretty fun one with Slime blocks. Additionally, they can slow down things that move over them, which makes them useful for traps. Finally, if water flows over a Slime block, it speeds up anything moving over it. Build a Slime block pathway with guardrails just under a river, and you have a perfect transport device. Have your character use it as a quick slide, or shift materials down the river like an old-fashioned logging operation.

Soul Sand

LOCATION	GATHERED WITH	USES
The Nether	Shovel	Traps, transportation, farming, making a Wither

The Nether holds a number of dangers, and wandering into a stretch of Soul Sand doesn't help. This gray-brown substance, often found near large Lava fields, slows down anything walking through it. It's also slightly smaller than most other blocks, adding a bit of a challenge to getting out of it.

However, Soul Sand's slowing property makes it perfect for traps! A track of Soul Sand around your property can slow down and corral large numbers of monsters, which you can then mow down en masse. This also works against players in PvP multiplayer situations.

Soul Sand is the only material on which to grow Nether Wart, the primary component of all Potions. If you're interested in brewing, make sure you have an ample supply of Soul Sand!

Finally, Soul Sand can also be used to summon a horrible monster called a Wither. But you should really know what you're facing before you do this; you don't want to mess with Withers unless you're prepared in advance.

Sponge

LOCATION	GATHERED WITH	USES
The Overworld (underwater)	Anything	Decoration, absorbing water

Sponges, when dry, absorb up to 65 Water blocks from the area that they're placed in. Once full, they become Wet Sponges and won't absorb any more water until they've been dried out in a Furnace.

Sponges are sometimes found when you kill Elder Guardians near an Ocean Temple. There are also rooms in some of these Temples that have Wet Sponges already inside them. Break them to steal these rare items, and take them home as loot!

Stone

LOCATION	GATHERED WITH	USES
The Overworld	Pickaxe	Construction, some specialty components

Stone is something you seek out in your early days of *Minecraft*. It's one of the most common materials in the Overworld, but sometimes you have to dig before you get to it, depending on your circumstances. From that point on, though, you face no shortage of Stone and Cobblestone (the material produced when you break Stone).

If you want to form your Cobblestone back into Stone, all you have to do is smelt it in a Furnace, turning it back into Stone blocks. You can use these to make Stone Slabs or Stone Bricks. You can also make a few specialty components: Redstone Comparators and Redstone Repeaters.

The most common use for Stone is as a general construction material. It's pretty durable and fairly nice-looking, and it has a realistic appearance. Try using Stone to make a truly impressive castle or bridge!

Stone Brick

LOCATION	GATHERED WITH	USES
Crafted item	Pickaxe, Furnace	Construction, decoration

Stone Brick is a decorative material made from Stone, and it provides a different look from other building materials. Stone Bricks are similar to Clay Bricks, except they require slightly less material and time to make.

Strongholds and Temples use Stone Bricks in their construction, so you can get an idea of what they look like when you visit these locations. Additionally, Stone Bricks can be chiseled (Chiseled Stone Bricks) or covered in moss (Mossy Stone Bricks) for even more decor choices.

Sugar Cane

LOCATION	GATHERED WITH	USES
The Overworld, near water	Anything	Farming, making Paper and Sugar

You can find Sugar Cane growing as a series of three long, thin, green tubes anywhere near water. Farming your own supply is pretty simple: knock down the top two pieces and plant it along the water's edge. It grows as a stack, and you can harvest the top pieces as they become available. Of course, you can always make more impressive Sugar Cane farms. All you need is the Sugar Cane itself, water, something nice for it to grow on (Dirt and Sand), and your imagination.

It's a good idea to have a fair supply of Sugar Cane as your game progresses. You need Sugar Cane to make Paper, and without Paper, you can't make Bookcases. And without Bookcases, you can't have a fully powered Enchanting Table. Any excess Sugar Cane can be processed into Sugar, which is useful for making Cakes and some Potions.

Sugar Cane itself creates air pockets in water. You can intersperse Sugar Cane within water to make small airlocks. It can also block the flow of Lava, which is a pretty neat trick for a simple plant.

Sunflower

LOCATION	GATHERED WITH	USES
The Overworld, in Sunflower Plains	Anything	Decoration, making Dandelion Yellow Dye

These lovely yellow flowers are found only in special Sunflower Plains, where they add a bright counterpoint to the smooth green landscape. You can pick Sunflowers at your leisure, and they make a nice addition to your living space. If you want, you can crush them to make a yellow dye, the same dye made with Dandelions.

Tripwire

LOCATION	GATHERED WITH	USES
Anywhere	Anything	Traps

No trap would be complete without a Tripwire! Made when you place a piece of String, the small gray Tripwire connects signals from Redstone-powered Circuits to Tripwire Hooks on opposite ends. When something collides with the Tripwire, a pulse is sent to the Tripwire Hooks, triggering the trap.

It's difficult to see a Tripwire unless you really look for it. If you do see one, though, you can cut it with Shears, which disarms the trap.

Traps are much more common in multiplayer games, but they do occur in Jungle Temples in single-player. If you ever explore a Jungle Temple, it's best to keep your eyes open and your Shears ready for Tripwires! This can spare you from a painful Arrow to the knee or a falling rock pile.

Tulip

LOCATION	GATHERED WITH	USES
The Overworld	Anything	Decoration, making dyes

What flower grows between your nose and your chin? Easy! Tulips—get it? Two lips! Okay, well, maybe not… Instead, you can find Tulips on the plains, including Sunflower Plains, and in Flower Forests. They come in a wider variety than most other flowers; you can find white, pink, orange, and red Tulips.

Like other flowers, Tulips can be put around your house as decoration. You can also make dyes, depending on the color of your Tulips: Light Gray Dye from white Tulips, Orange Dye from orange Tulips, Pink Dye from pink Tulips, and Rose Red Dye from red Tulips.

Vines

LOCATION	GATHERED WITH	USES
The Overworld, in swamps and jungles	Shears	Transportation, decoration

Jungles and swamps are covered in dense vegetation, and the trees are surrounded by quickly growing Vines. However, these Vines provide some real benefits: they can be climbed, just like Ladders, and they can hide you or anything you build from sight.

To climb a Vine, simply move onto it from any solid block. "Sneaking" on a Vine causes you to stop; you can use this to hover in place. Falling onto a Vine greatly reduces falling damage, so they make a good safety system.

If you want to grow your own set of Vine "ladders," you have to harvest the Vines with Shears. Vines grow only on solid blocks, and they grow down into any empty space below them. They don't need light to grow, either. Vines are perfectly happy to take over any territory beneath them,

under any condition. Vines block line of sight, so monsters (even Endermen) and other players won't see things behind them. You can make secret passageways and hidden nooks using hanging Vines. They can even be placed over Chests, making them perfect for creating your own Jungle Temple.

Wood

LOCATION	GATHERED WITH	USES
The Overworld	Axe	Construction, making Wood tools, making crafting materials, fuel

Wood: it's what you gather your first day, every time. Most biomes have at least a reasonable supply of trees, and if you don't find any, it's worth running and searching for them. Wood comes from any type of tree (Oak, Spruce, Birch, Jungle, Acacia, and Dark Oak), and you need Wood (as Wood Planks) to make your Crafting Table. From there, you use Wood to make your first set of Wood tools, especially a Wooden Axe to get more Wood, and then to create other useful items, like Chests and Torches. Other useful items you make from Wood include Fences, Ladders, and Doors. If you can't find any Coal early on, Wood is your first means of making your own light; burning it in your Furnace helps stave off the darkness and creates Charcoal in the process.

As you become more comfortable with the game and gain access to additional materials, Wood becomes less valuable, but you never want to be completely without it. Even if you deforest the area around you, it's worth starting a Sapling farm. Without Wood, you can't make any tools at all, and that is a true problem.

COMMON ITEMS

Bone

LOCATION	GATHERED WITH	USES
The Overworld, the Nether	Weapons, Fishing Rod	Taming Wolves, fertilizer, making Bone Meal (white) Dye

You can tell that Skeletons and Wither Skeletons have a Bone to pick with you—they leave it behind when they die! But what can you do with this grisly trophy?

Bones can be turned into Bone Meal, and that's the best way to grow a huge number of plants and trees quickly. You can also use Bone Meal to dye Wool white, but this is a waste of its potential; there are much easier ways to get white Wool. Additionally, you can use Bones to tame Wolves. A tame Wolf will defend you from harm and makes a loyal companion, so if you want your own dog, be sure to keep some Bones around.

If you don't like the idea of hunting the Overworld for Skeletons or the Nether for Wither Skeletons, you can always make a Fishing Rod. You have a chance to fish up a Bone instead of a Fish during your fishing trip.

Bottle of Enchanting

LOCATION	GATHERED WITH	USES
The Overworld, in Villages	Trade from a Priest Villager	Gaining experience

The Bottle of Enchanting is also called an Experience Potion, because breaking it releases experience orbs (between 3 and 10 points). Unlike other Potions, you can't brew Bottles of Enchanting; they require a bit of diplomacy and some trading expertise. Bottles of Enchanting are made only in Villages, and only by specific Villagers at that. Priests offer two to four Bottles of Enchanting for one Emerald. Of course, Emeralds are pretty rare, and the best way to get them is to trade with other Villagers, who sometimes give Emeralds if you offer them something they want—Librarians who need Paper, for example. All of this necessitates, of course, that you've discovered a nearby Village, you have Villagers with the right mix of tradable items, and you have those items to trade.

However, if you do have that nice combination, Bottles of Enchanting are a good way to farm experience. They're an easy source of renewable experience that doesn't demand many risks.

Cactus Green

LOCATION	GATHERED WITH	USES
Crafted item	Furnace	Decoration, making dyes and Fireworks

Burning a piece of Cactus in your Furnace creates Cactus Green. You can use this material to color a number of products green, including Leather armor, Wool, and Glass (for Stained Glass). Other dyes use Cactus Green as an ingredient; Cyan Dye is made with Lapis Lazuli and Lime Dye with Bone Meal.

If Fireworks are your thing, add Cactus Green to Gunpowder to make a Firework Star. Like any other dye, Cactus Green can be added to Fireworks to create a "fade to color" effect.

Charcoal

LOCATION	GATHERED WITH	USES
Created by burning Wood	—	Burned in Furnaces, crafting Torches

Charcoal has the same general purpose as Coal. It's primarily used as a fuel for Torches and Furnaces in the early game, when you have better access to Wood but might not have much time to mine Coal out of the rocks below.

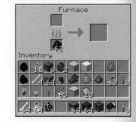

To make Charcoal, burn blocks of Wood inside your Furnace. Use Sticks or Wood tools to light your first fire. Burn a block of Wood to make a single piece of Charcoal, and then put that into your fuel slot. Now use that piece to burn even more blocks of Wood, and you're good to go from there.

Coal

LOCATION	GATHERED WITH	USES
Underground in the Overworld	Pickaxe	Fuel for Furnaces

Coal is a somewhat common sight in the Overworld's underground areas. You see chunks of this dark ore in the rocks, and they're easily mined with any Pickaxe. Mining Coal is a good way to get experience, because each block nets you a small chunk of XP.

Bring Coal back to your base to use in your Furnaces; it's a very efficient fuel. Coal Is also a major ingredient in Torches and Fire Charges.

Diamond

LOCATION	GATHERED WITH	USES
Deep underground in the Overworld	Iron or Diamond Pickaxes	High-quality tools and equipment

Diamond is one of the rarest materials in *Minecraft*. It's found only near bedrock, at the bottom of the Overworld. Make sure you're below 15 on the "Y" scale. Or dig down to the bedrock and go up about a dozen blocks from the bottom.

Search for this light ore and mine it with Iron or Diamond Pickaxes. Nothing else is strong enough to cut through the Diamond. Bring the ore home to use in tools, weapons, armor, and special crafting recipes: Enchantment Tables, Firework Stars, Jukeboxes, etc.

Ender Pearl

LOCATION	GATHERED WITH	USES
Carried by Endermen	Kill Endermen	Teleportation, crafting Eyes of Ender

Ender Pearls are dropped when you kill Endermen. These are important items for reaching the late game, because you can't find Strongholds without crafting Eyes of Ender, and those require Ender Pearls.

Used on their own, Ender Pearls are short-range teleportation devices. Use them to cross ravines or to save yourself if you're knocked off a high edge and react quickly. Even if you don't fall, Ender Pearls cause falling damage to your character when you use them, so be careful.

Explorer Map

LOCATION	GATHERED WITH	USES
Villages	Trading	Helping you find rare structures

Trade with any Cartographers you find in Villages. If you get up to Tier 4 with them, they'll offer you Explorer Maps from time to time. These items are very costly (requiring up to 28 Emeralds and a Compass), but they point you toward either a Woodland Mansion or an Ocean Monument.

Feather

LOCATION	GATHERED WITH	USES
Dropped by Chickens	Kill Chickens	Crafting

Feathers are a key ingredient in Arrows, a Book and Quill, and Firework Stars. Of these, Arrows are easily the most common item that you craft. It takes many Arrows to get through the game, and most targets are safer to kill with Bows than with Swords.

To ensure you have a huge supply of Feathers, create a pen or barn for any Chickens you find in the wilderness. Don't kill them! Use Seeds to lure them home and keep them safe in your pen. Breed them, using Seeds, and only kill excess Chickens. This gets you plenty of Feathers over time.

Fireworks

LOCATION	GATHERED WITH	USES
Crafted item	Crafting	Fun

Firework Rockets require a special, complex crafting recipe. They have variable ingredients so you can alter the effect of the rocket when it's fired.

Firework Rockets need Paper and Gunpowder to work. Extra units of Gunpowder make the rockets go higher when they're fired. If you want an attractive explosive effect, add Firework Stars to the recipe as well. You're allowed to add as many Stars as you have room in the crafting box.

RECIPE

INGREDIENTS	CRAFTING RECIPE	RESULT
Paper, Gunpowder (1-3), Firework Star (0-7)		Firework Rocket

Flint

LOCATION	GATHERED WITH	USES
Found in Gravel	Shovels	Crafting

You sometimes find Flint when you dig through Gravel. It's a useful material, so bring a Shovel whenever you go out to mine, and don't dig around Gravel deposits. Slowly dig them out, don't get trapped when they fall, and collect all the Flint you find.

Flint is used to make Arrows, as well as Flint and Steel. Both of these are quite useful, so save all your Flint until it's needed!

Ghast Tear

LOCATION	GATHERED WITH	USES
In the eyes of sad Ghasts	Kill Ghasts	Brewing

Ghast Tears drop fairly often when you kill Ghasts. They're used to make Mundane Potions and Potions of Regeneration. The latter are quite useful in dangerous battles that take a long time to win.

Glowstone Dust

LOCATION	GATHERED WITH	USES
The Nether, often up high	Anything	Firework Stars, brewing

You gather Glowstone Dust by breaking Glowstone blocks in the Nether. You sometimes get it from killing Witches, but that's a hard way to get a decent amount. Instead, go to the Nether and look along the ceilings for large deposits of Glowstone. Each piece of Glowstone breaks into several Glowstone Dust.

Use Glowstone Dust to make Firework Stars, Thick Potions, or to increase the power of other Potions: Harming, Healing, Poison, Regeneration, Strength, Swiftness.

Gunpowder

LOCATION	GATHERED WITH	USES
Carried by Creepers	Kill Creepers	Crafting

Kill Creepers (without detonating them) to get Gunpowder. Ghasts and Witches also carry it, though both of these are harder to find and farm compared to Creepers.

Gunpowder itself is used to make Fire Charges, Fireworks, and TNT—boom! It's also useful in brewing to turn normal Potions into Splash Potions; these activate when thrown. They're great for fast-acting Healing Potions or as a way to attack targets with Potions of Harming, Weakness, or Poison.

Horse Armor

LOCATION	GATHERED WITH	USES
Special Treasure Chests	Open the Chest	Protecting your beloved Horse

Horse Armor cannot be crafted. You have to explore the world and find this barding. One usually finds it in Dungeon or Temple Chests. Sometimes Village Blacksmiths have it as well, or you bump into it in Nether Fortresses.

Once you have Horse Armor, interact with your Horse and equip the armor as you would your own. This makes it much harder for monsters to kill your mount. Horse Armor comes in Iron, Gold, and Diamond varieties. Interestingly, Gold Horse Armor is superior to Iron and doesn't have any durability to worry about!

Ink Sac

LOCATION	GATHERED WITH	USES
Carried by Squid	Kill Squid	Making dark dye

One normally acquires Ink Sacs by killing Squid in deep water, but you sometimes find them while fishing, too. As a crafting item, Ink Sacs are useful for making Gray Dye, Light Gray Dye, Black Wool, Black Stained Glass, Black Stained Clay, a Book and Quill, and Black Firework Stars.

Iron Ingot

LOCATION	GATHERED WITH	USES
Cooked item	Cook Iron Ore in a Furnace	Crafting

Iron Ingots are created when you smelt Iron Ore inside a Furnace. Iron Ore is brought up from the Overworld's underground areas, and is brownish in color.

Use Iron Ingots to create Iron weapons, armor, and tools. It's one of the most common items in the game for crafting purposes, so you need to mine a ton of it!

Leather

LOCATION	GATHERED WITH	USES
Carried by Cows and Horses	Kill Cows and Horses to harvest their Leather	Armor, Books, Item Frames

Leather is a required ingredient for Books, so it's a vital resource for enchanting. For people who are light on Iron, Leather is also a good resource for armor. You need a fair amount of material to create a full suit of Leather armor, but it's doable.

To harvest Leather, search for Cows or Horses. Breed these animals heavily until you have a large, working population of the beasts. Then slaughter a number of adults each time they successfully breed. Keep your Leather, and continue culling the population each time there are too many adults in your barn/pen.

Music Disc

LOCATION	GATHERED WITH	USES
Dungeon Chests, carried by Creepers	Search Dungeons or kill Creepers (*)	For playing in Jukeboxes to change the game's music

Music Discs are either hard to find or tricky to get. You find them in Dungeon Treasure Chests when you're lucky. Bring them home and craft a Jukebox. Then put your discs in a Chest next to the Jukebox and play music whenever you like. Neato!

For a more reliable way to gather these discs, go outside at night. Get away from your base to avoid damaging it during monster attacks, and look for Creepers and Skeletons. Lure the two into the same area, and wound the Creepers. Get them close to death and then stop attacking them. Sprint to get a Creeper between your character and a Skeleton. Keep backing up and wait for the Skeleton to accidentally snipe your Creeper buddy. This forces them to drop Music Discs. Huzzah!

Name Tag

LOCATION	GATHERED WITH	USES
Dungeon Chests, rare fishing treasure	Open the Chests or use a Fishing Rod on water	Naming creatures

Search through Dungeons or fish extensively to find Name Tags; they're rare loot, so you won't get too many of them. Use them in your Anvil to put a name on them. Then find a monster and use the Name Tag to assign that name to the creature. This uses up your Name Tag, but causes anyone who targets the creature to see the name you've given it.

Try naming something "Dinnerbone" or "Grumm" to see what happens. Naming a Sheep "jeb_" is rather interesting, too.

Redstone

LOCATION	GATHERED WITH	USES
Deep underground in the Overworld	Iron or Diamond Pickaxe	Brewing, crafting, machines

Redstone is the most complex material in the game. It's mined in the Overworld's darker tunnels, and then used to extend the length of Potions, to construct rare tools, and to activate machines. Redstone Dust transmits power, while Redstone blocks are used for power or decoration. There's an entire section of **Chapter 6** dedicated to Redstone.

Saddle

LOCATION	GATHERED WITH	USES
Chests or Villages	Open the Chests	Riding Horses

Saddles cannot be crafted. They're found inside Treasure Chests. Save any that you find, and use them after you tame Horses or Llamas. Saddled Horses are easily ridden and let you get around quickly. Make sure to breed your toughest and fastest Horses, so you have a good selection of animals to saddle. Pigs can also be saddled, but they're not quite as fast!

Shulker Shell

LOCATION	GATHERED WITH	USES
Shulkers	Kill Shulkers	Crafting Shulker Boxes

Hunt Shulkers in the End to get their shells. Once you have a couple of these items, you can craft a purple Shulker Box (which can later by dyed into other colors if you prefer). Shulker Boxes are extremely useful, and this makes Shulker hunting extremely rewarding.

Slimeball

LOCATION	GATHERED WITH	USES
Carried by Slimes	Kill Slimes	Crafting

Slimeballs are dropped when you kill Slimes. They're often found in swamps, but specific underground areas can also spawn them. If you find a place that has Slimes, mark it with Signs so you know where to find it again later. Slimeballs frequently spawn there, and you can harvest the area more than once.

With these items, you can craft blocks made of Slime, Leads to control animals, Magma Cream, and Sticky Pistons. These are pretty useful crafting recipes, so you should find a steady source of Slimes whenever you can.

String

LOCATION	GATHERED WITH	USES
Cobwebs, Spiders	Shears, or Kill Spiders	Crafting

Spiders and Cave Spiders drop String when slain, so they're very good sources of this material. Dark caves that are just a single block high are perfect for spawning Spiders, because they're one of the only creatures small enough to get through the space. If you cut down cobwebs in Abandoned Mineshafts, you get String from that, too.

Craft String into Bows, Fishing Rods, and Leads. It also makes white Wool, but this is a major waste of your String. It's better to use the default Wool that you get from most Sheep. It's already light in color and doesn't require you to use four String per piece!

String also forms a Tripwire when attached to Tripwire Hooks. This is a great way to set traps in your base or in tunnels where people have to follow a certain passage.

Totem of Undying

LOCATION	GATHERED WITH	USES
Woodland Mansions	Kill Evokers	Saves you from player death one time

Totems of Undying are gathered after you kill Evokers. To use these items, hold them (preferably in your offhand slot), and perform whatever risky behavior you wish. When you character falls to 0 health, the Totem is destroyed but raises you to 1 health, removes your status effects, and gives you Regeneration II and Absorption II for a short time.

This is helpful in long fights, when playing around at extreme heights, or anytime you know you're doing something that has a decent chance of knocking you off. That said, remember that you are still quite vulnerable after the Totem is destroyed. If you're fighting a hopeless battle, don't bother wasting your Totem. You'll just get killed a few seconds later, and that's really not worth the expense.

CRAFTING

Activator Rail

LOCATION	GATHERED WITH	USES
Crafted item	Crafting	Triggering Minecarts that are carrying Command blocks, Hoppers, or TNT

Activator Rails are used to set off explosions, turn off Hoppers, or for commands that are coded into Command blocks. Any monster or person riding in a Minecart that hits an Activator Rail is thrown out of the cart as it passes over the Rail. So, Activator Rails are also used to set up traps for invaders who try to use your Rail system to get into your base.

RECIPE

INGREDIENTS	CRAFTING RECIPE	RESULT
Iron Ingot (6), Stick (2), Redstone Torch		Activator Rail

Andesite

LOCATION	GATHERED WITH	USES
Underground in the Overworld	Pickaxe	Decoration

This newer type of rock is found in the Overworld, in any location where Stone blocks appear. Use it to decorate areas where you want more variety than Stone or Cobblestone blocks can offer.

RECIPE

INGREDIENTS	CRAFTING RECIPE	RESULT
Diorite, Cobblestone	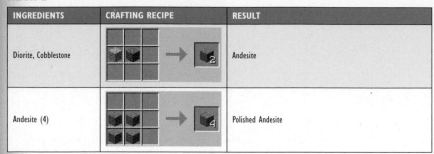	Andesite
Andesite (4)		Polished Andesite

Anvil

LOCATION	GATHERED WITH	USES
Crafted item	Crafting	Naming, repairing, and combining items

Anvils require a huge amount of Iron to craft. Investing over 30 Iron into anything is a big deal, especially in the early game. Don't craft one of these until you have a steady supply of Iron tools and armor.

When you craft an Anvil, it gives you a block to place. Put it somewhere safe in your base, and don't drop it on anyone you like; Anvils cause major damage if dropped on something.

Interact with the Anvil to name or repair items. It's possible to combine items of the same name/type. Like enchanting, it costs your character levels to use Anvils, but they offer the potential to make your powerful items last for a very long time.

RECIPE

INGREDIENTS	CRAFTING RECIPE	RESULT
Iron Ingot (4), Block of Iron (3)		Anvil

Armor Stand

LOCATION	GATHERED WITH	USES
Crafted item	Crafting	Holding and displaying wearable items

Armor Stands are crafted with simple materials and then can be placed around your home to make the space more visually exciting. Once placed, these structures hold armor or monster heads. You already know how to get armor, but heads are found when many types of enemies are killed by a charged Creeper explosion. In the case of Wither Skeletons, you can also simply farm their heads (but it's a slow process).

RECIPE

INGREDIENTS	CRAFTING RECIPE	RESULT
Stick (6), Stone Slab	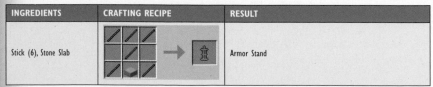	Armor Stand

Beacon

LOCATION	GATHERED WITH	USES
Crafted item	Crafting	Beneficial effects

Beacons are crafted with special materials. The Glass and Obsidian aren't too hard to get, but Nether Stars certainly are. You get these from killing Withers, a type of boss monster that cannot be summoned or killed easily. **Chapter 6** has a section explaining how to create one of these monsters, and a section on using Beacons as well.

Beacon (Continued)

After you craft a Beacon, it provides special powers to nearby characters, as long as it's activated and placed on top of a pyramid of Iron, Emerald, Diamond, etc. Building a functional Beacon is a huge investment in time and resources, but it's awesome once you make it work.

RECIPE

INGREDIENTS	CRAFTING RECIPE	RESULT
Glass (5), Obsidian (3), Nether Star		Beacon

Bed

LOCATION	GATHERED WITH	USES
Crafted item	Crafting	Advancing night to day

Beds are pieces of furniture that you can use only at night or during thunderstorms. Sleeping in a Bed lets you advance until the night/storm is over, and it also saves your location. Should your character be killed, you reappear in the last place where your character slept.

Beds cannot be used in the Nether or the End; they turn into massive explosives.

RECIPE

INGREDIENTS	CRAFTING RECIPE	RESULT
Wool (3), Wood Plank (3)	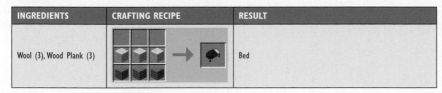	Bed

Blaze Powder

LOCATION	GATHERED WITH	USES
Crafted item	Crafting	Brewing, special recipes

It's easy to create Blaze Powder by breaking a Blaze Rod in your inventory or at a Crafting Table. This gets you two pieces of Blaze Powder. They can then be used to craft Eyes of Ender, Fire Charges, or Magma Cream.

Blaze Powder is also a direct ingredient in brewing. It's used to make Mundane Potions and Potions of Strength, the latter of which are amazingly useful!

RECIPE

INGREDIENTS	CRAFTING RECIPE	RESULT
Blaze Rod		Blaze Powder (2)

Block of Quartz

LOCATION	GATHERED WITH	USES
Crafted item	Crafting	Decoration

Blocks of Quartz are crafted from several pieces of Nether Quartz, as found in the Nether. These blocks make lovely decoration for any building you're working on; the stone has a light color that is really attractive.

You can craft these even if you aren't at a Crafting Table.

RECIPE

INGREDIENTS	CRAFTING RECIPE	RESULT
Nether Quartz (4)		Block of Quartz

Boat

LOCATION	GATHERED WITH	USES
Crafted item	Crafting	Sailing the seven seas

Boats are wooden objects that you place in the water and ride inside—no surprise there. They're crafted with five Wood Planks, so they don't require a big investment. Make a Boat anytime you have to cross a large body of water. Try not to run into anything, because Boats shatter if they run aground or bump into anything substantial.

Interact with Boats to start riding in them, and use the Sneak command if you have to get out of the Boat.

RECIPE

INGREDIENTS	CRAFTING RECIPE	RESULT
Wood Plank (5)		Boat

Bone Meal

LOCATION	GATHERED WITH	USES
Crafted item	Crafting	Fertilizing crops

Break a single Bone into a few pieces of Bone Meal, and use those to make crops or other vegetation grow quickly. It sometimes takes a few Bone Meal applications to get something to mature, but the process is still extremely efficient.

Save your Bone Meal for new crops that you don't already have in abundance. That way, you can kick-start a major farming effort without spending a few hours getting up to speed.

Try Bone Meal on trees for an impressive effect. Making an orchard has never been so easy.

RECIPE

INGREDIENTS	CRAFTING RECIPE	RESULT
Bone		Bone Meal (3)

Book

LOCATION	GATHERED WITH	USES
Crafted item	Crafting	Enchanting

Books let you make an Enchanting Table, and they're the backbone of Bookshelves, which you also need for high-tier enchanting. You have to craft quite a few Books if you plan on becoming a great enchanter.

RECIPE

INGREDIENTS	CRAFTING RECIPE	RESULT
Paper (3), Leather		Book

Book and Quill

LOCATION	GATHERED WITH	USES
Crafted item	Crafting	Entertainment, trading

You use a Book and Quill to make a Written Book. These let you create lore for the world you're building (to show to other people), or they're traded to Villagers at a very nice rate.

Equip a Book and Quill in your hotbar, use it to open the Book, and start writing.

RECIPE

INGREDIENTS	CRAFTING RECIPE	RESULT
Book, Ink Sac, Feather	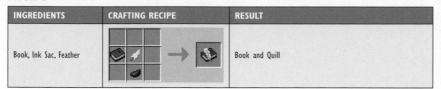	Book and Quill

Bookshelf

LOCATION	GATHERED WITH	USES
Crafted item	Crafting	Enchanting

Bookshelves make your Enchanting Table even stronger; your table can put higher-level enchantments onto items if it's two blocks away from your Bookshelves. Craft 15 Bookshelves and place them close to your Enchanting Table to give it maximum power.

Bookshelves are fairly expensive. The investment of Wood isn't too big a deal, but making three Books per Bookshelf is painful. Get a large ranch of Cows or Horses before you start this, and breed them well. You need tons of Leather to make all of those Books.

RECIPE

INGREDIENTS	CRAFTING RECIPE	RESULT
Book (3), Wood Plank (6)	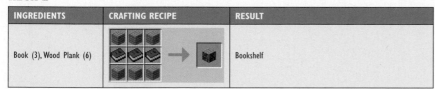	Bookshelf

Brewing Stand

LOCATION	GATHERED WITH	USES
Crafted item	Crafting	Brewing

Brewing Stands are required for making Potions. You have to find Nether Fortresses before you make these, because Blaze Rods are required to make a Brewing Stand. Plus, Nether Wart is the primary ingredient for all useful Potions, and Nether Wart is also located in Nether Fortresses.

Once you have a Brewing Stand, find a safe place for it inside your base. Keep a Chest there for special ingredients, and a Cauldron for decoration and filling up Water Bottles.

RECIPE

INGREDIENTS	CRAFTING RECIPE	RESULT
Cobblestone (3), Blaze Rod		Brewing Stand

Brick and Blocks of Bricks

LOCATION	GATHERED WITH	USES
Cooked item	Put Clay in a Furnace	Decoration

Cook Clay to turn it into a single Brick. Turn your Bricks into a block of Bricks by crafting four of them together, or make them into Flower Pots with only three Bricks.

RECIPE

INGREDIENTS	CRAFTING RECIPE	RESULT	
Brick (4)		Bricks	

Button

LOCATION	GATHERED WITH	USES
Crafted item	Crafting	Burst of power

Buttons trigger power for a short period, making them useful for opening Doors, triggering traps, and other sudden activities. It's possible to make Buttons out of Stone or Wood, so you can have them stand out against the wall to which they're attached. Or you can try to have them blend in if you're trying to be subtle.

After placing a Button on a surface, interact with it to trigger the Button and anything that's attached to it: nearby mechanisms or Redstone Dust.

RECIPE

INGREDIENTS	CRAFTING RECIPE	RESULT	
Stone or Wood Plank		Button	

Carpet

LOCATION	GATHERED WITH	USES
Crafted item	Crafting	Decoration

Use any two pieces of Wool to make three sections of Carpet. Lay them on top of blocks to add a neat decoration to your room. Dyed Wool lets you spruce up your base with a variety of colors.

RECIPE

INGREDIENTS	CRAFTING RECIPE	RESULT	
Wool (2)	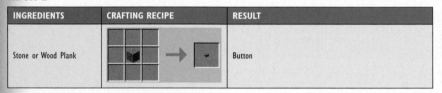	Carpet (3)	

Carrot on a Stick

LOCATION	GATHERED WITH	USES
Crafted item	Crafting	Leading Pigs

Use a Saddle to get onto a Pig, and then equip a Carrot on a Stick to lead the Pig wherever you like. You end up with a slow mount that isn't terribly effective, but it's pretty darn funny.

If you use the Carrot on a Stick actively, its durability decreases by a fair amount but gets your Pig moving much faster for 40 seconds or so.

RECIPE

INGREDIENTS	CRAFTING RECIPE	RESULT	
Fishing Rod, Carrot		Carrot on a Stick	

Cauldron

LOCATION	GATHERED WITH	USES
Crafted item	Crafting	Holding water

Cauldrons are a nice, decorative way to hold water. They're great to keep near Brewing Stands to give your setup an air of authenticity. However, Cauldrons aren't required for this. Any source of water is good for brewers. Using a Cauldron is more a matter of taste than necessity.

RECIPE

INGREDIENTS	CRAFTING RECIPE	RESULT
Iron Ingot (7)	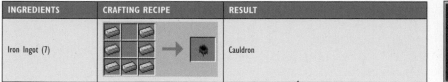	Cauldron

Chest

LOCATION	GATHERED WITH	USES
Crafted item	Crafting	Holding items

Chests are storage devices that help you sort items and keep your inventory organized. Drop off valuable or unneeded goods in your Chests by interacting with them, and then you don't have to worry about losing anything if your character dies.

For added storage, place two Chests next to each other. They merge, giving your character even more storage in one shared super Chest!

RECIPE

INGREDIENTS	CRAFTING RECIPE	RESULT
Wood Plank (8)		Chest

Chiseled Quartz Block

LOCATION	GATHERED WITH	USES
Crafted item	Crafting	Decoration

Chiseled Quartz blocks are attractive Stone blocks that require some crafting work to prepare. Use Nether Quartz to make several Nether Quartz blocks. Turn those into Slabs, and then use two of those Slabs to produce Chiseled Quartz blocks. Functionally, they aren't much different from other Quartz blocks, but they have a more intricate texture.

RECIPE

INGREDIENTS	CRAFTING RECIPE	RESULT
Quartz Slab (2)		Chiseled Quartz block

Chiseled Sandstone

LOCATION	GATHERED WITH	USES
Crafted item	Crafting	Decoration

Use two Sandstone Slabs to craft these neat-looking blocks. They're perfect for pyramids and other desert-inspired buildings.

RECIPE

INGREDIENTS	CRAFTING RECIPE	RESULT
Sandstone Slab (2)	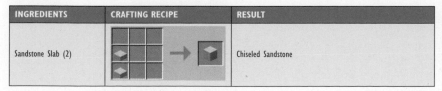	Chiseled Sandstone

Clay Block

LOCATION	GATHERED WITH	USES
Crafted item	Crafting	Decoration

Clay blocks are soft and easily dug out or damaged. However, they look nice and are useful as interior blocks for your base. Decorate rooms with them for fun. Or cook Clay blocks to harden them, and then use dyes to turn the Hardened Clay into Stained Clay for even more visual options.

RECIPE

INGREDIENTS	CRAFTING RECIPE	RESULT
Clay (4)		Clay block

Crafting Table

LOCATION	GATHERED WITH	USES
Crafted item	Crafting	Making more elaborate items

Use the default space for crafting in your inventory to make a Crafting Table by using four Wood Planks. Set up your table somewhere accessible, and interact with it to open far more crafting options.

RECIPE

INGREDIENTS	CRAFTING RECIPE	RESULT
Wood Plank (4)		Crafting Table

Cyan Dye

LOCATION	GATHERED WITH	USES
Crafted item	Crafting	Light-blue staining

This pleasing light-blue dye is used to change the color of Wool, Sheep, Stained Clay, etc.

RECIPE

INGREDIENTS	CRAFTING RECIPE	RESULT
Lapis Lazuli, Cactus Green		Cyan Dye

Dandelion Yellow Dye

LOCATION	GATHERED WITH	USES
Crafted item	Crafting	Yellow staining

Turn a single Dandelion or Sunflower into this yellow dye. It's used for changing the color of Wool, Sheep, Stained Clay, armor, etc.

RECIPE

INGREDIENTS	CRAFTING RECIPE	RESULT
Dandelion or Sunflower		Dandelion Yellow Dye

Daylight Sensor

LOCATION	GATHERED WITH	USES
Crafted item	Crafting	Outputting power based on the time of day/night

Daylight Sensors that are exposed to the sky put out a Redstone signal based on the time of day. It gets stronger as the day progresses, and shuts down at night. Used with a Redstone Torch, the Daylight Sensor can be inverted, making it into a Nighttime Sensor instead.

These are used to automate machines around your base depending on the time of day. People often use them to close Fences and Doors or to turn on lights when the sky starts to darken.

RECIPE

INGREDIENTS	CRAFTING RECIPE	RESULT
Glass (3), Wood Slab (3), Nether Quartz (3)	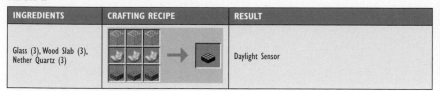	Daylight Sensor

Detector Rail

LOCATION	GATHERED WITH	USES
Crafted item	Crafting	Creating a signal if a Minecart passes over it

Detector Rails allow you to trigger machines based on the approach of a Minecart. Use them to set off traps, alert people (with Note blocks, Door opening/closing, etc.), or to make sure carts speed through in only one direction.

RECIPE

INGREDIENTS	CRAFTING RECIPE	RESULT
Iron Ingot (6), Redstone, Stone Pressure Plate		Detector Rail (6)

Diorite

LOCATION	GATHERED WITH	USES
Crafted item	Crafted	Decoration

Blocks of Diorite are used to decorate people's homes and tunnels. They're made with Cobblestone and Nether Quartz, so they're much more costly than basic Stone-based blocks.

Put four blocks of Diorite together to check out Polished Diorite for even more visual options.

RECIPE

INGREDIENTS	CRAFTING RECIPE	RESULT
Cobblestone (2), Nether Quartz (2)		Diorite (2)
Diorite (4)		Polished Diorite (4)

Dispenser

LOCATION	GATHERED WITH	USES
Crafted item	Crafting	Shooting items

Dispensers hold items, such as a Chest, but shoot them back out if they receive power from any source. Use Redstone to trigger Dispensers so they fire Arrows, Fire Charges, Potions, or anything else you want to send at friends or enemies. You can even set up armor Dispensers so you quickly armor yourself by walking over a series of Pressure Plates.

Use only new Bows to craft Dispensers. The recipe won't work if you try to craft one using a Bow that's taken any durability damage, even from a single firing.

RECIPE

INGREDIENTS	CRAFTING RECIPE	RESULT
Cobblestone (7), Restone, Bow	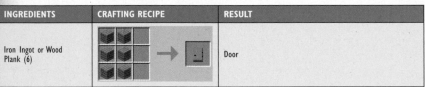	Dispenser

Door

LOCATION	GATHERED WITH	USES
Crafted item	Crafting	Limiting accessibility

Doors allow you to block off areas without totally sealing them. Wood Doors are easy to open and close; interact with them to toggle between these two settings, and walk through the opening whenever you want. Wood Doors keep out enemies fairly well, but concerted attacks can break through them.

Iron Doors require Redstone power to open and close, so they're a bigger hassle to build. However, they keep out almost any type of attacker, except for other players. Use Pressure Plates or Buttons to operate Iron Doors and have them shut automatically.

Note that the type of wood you use to create a standard Door determines the visual appearance of that Door. Try this to see which styles of Door you enjoy the most. This controls the color AND the texture of the Door, including changes in the windows and style of the entire item.

RECIPE

INGREDIENTS	CRAFTING RECIPE	RESULT
Iron Ingot or Wood Plank (6)		Door

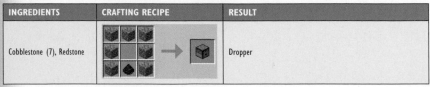

Dropper

LOCATION	GATHERED WITH	USES
Crafted item	Crafting	Moving items

Droppers drop items from their inventory whenever they are powered by a Redstone signal. Because they have inventories and the ability to push items into another block, Droppers can be chained together.

RECIPE

INGREDIENTS	CRAFTING RECIPE	RESULT
Cobblestone (7), Redstone		Dropper

Dyed Wool

LOCATION	GATHERED WITH	USES
Crafted item	Crafting	Decorative Wool

Use a dye to change Wool to another color and make Wool items that are whatever color you like. Another way to do this is to dye Sheep before shearing them. The Wool you receive is colored the same as the dye you use. This is more efficient than dyeing Wool directly, because you get multiple colored pieces per dye.

RECIPE

INGREDIENTS	CRAFTING RECIPE	RESULT
Wool + Dye	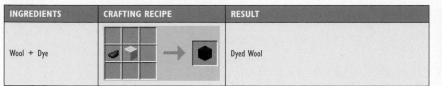	Dyed Wool

Enchanted Book

LOCATION	GATHERED WITH	USES
Crafted item	Crafting	Putting specific effects onto your tools or equipment

Regular Books can be enchanted just like your armor, tools, and weapons. Use an Enchantment Table to put special effects onto your Books to turn them into Enchanted Books. This process can be done multiple times, adding more abilities onto the Enchanted Book each time.

When an Enchanted Book is taken to an Anvil, its powers are added to another item, and the Enchanted Book is destroyed. Any powers that are allowed to go onto the item will do so, but powers that are not allowed on the item type are lost and wasted. This is a costly but useful process when you want to create extremely powerful items.

Enchantment Table

LOCATION	GATHERED WITH	USES
Crafted item	Crafting	Improving tools, weapons, and armor

Craft an Enchantment Table once you have access to Diamonds and Obsidian. Place the table in your base, and bring items to it once your character is higher in level. You're allowed to spend your levels to add special abilities to your items and equipment. Place the desired item into the Enchantment Table interface, and use the table on the right when deciding how many levels to invest in the object.

Surround your Enchantment Table with 15 Bookshelves to give it even more enchanting power. This lets you place much stronger enchantments on your equipment.

RECIPE

INGREDIENTS	CRAFTING RECIPE	RESULT
Book, Diamond (2), Obsidian (4)	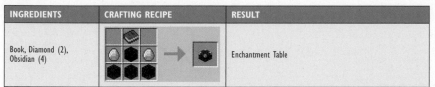	Enchantment Table

Ender Chest

LOCATION	GATHERED WITH	USES
Crafted item	Crafting	Storing items in multiple places

Ender Chests are more expensive than regular Chests because they require Obsidian and Eyes of Ender. However, they have a powerful special ability; all Ender Chests are connected. Anything you put inside one Ender Chest is available in every Ender Chest you own.

Place these by your remote mining operations or in the Nether and the End as a way to safely keep items whether you live or die. You can plop down an Ender Chest, load it with goodies, and then break it with a Pickaxe to keep carrying it with you. The items remain in the Ender space between worlds and appear when you put the Chest down anywhere else.

RECIPE

INGREDIENTS	CRAFTING RECIPE	RESULT
Obsidian (8), Eye of Ender		Ender Chest

Eye of Ender

LOCATION	GATHERED WITH	USES
Crafted item	Crafting	Finding Strongholds and activating the End Portal

Craft Eyes of Ender when you're ready to face *Minecraft*'s late game. Use these items to find Strongholds (massive Dungeons located in the Overworld). These Dungeons are quite hard to find on their own, and following Eyes of Ender makes locating them so much easier. Trace the steps of the Eyes of Ender, pick them up when you can, and reuse them until you get to the Stronghold.

Within each Stronghold is a room with a Portal to the End. Use Eyes of Ender to activate these Portals; completing a Portal requires many Eyes of Ender, so bring as many as you can. Afterward, the Portal allows travel between the Overworld and the End. Until you kill the Ender Dragon, it's a one-way trip, so watch out.

RECIPE

INGREDIENTS	CRAFTING RECIPE	RESULT
Blaze Powder, Ender Pearl	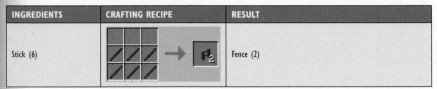	Eye of Ender

Fence

LOCATION	GATHERED WITH	USES
Crafted item	Crafting	Blocking movement but not sight

Fences corral animals and monsters so they can't move around or jump over your barricade. Though Fences look like they're one block high, they're a tiny bit taller than that. This prevents normal jumps from clearing them.

Like Doors, you can change the visual appearance of a Fence by using different wood in its creation.

RECIPE

INGREDIENTS	CRAFTING RECIPE	RESULT
Stick (6)		Fence (2)

Fence Gate

LOCATION	GATHERED WITH	USES
Crafted item	Crafting	Allowing movement into fenced areas

Use Fence Gates to act as Doors into fenced-off areas. These open and close just like Wood Doors, so they're easy to use. Try different types of wood when crafting a Fence Gate to change its visual appearance.

RECIPE

INGREDIENTS	CRAFTING RECIPE	RESULT
Stick (4), Wood Plank (2)		Fence Gate

Fermented Spider Eye

LOCATION	GATHERED WITH	USES
Crafted item	Crafting	Brewing

Craft Spider Eyes into this enhanced brewing item. Fermented Spider Eyes are used in a variety of Potions, with Potions of Harming and Invisibility being two of the most fun. Potions of Slowness, combined with a well-trapped area, wreak havoc on enemy players.

RECIPE

INGREDIENTS	CRAFTING RECIPE	RESULT
Brown Mushroom, Sugar, Spider Eye		Fermented Spider Eye

Flower Pot

LOCATION	GATHERED WITH	USES
Crafted item	Crafting	Decoration

Flower Pots act like decorative blocks for flowers, trees, and other plant life. Though these items have no functional value, they're nice-looking when you want to create a homey feel to your outdoor or indoor areas.

RECIPE

INGREDIENTS	CRAFTING RECIPE	RESULT
Brick (3)		Flower Pot

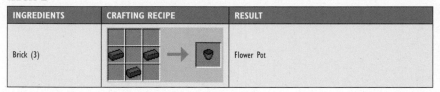

Furnace

LOCATION	GATHERED WITH	USES
Crafted item	Crafting	Cooking

Furnaces are easy to make because they require only Cobblestone. Make one or two of them for your base as soon as you can, and bake Wood and Sticks to make Charcoal. Use the Charcoal as a superior fuel to burn more Wood until you accumulate an ample supply of Charcoal.

Use your Furnace to prepare food and smelt raw ore that you bring up from the mines. Furnaces that are burning items also provide light if you're out of Torches and need to see what you're doing.

RECIPE

INGREDIENTS	CRAFTING RECIPE	RESULT
Cobblestone (8)		Furnace

Glass Bottle

LOCATION	GATHERED WITH	USES
Crafted item	Crafting	Brewing

Craft Glass Bottles to use with your Brewing Stand. They're required for every base Potion. Use a Glass Bottle while you're facing a supply of water to transform the item into a Water Bottle.

RECIPE

INGREDIENTS	CRAFTING RECIPE	RESULT
Glass (3)		Glass Bottle (3)

Glass Pane

LOCATION	GATHERED WITH	USES
Crafted item	Crafting	Decoration, light

You don't have to use Glass blocks to make windows in your home. Instead, craft Glass into Glass Panes. You get more bang for your buck this way, because you get 16 items to work with instead of six. Cut holes in your wall and install the Glass Panes to make windows.

RECIPE

INGREDIENTS	CRAFTING RECIPE	RESULT
Glass (6)	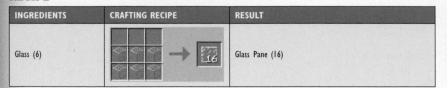	Glass Pane (16)

Glistering Melon

LOCATION	GATHERED WITH	USES
Crafted item	Crafting	Brewing

Use Gold Nuggets to turn a regular Melon into a Glistering Melon. The final product is a major ingredient in Mundane Potions and Potions of Healing.

RECIPE

INGREDIENTS	CRAFTING RECIPE	RESULT
Gold Nugget (8), Melon		Glistering Melon

Glowstone

LOCATION	GATHERED WITH	USES
Crafted item	Crafting	Light, broken into Glowstone Dust

Glowstone forms in the Nether, near that world's massive ceiling. Create pillars to climb up there, and cut down the Glowstone. When you break a Glowstone block, it shatters and drops Glowstone Dust, a useful brewing ingredient.

For a powerful light source that even works underwater, use Glowstone and Redstone to make a Redstone Lamp. It's brighter than a Torch.

Gold Ingot

LOCATION	GATHERED WITH	USES
Crafted item	Crafting	Making tools, equipment, decorations, and more

Smelt Gold Ore in a Furnace to make Gold Ingots. These Ingots are used for crafting Gold tools, armor, and weapons. They're also required for Clocks, Powered Rails, Weighted Pressure Plates, and Golden Apples.

In general, Gold tools aren't very good. They're fast to use but break much too quickly to be practical.

RECIPE

INGREDIENTS	CRAFTING RECIPE	RESULT
Gold Nugget (9)	(crafting grid)	Gold Ingot

Gold Nugget

LOCATION	GATHERED WITH	USES
Carried by Zombie Pigmen	Kill Zombie Pigmen	Creating Gold Ingots, crafting

Gold Nuggets are made either by breaking Gold Ingots or hunting groups of Zombie Pigmen. The nuggets are used when crafting Firework Stars, Glistering Melon, and Golden Carrots.

If you have more Gold Nuggets than you need, combine them back into Gold Ingots for more compact storage!

RECIPE

INGREDIENTS	CRAFTING RECIPE		RESULT
Gold Ingot			Gold Nugget (9)

Granite

LOCATION	GATHERED WITH	USES
Anywhere that Stone forms	Pickaxe	Decoration

Granite is naturally occurring rock that's harvested like normal Stone—it just looks different. Use Granite to make a Stone building or floor look brownish in color, for a southwestern feel.

RECIPE

INGREDIENTS	CRAFTING RECIPE		RESULT
Diorite, Nether Quartz			Granite
Granite (4)			Polished Granite (4)

Gray Dye

LOCATION	GATHERED WITH	USES
Crafted item	Crafting	Gray staining

Use this dye to stain Wool, Stained Glass, Stained Clay, Leather armor, and other items a grim gray color.

RECIPE

INGREDIENTS	CRAFTING RECIPE		RESULT
Ink Sac, Bone Meal			Gray Dye (2)

Hay Bale

LOCATION	GATHERED WITH	USES
Crafted item	Crafting	Feeding Horses, Donkeys, and Mules

A full Crafting Table of Wheat makes a single Hay Bale. Feed these bales to your Horses, Donkeys, or Mules to heal them from injuries. Or break the Hay Bale in a crafting window to make it back into nine Wheat. Store large amounts of excess Wheat in a compact space by leaving it in Hay Bales.

RECIPE

INGREDIENTS	CRAFTING RECIPE		RESULT
Wheat (9)			Hay Bale

Hopper

LOCATION	GATHERED WITH	USES
Crafted item	Crafting	Moving items

Hoppers pull items from containers above them and push the items down into anything below them. Put a Hopper under a Furnace to immediately have cooked/smelted items fall into your Hopper. Similarly, Hoppers above a Chest or Furnace fill those objects with whatever you put into the Hopper.

Brewing Stands and Furnaces can also be fed from their sides. A Hopper beside these objects loads their fuel/ingredient slots. It's pretty neat.

RECIPE

INGREDIENTS	CRAFTING RECIPE	RESULT	
Iron Ingot (5), Chest		Hopper	

Iron Bars

LOCATION	GATHERED WITH	USES
Crafted item	Crafting	Barriers

Iron Bars let you wall off an area without restricting your view. They're nice when you need to secure a compound and give the appearance of a jail or fortress.

RECIPE

INGREDIENTS	CRAFTING RECIPE	RESULT	
Iron Ingot (6)		Iron Bars (16)	

Item Frame

LOCATION	GATHERED WITH	USES
Crafted item	Crafting	Decoration

An Item Frame stores an object inside it. Make the frame and place it somewhere in your home. This locks the Item Frame onto a wall, Fence, tree, or whatever else is appropriate. Then slot one of your items and interact with the empty Item Frame to put the object inside.

There, you have something nice hung in your house. Use this with Clocks to see the time when you're walking around your home. Maps and weapons are fun, too. To get your item back, attack the Item Frame to knock the object out of it.

RECIPE

INGREDIENTS	CRAFTING RECIPE	RESULT	
Stick (8), Leather		Item Frame	

Jack-o'-Lantern

LOCATION	GATHERED WITH	USES
Crafted item	Crafting	Light, decoration

Use spare Pumpkins as bright light sources by adding a Torch to them. These blocks make your home safer yet add a spooky air when you're in a holiday mood. Perfect for Halloween.

RECIPE

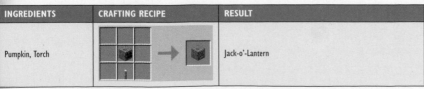

INGREDIENTS	CRAFTING RECIPE	RESULT	
Pumpkin, Torch		Jack-o'-Lantern	

Jukebox

LOCATION	GATHERED WITH	USES
Crafted item	Crafting	Playing music

Jukeboxes play Music Discs to add fun ambient music to your home. Music Discs are found in special Chests, or are gained by causing Skeletons to shoot Creepers to death. Once you have these discs, hold them in your hand and interact with the Jukebox to turn it on.

RECIPE

INGREDIENTS	CRAFTING RECIPE	RESULT
Wood Plank (8), Diamond		Jukebox

Ladder

LOCATION	GATHERED WITH	USES
Crafted item	Crafting	Safe climbing

Craft quite a few Ladders when you plan to work on pillars, ravines, mineshafts, and other vertical surfaces. Install Ladders on the sheer walls of these areas so your character can safely climb up or down from them.

If you fall near a Ladder, push toward it. Your character catches the Ladder and stops his or her fall without taking damage. This is a useful trick.

RECIPE

INGREDIENTS	CRAFTING RECIPE	RESULT
Stick (7)	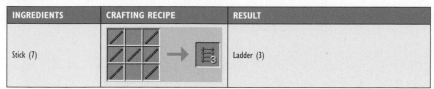	Ladder (3)

Lead

LOCATION	GATHERED WITH	USES
Crafted item	Crafting	Grab and control animals

Leads are great for pulling animals back to your home. Using food to lure creatures is acceptable for the same task, but it takes a long time to entice the animals. They sometimes lose interest. Leads are much more efficient. Walk up to the animal that you want to guide, and use the Lead on it. Once it's tethered, walk back toward home. Use additional Leads to gather even more animals as you go.

Leads can also be attached to Fences to tether your animals while you're away.

RECIPE

INGREDIENTS	CRAFTING RECIPE	RESULT
String (4), Slimeball		Lead (2)

Lever

LOCATION	GATHERED WITH	USES
Crafted item	Crafting	Creating On/Off switches

Levers create power as an On or Off switch. Pull them to activate their power and channel it through nearby machines or Redstone Dust, and turn off the power with a second flip of the switch.

RECIPE

INGREDIENTS	CRAFTING RECIPE	RESULT
Stick, Cobblestone		Lever

Light Blue Dye

LOCATION	GATHERED WITH	USES
Crafted item	Crafting	Light-blue staining

Stain Leather armor, Sheep, Wool, and various other objects a sky-blue color.

RECIPE

INGREDIENTS	CRAFTING RECIPE	RESULT
Blue Orchid or Bone Meal and Lapis Lazuli		Light Blue Dye

Light Gray Dye

LOCATION	GATHERED WITH	USES
Crafted item	Crafting	Gray staining

Use this to stain Leather armor, Sheep, Wool, Clay, and Glass a mild gray color.

RECIPE

INGREDIENTS	CRAFTING RECIPE	RESULT
Azure Bluet or Oxeye Daisy or White Tulip		Light Gray Dye
Gray Dye, Bone Meal		Light Gray Dye (2)
Ink Sac, Bone Meal		Light Gray Dye (3)

Lime Dye

LOCATION	GATHERED WITH	USES
Crafted item	Crafting	Bright green staining

Use Lime Dye to stain Leather armor, Sheep, Wool, Clay, and Glass a bright green color.

RECIPE

INGREDIENTS	CRAFTING RECIPE	RESULT
Cactus Green, Bone Meal		Lime Dye (2)

Magenta Dye

LOCATION	GATHERED WITH	USES
Crafted item	Crafting	Darker pink staining

Magenta Dye stains Leather armor, Sheep, Wool, Clay, and Glass a darker, saturated pink color.

RECIPE

INGREDIENTS	CRAFTING RECIPE	RESULT
Allium or Lilac		Magenta Dye

Magma Cream

LOCATION	GATHERED WITH	USES
Crafted item	Crafting	Brewing

Magma Cream is either crafted or found when you kill Magma Cubes in the Nether. It's used as an ingredient in Mundane Potions and Potions of Fire Resistance. The latter is a powerful defensive Potion when battling in the Nether.

RECIPE

INGREDIENTS	CRAFTING RECIPE	RESULT
Blaze Powder, Slimeball		Magma Cream

Melon Block

LOCATION	GATHERED WITH	USES
Crafted item	Crafting	Food, brewing

Combine a full set of Melons to make a Melon block, or break Melon blocks to get Melons. Either way, these blocks grow from Melon Seeds and are similar to Pumpkins in terms of their farming methods.

RECIPE

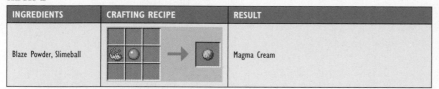

INGREDIENTS	CRAFTING RECIPE	RESULT
Melon (9)		Melon block

Minecart

LOCATION	GATHERED WITH	USES
Crafted item	Crafting	Transportation

There are several types of Minecarts in the game, and all of them are useful at different times. The base Minecart is a means of transport that rides along railways both aboveground and underneath it. Use downward slopes or occasional Powered Rails to keep your Minecarts moving at high speed, traveling from one end of the track to the other as quickly as possible.

Minecarts with Chests give you storage options. Place items in the Minecart and send it on its way using a Powered Rail system. Because the cart is full, you can't ride along in it. Either use another Minecart to follow, or use another means of transport.

Minecarts with Hoppers are pretty cool. They grab any items along the railway as they travel (unless they hit an Activator Rail). Set up areas where monsters are slain and farmed for items, and run your Minecart with Hopper through it to collect your treasure.

Minecarts with TNT are mobile explosives that detonate if they touch an Activator Rail—very nice.

Minecarts with Furnaces push other carts ahead of themselves. Add fuel to make them work, and it's full speed ahead for your new train of Minecarts.

(Recipes on next page.)

INGREDIENTS	CRAFTING RECIPE	RESULT
Iron Ingot (5)		Minecart
Minecart, Chest		Minecart with Chest
Minecart, TNT		Minecart with TNT
Minecart, Furnace		Minecart with Furnace
Minecart, Hopper		Minecart with Hopper

Note Block

LOCATION	GATHERED WITH	USES
Crafted item	Crafting	Making some noise

Note blocks make a brief noise when something powers them. Interact with the blocks to change the pitch of their noise and customize how they sound. If arranged carefully, this allows people to make music with them.

The instrument played by a Note block is actually determined by the type of block underneath it. Wood blocks produce a bass guitar noise. Sand and Gravel yield a snare drum sound. Stones are for a bass drum. Dirt does a synth piano.

INGREDIENTS	CRAFTING RECIPE	RESULT
Wood Plank (8), Redstone		Note block

Orange Dye

LOCATION	GATHERED WITH	USES
Crafted item	Crafting	Orange staining

Orange Dye stains Leather armor, Sheep, Wool, Glass, and other items a simple orange color.

INGREDIENTS	CRAFTING RECIPE	RESULT
Orange Tulip		Orange Dye
Rose Red, Dandelion Yellow		Orange Dye (2)

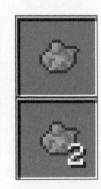

TOOLS, RESOURCES, AND CONSUMABLES

Painting

LOCATION	GATHERED WITH	USES
Crafted item	Crafting	Decoration

Paintings can improve the look of your home. Place them on walls to make your base impressive. Sometimes people put secret passages behind Paintings because you're allowed to walk through them as long as a solid block isn't on the other side. Experienced players are used to this and often search behind Paintings; this is why you might want to put a pit trap behind a Painting, in case someone runs straight through it.

RECIPE

INGREDIENTS	CRAFTING RECIPE	RESULT
Stick (8), Wool		Painting

Paper

LOCATION	GATHERED WITH	USES
Crafted item	Crafting	Enchanting, crafting

Paper is made into Books, Maps, and Fireworks. It's made from Sugar Cane, which you can grow in large quantities as long as you have plenty of water in the area. Turn Paper into Books once you have enough Leather, and use Books to make an Enchantment Table and tons of Bookshelves. That's the route to better enchanting and superior equipment.

RECIPE

INGREDIENTS	CRAFTING RECIPE	RESULT
Sugar Cane (3)		Paper (3)

Pillar Quartz Block

LOCATION	GATHERED WITH	USES
Crafted item	Crafting	Decoration

Use two Quartz blocks to make Pillar Quartz blocks; they're striated in such a way that they look a bit like marble pillars. If you're making arches or other pieces of architectural flair, Pillar Quartz blocks are perfect for the task.

RECIPE

INGREDIENTS	CRAFTING RECIPE	RESULT
Block of Quartz (2)		Pillar Quartz block (2)

Pink Dye

LOCATION	GATHERED WITH	USES
Crafted item	Crafting	Pink staining

Use Pink Dye to give a gentler appeal to Leather armor, Wool, Sheep, Stained Glass, and other items.

RECIPE

INGREDIENTS	CRAFTING RECIPE	RESULT
Pink Tulip		Pink Dye
Peony		Pink Dye (2)
Rose Red, Bone Meal		Pink Dye (2)

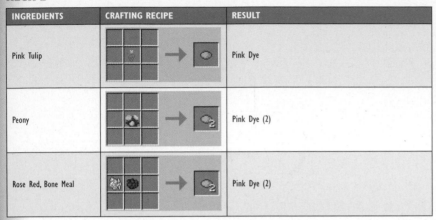

Piston

LOCATION	GATHERED WITH	USES
Crafted item	Crafting	Pushing objects

Pistons that receive power push blocks one space in a single direction. They can move an entire line of blocks that's up to 12 deep. When Pistons retract, they leave empty air behind. This resets their action, making it possible to push additional blocks forward if something new moves in front of them.

Pistons are often placed in areas where Cobblestone forms (from a Cobblestone generator) or in spots where enemies get trapped. For the enemy scenario, use Pistons to shove blocks through the enemies' heads. This begins the suffocation process.

RECIPE

INGREDIENTS	CRAFTING RECIPE	RESULT
Wood Plank (3), Cobblestone (4), Redstone, Iron Ingot		Piston

Powered Rail

LOCATION	GATHERED WITH	USES
Crafted item	Crafting	Fast railways

Regular Rails keep your Minecarts moving quickly only if they lead down a slope. Otherwise, you lose speed over time, especially if you try to ascend an upward slope. Powered Rails are a way to combat this problem. Place a Powered Rail every 32 blocks once a Minecart is up to speed, and use a trio of Powered Rails to start off your journey from either end. Add Powered Rails more frequently during steep upward sections of Rail.

To provide power, use a Redstone Torch next to the Powered Rails. This provides constant energy to them.

RECIPE

INGREDIENTS	CRAFTING RECIPE	RESULT
Gold Ingot (6), Stick, Redstone		Powered Rail (6)

Pressure Plate

LOCATION	GATHERED WITH	USES
Crafted item	Crafting	Triggering power

Put Pressure Plates on the ground when you need to trigger a mechanism based on a monster's or person's position. Use them in front of internal Doors to let people run outside without having to stop and open the Door. In more dangerous areas, use Pressure Plates to trigger traps.

RECIPE

INGREDIENTS	CRAFTING RECIPE	RESULT
Stone (2) or Wood Plank (2)		Pressure Plate

Purple Dye

LOCATION	GATHERED WITH	USES
Crafted item	Crafting	Purple staining

Purple Dye stains Leather armor, Sheep, Wool, Stained Glass, and so forth a pretty purple color.

RECIPE

INGREDIENTS	CRAFTING RECIPE	RESULT
Lapis Lazuli, Rose Red		Purple Dye (2)

Rail

LOCATION	GATHERED WITH	USES
Crafted item	Crafting	Minecart transportation

Rails create a path for Minecarts. You have to make these yourself most of the time, but you can find them naturally in Abandoned Mineshafts in the Overworld. Once you lay a line of Rails between two points, Minecarts with Furnaces can ride between them without much trouble.

Add Powered Rails to a system, give them power, and you won't have to rely on Minecarts with Furnaces or their fuel. Powered Rails accelerate Minecarts as long as they're supplied with power, as from a Redstone Torch.

RECIPE

INGREDIENTS	CRAFTING RECIPE	RESULT
Iron Ingot (6), Stick		Rail (16)

Redstone Comparator

LOCATION	GATHERED WITH	USES
Crafted item	Crafting	Making more complex power transmission systems

Redstone Dust carries power from a source, such as a Lever or Pressure Plate, to a machine that needs that power to operate. Redstone Comparators are more complex. They take power from the rear of the unit and transmit it to the front of the unit. Any power that comes in from the sides of the Comparator is used either to stop the back-to-front power entirely or to diminish it.

Use a Redstone Comparator in Comparison Mode to stop power if the side input is higher than the rear input. Otherwise, Comparison Mode does not affect power that comes out of the unit.

Use a Redstone Comparator in Subtraction Mode to reduce power output by the level of power coming in from the sides of the unit.

RECIPE

INGREDIENTS	CRAFTING RECIPE	RESULT
Redstone Torch (3), Nether Quartz, Stone (3)		Redstone Comparator

Redstone Lamp

LOCATION	GATHERED WITH	USES
Crafted item	Crafting	Light

Redstone Lamps require power to operate, but they produce light that's stronger than a Torch. They function all day and night, provided power isn't interrupted. Fiddle with Daylight Sensors if you'd like to have lamps that turn on only at night.

RECIPE

INGREDIENTS	CRAFTING RECIPE	RESULT
Redstone (4), Glowstone		Redstone Lamp

Redstone Repeater

LOCATION	GATHERED WITH	USES
Crafted item	Crafting	Strengthening Redstone signals

Redstone Repeaters let you transmit Redstone power across greater distances. They take the signal coming into the rear of their unit and spit it out the front with greater strength. This causes a brief delay in signal propagation, which is sometimes useful for making complex machine timings, as with Note blocks and timed music.

RECIPE

INGREDIENTS	CRAFTING RECIPE	RESULT
Redstone Torch (2), Redstone, Stone (3)		Redstone Repeater

Redstone Torch

LOCATION	GATHERED WITH	USES
Crafted item	Crafting	Power source, power inversion

Redstone Torches don't yield much light, so they're great for vision only if you put them intentionally in a shady area, like a Mushroom garden. Otherwise, they're good for providing power. A Redstone Torch next to any machine gives that device continuous power. This is useful when you want to ensure that something is always functioning.

In other cases, you might want to invert a signal, and that's where Redstone Torches get exciting. If you supply external power to a Redstone Torch, it turns off! This is known as an inverter, because it turns off with power instead of turning on.

Complex machines are possible thanks to interactions like this. You can have a device that gets power only under certain circumstances. The classic example is a Daylight Sensor that spits out power during the day. Draw a line of Redstone Dust from the Sensor over to a block with a Redstone Torch and a Redstone Lamp on the other side of it. The Redstone Dust carries power to the Redstone Torch during the day, and that disables the power. When the light level falls, the signal does as well, and the Redstone Torch resumes its normal function. This turns the Redstone Lamp back on.

RECIPE

INGREDIENTS	CRAFTING RECIPE	RESULT
Redstone, Stick	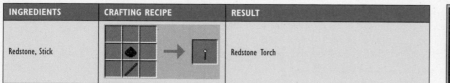	Redstone Torch

Rose Red Dye

LOCATION	GATHERED WITH	USES
Crafted item	Crafting	Red staining

Rose Red Dye turns Leather armor, Sheep, Wool, Stained Glass, and other items a deep red color.

RECIPE

INGREDIENTS	CRAFTING RECIPE	RESULT
Poppy, Red Tulip, or Beetroot		Rose Red Dye
Rose Bush		Rose Red Dye (2)

Sandstone

LOCATION	GATHERED WITH	USES
Deserts, sandy areas	Pickaxe	Decoration

Sandstone forms beneath sandy areas. Use a Shovel to dig through the upper, sandy layers and search for the harder Sandstone below. This material is quick to harvest with a Pickaxe, and it looks very nice. For color differentiation, use Red Sand to create the same types of blocks but in a much deeper color.

RECIPE

INGREDIENTS	CRAFTING RECIPE	RESULT
Sand (4)		Sandstone
Sandstone (4)		Smooth Sandstone (4)

Sea Lantern

LOCATION	GATHERED WITH	USES
Crafted item	Crafting	Underwater light source

You rarely find Sea Lanterns when exploring the deep oceans of the Overworld. Limited to Ocean Temples, these are items that you are only going to see on extremely rare occasions. They're destroyed if you try to mine them normally; only use items with Silk Touch if you're trying to harvest your own Sea Lanterns.

Lacking that enchantment, you can get enough Prismarine Crystals by breaking a couple of Sea Lanterns to craft one of your own. Though inefficient, this is still effective enough if you can't otherwise get these nifty underwater lamps for yourself.

RECIPE

INGREDIENTS	CRAFTING RECIPE	RESULT
Prismarine Crystal (5), Prismarine Shard (4)		Sea Lantern

Sign

LOCATION	GATHERED WITH	USES
Crafted item	Crafting	Leaving messages

Signs are normally used to alert or remind players about areas that they're moving through. "This Chest has food." "This Chest has metal." "Lava ahead!" You can write several lines on each Sign, conveying a fair amount of information. Use arrows in the text to indicate directions.

```
<--- Home
Village --->
```

Your characters can walk through Signs without any problems, but Lava and water won't flow through them. Use this trick to create air pockets underwater.

RECIPE

INGREDIENTS	CRAFTING RECIPE	RESULT
Wood Plank (6), Stick		Sign (3)

Shulker Box

LOCATION	GATHERED WITH	USES
Crafted item	Crafting	Storage

These special "chests" can hold 27 items and still be stored in your inventory or inside normal Chests while holding on to all of those objects. This allows you to greatly increase your carrying capacity by holding on to Shulker Boxes full of stored goodies. For pure insanity, you can walk around with an Ender Chest that has access to Shulker Boxes. That lets you get ahold of almost anything, at any time. Find a safe place for yourself, deploy the Ender Chest, and then look through your Shulker Boxes to get whatever you need.

RECIPE

INGREDIENTS	CRAFTING RECIPE	RESULT
Shulker Shell (2), Chest		Shulker Box

Slab

LOCATION	GATHERED WITH	USES
Crafted item	Crafting	Decoration

Slab (continued)

Slabs of material create half blocks that can be placed on an area's ground or ceiling. Though you don't have to jump to get onto Slabs, they still restrict movement if there isn't enough room overhead, so it's *almost* like you're walking on top of a full block even if it doesn't look that way.

You can place Redstone Dust trails underneath Slabs, allowing you to obscure your traps and machinery in subtle ways. Lay your power lines, test them, and then bury as much of their length as possible under a single layer of Slabs so that it looks like nothing is there.

RECIPE

INGREDIENTS	CRAFTING RECIPE	RESULT
Three blocks of the following: Stone, Sandstone, Cobblestone, Brick, Wood Plank, Nether Brick, Quartz, Granite, Diorite, Andesite, Polished Stone	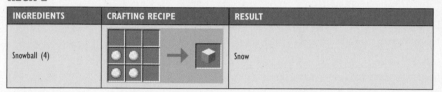	Slab (6)

Snow

LOCATION	GATHERED WITH	USES
Crafted item	Crafting	Decoration

Use groups of Snowballs to craft entire blocks of Snow. Place these in and around your home to add a wintry appeal. Because Snow is packed nice and tight, it won't melt even in the sun, regardless of the biome you take it to.

RECIPE

INGREDIENTS	CRAFTING RECIPE	RESULT
Snowball (4)		Snow

Snowball

LOCATION	GATHERED WITH	USES
Crafted item	Crafting	Crafting, thrown for fun

Break Snow blocks or ground cover to gather Snowballs. These items are crafted into Snow blocks or can be equipped and thrown at targets for fun. They don't hurt most targets, but Blazes and the Ender Dragon are an exception to this; both of them are vulnerable to Snowball attacks.

Stained Clay

LOCATION	GATHERED WITH	USES
Crafted item	Crafting	Decoration

Go to a Crafting Table with eight blocks of Hardened Clay, which is made by cooking regular Clay blocks in a Furnace. Craft Stained Clay by adding any dye that you like to this batch of Hardened Clay. The result can be any color in the game, determined by the dye you use.

Decorate your house any way you like with this method of coloring.

RECIPE

INGREDIENTS	CRAFTING RECIPE	RESULT
Hardened Clay (8), any dye		Stained Clay (8)

Stained Glass

LOCATION	GATHERED WITH	USES
Crafted item	Crafting	Decoration

Combine eight normal blocks of Glass with any dye to produce blocks of Stained Glass. Make a chapel, get some privacy, or set up neat windows for fun.

RECIPE

INGREDIENTS	CRAFTING RECIPE	RESULT
Glass (8), any dye		Stained Glass (8)

Stained Glass Panes

LOCATION	GATHERED WITH	USES
Crafted item	Crafting	Decoration

Stain your Glass any color you like, and then craft the results into Glass Panes. They retain their color. Now you have even more decorating options.

RECIPE

INGREDIENTS	CRAFTING RECIPE	RESULT
Stained Glass (6)		Stained Glass Panes (16)

Stairs

LOCATION	GATHERED WITH	USES
Crafted item	Crafting	Saving energy when climbing

You can craft Stairs out of a variety of materials. Create a crude set of blocks that goes up one block and then over one block. Repeat this until you have a crummy series of "steps" that allows characters to jump up until they reach the top. Then descend these natural steps and place your Stairs on the lower side of each block. If you try to place the Stairs too high, they come in upside down and aren't useful for climbing.

A real set of Stairs reduces jumping and saves you a huge amount of energy when you climb a long flight. Jumping burns through your hunger meter, so this is a worthwhile endeavor. Stairs look nice, too, so there's an aesthetic consideration as well.

RECIPE

INGREDIENTS	CRAFTING RECIPE	RESULT
Any six blocks of the following: Wood Plank, Cobblestone, Brick, Stone Brick, Nether Brick, Sandstone, Quartz	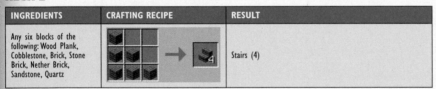	Stairs (4)

Stick

LOCATION	GATHERED WITH	USES
Crafted item	Crafting	Crafting

Divide Wood Planks into Sticks for a wide range of crafting options. Sticks are required for Swords, almost all tools, Rails, Fences, Gates, Signs, Ladders, Item Frames, and more. They're invaluable. Unless your inventory is filling up quickly, having Sticks on hand is a nice time-saver for replacing broken tools or making new Torches without taking extra steps.

RECIPE

INGREDIENTS	CRAFTING RECIPE	RESULT
Wood Plank (2)		Stick (4)

Sticky Piston

LOCATION	GATHERED WITH	USES
Crafted item	Crafting	Pushing and pulling objects

Sticky Pistons have the same general function as Pistons in that they push blocks one space forward. However, Sticky Pistons pull back the block to which they're attached. They're fun for making doors out of solid blocks. Trigger a Sticky Piston, let it open the makeshift door for you, and then cut the power to put the wall back in place. How cool is that for a secret lair?

RECIPE

INGREDIENTS	CRAFTING RECIPE	RESULT
Piston, Slimeball		Sticky Piston

Terracotta

LOCATION	GATHERED WITH	USES
Mesa	Pickaxe	Lovely decoration

Terracotta is a type of Hardened Clay found in the Overworld, in mesa biomes. You can craft this material using Clay in a Furnace to generate Terracotta reliably. Terracotta is quite lovely and can be dyed into many colors, making it a good source of decoration for your buildings.

Glazed Terracotta is even prettier. If you craft Terracotta with some type of dye and then cook it again in a Furnace, you end up with Glazed Terracotta. This variant of the material is way more fragile, but it's splendid-looking (having a textured surface).

RECIPE

INGREDIENTS	CRAFTING RECIPE	RESULT
Terracotta, Fuel in a Furnace		Glazed Terracotta

TNT

LOCATION	GATHERED WITH	USES
Crafted item	Crafting	Blowing stuff up

Craft blocks of TNT to use in traps, mining, or simply to have fun. The ingredients are easy to come by when you hunt Creepers. Carry TNT to a room you want to demolish, and place the block of explosives in the middle. Ignite TNT with a power source or something that creates fire (e.g., Flint and Steel), but make sure you don't stand nearby for the blast. TNT delivers a huge amount of damage.

RECIPE

INGREDIENTS	CRAFTING RECIPE	RESULT
Gunpowder (5), Sand (4)		TNT

Torch

LOCATION	GATHERED WITH	USES
Crafted item	Crafting	Light

Get a supply of Coal and Wood, and you can make Torches by the bundle. They're great for lighting your house, keeping your property clear of monster spawns, and for lighting tunnels as you mine and explore. Put Torches on the walls or the ground wherever you need to create light. They aren't the strongest light source in the game, but they're close, and they're inexpensive.

RECIPE

INGREDIENTS	CRAFTING RECIPE	RESULT
Stick, Coal/Charcoal		Torch (4)

Trapdoor

LOCATION	GATHERED WITH	USES
Crafted item	Crafting	Covering shafts

Use Trapdoors to conceal pits and prevent creatures from falling into them. Trapdoors open manually but can also be opened or closed with Redstone power. Use trails of Redstone Dust to activate Trapdoors from safety to drop monsters down into deadly pits. You can craft Trapdoors with either Wood or Iron Ingots, depending on the visual look of the item you're interested in making.

RECIPE

INGREDIENTS	CRAFTING RECIPE	RESULT
Wood Plank or Iron Ingot (6)		Trapdoor (2) or Iron Trapdoor (1)

Trapped Chest

LOCATION	GATHERED WITH	USES
Crafted item	Crafting	Interesting traps and secrets

Trapped Chests produce Redstone power when they're opened. They have a red tinge around their lock, so careful players spot them before they open the Chests. Signals from Trapped Chests are used to activate TNT, pits, and other defenses.

RECIPE

INGREDIENTS	CRAFTING RECIPE	RESULT
Chest, Tripwire Hook		Trapped Chest

Tripwire Hook

LOCATION	GATHERED WITH	USES
Crafted item	Crafting	Trap activation

Places two Tripwire Hooks across from each other in a passage; use a piece of String to connect them. This arms your trap, producing a pulse of energy if anything walks over the String or cuts it without using Shears.

Attach your Tripwire Hooks to a Redstone trail and concoct a nasty device to punish intruders: Lava from the ceiling, pits below, Pistons to close the corridor around someone, etc.

RECIPE

INGREDIENTS	CRAFTING RECIPE	RESULT
Iron Ingot, Stick, Wood Plank		Tripwire Hook (2)

Wall

LOCATION	GATHERED WITH	USES
Crafted item	Crafting	Decoration, defense

Walls protect areas from ingress by monsters, animals, and players. They can't be jumped over, so people have to break them or go around. They still allow a line of sight over the top edge, so you can see the areas outside your defensive perimeter. Shoot over your wall to safely kill monsters when they approach.

RECIPE

INGREDIENTS	CRAFTING RECIPE	RESULT
Cobblestone (6) or Mossy Cobblestone (6)		Wall (6)

Weighted Pressure Plate

LOCATION	GATHERED WITH	USES
Crafted item	Crafting	Sending a variable Redstone signal

Weighted Pressure Plates don't send a maximum-strength Redstone signal unless a certain amount of weight is placed upon them. Gold makes a plate that triggers more easily and sends a full-strength signal if there are 15 entities on top of it. Iron plates require much more weight to give off a strong signal; it takes over 140 items and creatures to fully trigger these plates.

RECIPE

INGREDIENTS	CRAFTING RECIPE	RESULT
Iron Ingot (2) or Gold Ingot (2)		Weighted Pressure Plate

Wood Plank

LOCATION	GATHERED WITH	USES
Crafted item	Crafting	Crafting, construction

Create Wood Planks by crafting any type of Wood in your inventory. You can then break down the resulting Planks even further into Sticks, or use the Planks to make a wide range of Wood-based items. Wood Planks are critical for Wood tools and equipment, the first tier of these implements that you can access.

Wood Planks are also used to make a vast range of furniture. At no point in the game do you stop using Wood or Wood Planks. Always keep a large supply in your Chests, and carry a full stack with you when you leave home.

RECIPE

INGREDIENTS	CRAFTING RECIPE	RESULT
Wood	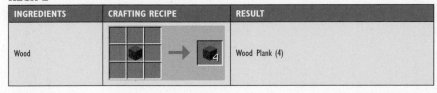	Wood Plank (4)

Wool

LOCATION	GATHERED WITH	USES
Worn by Sheep	Shears	Crafting

Gather Wool by using Shears on Sheep. Killing them yields less Wool, and live Sheep can regrow their Wool as long as they have access to yummy grass.

Wool is one of the most easily customized items in the game. Use dyes to change the color of your Wool, and then make custom blocks of Wool or craft colored Carpet. Wool is used to craft Beds and Paintings as well.

Written Book

LOCATION	GATHERED WITH	USES
Crafted item	Use a Book and Quill to write in it	Conveying information

Craft a Book and Quill, and then use this item from your hotbar. This lets you edit the text in the Book and Quill and turn it into a Written Book. Villagers trade Emeralds for these, when you're lucky, and they're also good for writing down stories for other players.

To copy a Written Book that you've edited, craft your existing one with another Book and Quill.

RECIPE

INGREDIENTS	CRAFTING RECIPE	RESULT
Written Book, Book and Quill		Written Book (2)

TOOLS, RESOURCES, AND CONSUMABLES

FOOD AND FOOD INGREDIENTS

Apple

LOCATION	GATHERED WITH	USES
Grows on trees	Anything	Food

Apples sometimes drop when you drop leaves, either by breaking them manually or when you destroy the Wood that the leaves are associated with. After the leaves break or decay naturally, an Apple is sometimes left behind. This happens only when you work with Oak leaves; other trees don't leave Apples.

Apples are an adequate food for the early game, when you're looking for something—anything—to eat. Their rarity makes them a poor choice for long-term hunger management. Breed animals or farm to provide for your feeding needs.

You can also craft Apples into Golden Apples or Enchanted Golden Apples when you want to get powerful effects for your character, but both of these items are costly.

Baked Potato

LOCATION	GATHERED WITH	USES
Cooked item	Cook Potatoes in a Furnace	Food

Throw a Potato into a Furnace and cook it. The result is a Baked Potato. Potatoes are extremely renewable because they're easy to grow.

Beetroot

LOCATION	GATHERED WITH	USES
Villages	Anything	Food

Beetroot can be eaten raw to reduce your hunger by a minimal amount. Or you can craft six Beetroot with a Wood Bowl to make Beetroot Soup.

Beetroots can also be broken down into Rose Red Dye.

Beetroot Soup

LOCATION	GATHERED WITH	USES
Crafted item	Crafting	Food

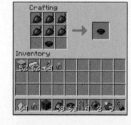

Cook Beetroot Soup to restore hunger faster than eating six regular Beetroots in a row.

Bowl

LOCATION	GATHERED WITH	USES
Crafted item	Crafting	Making Mushroom Stew

Bowls are used to carry Mushroom Stew. It takes only a few Planks to make your Bowl, so they're fairly easy to craft even out in the wilderness, though you need a Crafting Table as well.

Beetroots are also used with Bowls to make Beetroot Soup, a healing food.

RECIPE

INGREDIENTS	CRAFTING RECIPE	RESULT
Wood Plank (3)		Bowl

Bread

LOCATION	GATHERED WITH	USES
Crafted item	Crafting	Food

Combine three Wheat in order to craft a loaf of Bread. It's not an ideal food item, because it doesn't fill your hunger meter as much as cooked meat. However, Bread is extremely easy to make, and Wheat is renewable on a large scale. Make large Wheat farms to ensure you have food at your fingertips, regardless of the occasion.

RECIPE

INGREDIENTS	CRAFTING RECIPE	RESULT
Wheat (3)		Bread

Brown Mushroom

LOCATION	GATHERED WITH	USES
Swamps, shaded areas, the Nether	Anything	Food (Mushroom Stew)

Brown and Red Mushrooms combine to make Mushroom Stew. Carry a Wood Bowl around so you can make Mushroom Stew often while you explore swamps and various underground areas, including the Nether.

Cake

LOCATION	GATHERED WITH	USES
Crafted item	Crafting	Food

Cake isn't a very powerful food item, but it's fun to eat because you can share it with friends. Once crafted, Cake becomes a block that you have to place somewhere before it can be eaten. Stack the Cake on top of a higher block so it's easy to see, and to keep it off the ground. Then up to six people can take a bite out of it. Each bite restores only a tiny amount of hunger.

RECIPE

INGREDIENTS	CRAFTING RECIPE	RESULT
Milk (3), Sugar (2), Egg, Wheat (3)		Cake

Carrot

LOCATION	GATHERED WITH	USES
Carried by Zombies	Anything	Food, Pig breeding

Zombies drop Carrots on rare occasions. You sometimes find them in Villages as well. They're a useful crop to farm, and don't require any new locations or methods compared to Potatoes or Wheat. Develop Farmland, irrigate it, and start growing Carrots as soon as you find one of them.

Carrots lure Pigs and Rabbits if you're holding them, and are also used to breed Pigs once you have a few of them.

In crafting, Carrots make Carrots on a Stick and Golden Carrots.

Chorus Fruit

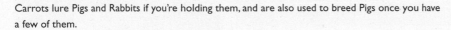

LOCATION	GATHERED WITH	USES
The End	Anything	Food

After breaking a Chorus Plant, you get Chorus Flowers (to make new plants) and Chorus Fruits (to eat). Chorus Fruit is a fairly decent source of food, though there's a chance that you will be teleported after eating a piece of it.

Chorus Fruit can be cooked in a Furnace to turn it into building material (Popped Chorus Fruit).

Clownfish

LOCATION	GATHERED WITH	USES
Water blocks	A Fishing Rod	Food and Ocelot taming

Clownfish isn't very tasty. There isn't any way to cook it properly, and it doesn't restore much health. Save these until you find Ocelots, and then use them to tame kitties. Ocelots like them as well as any other raw variety of fish.

Cooked Chicken

LOCATION	GATHERED WITH	USES
Cooked item	Cook Raw Chicken in a Furnace	Food

Kill Chickens with fire or cook Raw Chicken in a Furnace to produce Cooked Chicken. This eliminates the chance of food poisoning that Raw Chicken poses.

Cooked Porkchop

LOCATION	GATHERED WITH	USES
Cooked item	Cook Raw Porkchops in a Furnace	Food

Cook Raw Porkchops in a Furnace, or use fire to kill Pigs. Either of these methods produces Cooked Porkchops. They restore a fair amount of hunger.

Cooked Salmon

LOCATION	GATHERED WITH	USES
Cooked item	Cook Raw Salmon in a Furnace	Food

Take Raw Salmon and cook it in a Furnace. That's it; you now have some yummy food to eat.

Cookie

LOCATION	GATHERED WITH	USES
Crafted item	Crafting	Food

Cookies are made from Wheat and Cocoa Beans. They're made in large batches, and it takes quite a few to fill you up. They don't leave you satisfied for long, but having large stacks of them makes it easy to eat only as much as you need so nothing gets wasted.

All in all, Cookies are useful if you have Cocoa Beans and Wheat. They're a reliable food source, despite several minor drawbacks, such as long eating time for the amount of hunger restored.

RECIPE

INGREDIENTS	CRAFTING RECIPE	RESULT
Cocoa Bean, Wheat (2)	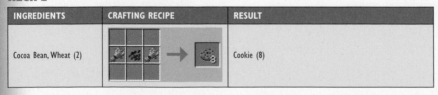	Cookie (8)

Egg

LOCATION	GATHERED WITH	USES
Near Chickens	Pick them up	Baking

Chickens lay Eggs once or twice every ten minutes. They pop out, making a sound when it happens, and you can grab the Egg anytime after that. Eggs are ingredients for Cakes and Pumpkin Pie.

It's also possible to throw Eggs. Equip them on your hotbar and use the Eggs as projectile weapons. They don't inflict any substantial damage, but they sometimes spawn a baby Chicken when they hit something.

Enchanted Golden Apple

LOCATION	GATHERED WITH	USES
Crafted item	Crafting	Special food

Enchanted Golden Apples require nine times more Gold to create than a Golden Apple. They're brutal to craft. However, they add 30 seconds of Regeneration V, the same amount of Absorption as a Golden Apple, and five minutes of Resistance and Fire Resistance. You become almost an un-killable god after eating one. Save Enchanted Golden Apples for boss fights against the Wither or Ender Dragon. Otherwise, you're spending too much Gold to be worthwhile.

RECIPE

INGREDIENTS	CRAFTING RECIPE	RESULT
Apple, Gold Block (8)	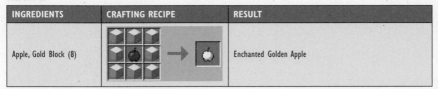	Enchanted Golden Apple

Gold Block

LOCATION	GATHERED WITH	USES
Crafted item	Crafting	Decoration, crafting an Enchanted Golden Apple

Put together a full set of nine Gold Ingots to craft a Gold block. It looks nice, but it's very expensive. You won't use them to decorate your house unless you've been playing for a long time or are working in Creative Mode.

Gold blocks are ingredients for Enchanted Golden Apples, the most expensive and most useful food in the game.

RECIPE

INGREDIENTS	CRAFTING RECIPE	RESULT
Gold Ingot (9)		Gold block

Golden Apple

LOCATION	GATHERED WITH	USES
Crafted item	Crafting	Special food

One sometimes finds Golden Apples in Chests, but you often have to craft them yourself. Golden Apples act as food items that also provide beneficial effects to your character. Golden Apples give you Regeneration II for several seconds, and add Absorption for a couple minutes. For major battles, Golden Apples are worthwhile items to use.

RECIPE

INGREDIENTS	CRAFTING RECIPE	RESULT
Apple, Gold Ingot (8)		Golden Apple

Golden Carrot

LOCATION	GATHERED WITH	USES
Crafted item	Crafting	Food, brewing

Golden Carrots are expensive. Get a Carrot from a Zombie and start a Carrot garden. Then craft one of your Carrots with eight Gold Nuggets to make one Golden Carrot. Golden Carrots are used in Potions of Night Vision, or they're eaten to restore a large amount of hunger.

RECIPE

INGREDIENTS	CRAFTING RECIPE	RESULT
Carrot, Gold Nugget (8)		Golden Carrot

Melon

LOCATION	GATHERED WITH	USES
Jungle biomes	Anything	Food, brewing

Melons are naturally found in jungles, though they're also available for trade in some Villages. Once you find Melons or Melon Seeds, create a garden back at your base. A steady supply of Melons is extremely handy because of their use in brewing.

Combine Gold Nuggets and a Melon to make a Glistering Melon. This is a major brewing ingredient thanks to its use in Potions of Healing!

Milk

LOCATION	GATHERED WITH	USES
Inside Cows	Bucket	Removing Poison and other effects

Cows and Mooshrooms provide Milk if you use a Bucket on either of them. This liquid doesn't fill up your hunger meter, but it's useful for removing a variety of effects. Use Milk after you eat foods that poison you to negate their negative effects.

When fighting against creatures that cause Poison, it's smart to keep a Bucket of Milk on hand. Use it after battle to reduce the damage you've taken.

Mushroom Stew

LOCATION	GATHERED WITH	USES
Crafted item	Crafted in a Bowl	Snacks

Mushroom Stew requires you to harvest a Red Mushroom and a Brown Mushroom. Combine these in your inventory with a Bowl, and you end up with this stew. Eating it frees up your Bowl to be reused as many times as you like. Carry a Bowl when you travel through swamps or the Nether to get free food on the fly without wasting much time.

Use Bowls to "milk" Mooshrooms to receive this stew. Mooshrooms are insanely useful animals to keep around.

RECIPE

INGREDIENTS	CRAFTING RECIPE	RESULT
Red Mushroom, Brown Mushroom, Bowl		Mushroom Stew

Poisonous Potato

LOCATION	GATHERED WITH	USES
Potato farms	Anything	None

When you harvest Potatoes, you sometimes (rarely) end up with Poisonous Potatoes as well. Don't eat these; they've gone bad. Throw them away, give them to friends you don't like, or leave them in a Chest in case someone ever comes up with a fun use for them.

TOOLS, RESOURCES, AND CONSUMABLES

Potato

LOCATION	GATHERED WITH	USES
Zombie treasures or Villages	Kill Zombies or steal from Village Farmers	Food

If you want to get a Carrot or Potato, kill Zombies often. These rare drops provide an entirely new type of crop to plant in your garden. Potatoes are planted directly into Farmland and grow in a way that's similar to Wheat. When they fully pop out of the soil, harvest them and cook them in a Furnace. You end up with Baked Potatoes.

Pufferfish

LOCATION	GATHERED WITH	USES
Water blocks	A Fishing Rod	Brewing Potions of Water Breathing

Fishing Rods occasionally grab Pufferfish from the water. These are not edible in any safe way; they make your character very sick. However, they're the main ingredient for Potions of Water Breathing. Save your Pufferfish in a Chest with brewing ingredients in case you ever want to perform involved underwater exploration or construction.

Pumpkin

LOCATION	GATHERED WITH	USES
Found rarely throughout the Overworld	Axe	Helmets, cooking, crafting

Pumpkins are hard to find. They grow naturally in a number of biomes, but they're rare enough that you don't always find them within a minute or two of your home. Getting these plants requires a fair amount of exploration unless you're really lucky!

Once you find Pumpkins, chop them down with an Axe and bring them home. Break your Pumpkins into Pumpkin Seeds, and plant those. Let your Pumpkin garden grow on its own for a while, and then use your excess Pumpkins for pies, Pumpkin Helmets (which don't enrage Endermen), and Jack-o'-Lanterns (good mood lighting).

Pumpkin Pie

LOCATION	GATHERED WITH	USES
In a baker's oven	Crafting	Dessert

Pumpkin Pie is made when you craft an Egg, Sugar, and a Pumpkin together. If you have a Chicken pen and gardens for Sugar Cane and Pumpkins, this is an easy item to make. Cooked meats are better at filling up your character, but Pumpkin Pie still fills a satisfying number of bars on your hunger meter. You just end up hungry again sooner than if you eat cooked meats.

RECIPE

INGREDIENTS	CRAFTING RECIPE	RESULT
Pumpkin, Sugar, Egg	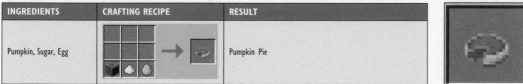	Pumpkin Pie

Raw Beef

LOCATION	GATHERED WITH	USES
On Cows	Kill Cows with a Sword	Cooking

Each Cow can drop up to several pieces of Raw Beef. Cook these in a Furnace to produce Steak, a very nice food item. If you use fire to kill a Cow, they drop Steak instead of Raw Beef.

Raw Chicken

LOCATION	GATHERED WITH	USES
On Chickens	Kill Chickens with a Sword	Cooking

You earn Raw Chicken by hunting Chickens. Kill them with a Sword to get raw meat, or use Flint and Steel to get your Chickens cooked immediately. Always cook Raw Chicken in a Furnace; raw meat from these birds has a chance to make your character sick from food poisoning.

Raw Fish

LOCATION	GATHERED WITH	USES
Water blocks	A Fishing Rod	Cooking

Use a Fishing Rod to harvest fish and other useful items from Water blocks. Pull the Fishing Rod out of the water when you see bubbling, and hope that you get something good. Raw Fish are cooked in Furnaces to produce Cooked Fish.

If you want a house cat, feed Raw Fish to Ocelots to tame them. Bring several pieces of Raw Fish, because you won't always impress them with your first gift!

Raw Porkchop

LOCATION	GATHERED WITH	USES
On Pigs	Kill Pigs with Swords	Cooking

One finds Pigs in small groups throughout the Overworld. Kill them with your Sword to grab a few Raw Porkchops. Cook them in your Furnace to turn them into yummy Porkchops.

If you kill Pigs with fire, they'll drop Cooked Porkchops instead.

Raw Salmon

LOCATION	GATHERED WITH	USES
Water blocks	A Fishing Rod	Food

Gather Raw Salmon by using your Fishing Rod on Water blocks. This takes time and patience, so it isn't as efficient as farming. Once you get Raw Salmon or other edible fish, take it to a Furnace and cook it. Eat the Cooked Salmon whenever you get hungry.

Red Mushroom

LOCATION	GATHERED WITH	USES
Dark areas in forests or the Nether	Anything	Food (Mushroom Stew)

Red Mushrooms and Brown Mushrooms are combined with Bowls to make Mushroom Stew. This is a good food source for people working with shade gardens. It's also nice in the Nether, because there aren't many ways to feed your character in that dimension. Mushrooms grow in the Nether's dim light, so they're a renewable food source. Just bring a Bowl and you're good to go.

Rotten Flesh

LOCATION	GATHERED WITH	USES
On Zombies	Kill Zombies	Healing and taming Wolves

Rotten Flesh is bad for your health. Eating it often gives your character food poisoning, which drains points from your hunger meter. Eat Rotten Flesh only if you're desperate. Even then, save several Rotten Flesh and eat them all at once. Food poisoning doesn't stack, so you won't be any worse off eating five Rotten Flesh than you would be eating one or two pieces.

It's better to save Rotten Flesh for Wolves you meet. Feed them to earn their trust, and use Rotten Flesh to heal them or get them breeding once they're already tamed.

Spider Eye

LOCATION	GATHERED WITH	USES
Spiders' heads	Kill Spiders with any weapon	Brewing

Spider Eyes are fermented with Brown Mushrooms and Sugar to make Fermented Spider Eyes. These are very useful in high-end brewing. Regular Spider Eyes only help to make Potions of Poison and Weakness, so they're nice but slightly limited.

It is possible to eat Spider Eyes in an act of complete desperation if you're starving. However, they're poisonous. Drink Milk immediately after eating your Spider Eyes, or avoid eating them unless you're already at such low health that the Poison won't do any additional damage.

Steak

LOCATION	GATHERED WITH	USES
Cooked item	Cook Raw Beef in a Furnace	Dinner

Slay Cows to collect Raw Beef. Put this inside a Furnace and use any type of fuel to cook the beef into Steak. Alternatively, kill Cows with fire to cook their meat instantly and get Steak straight from the source.

Steak is very filling, so it's a great food item to carry around when you go far away from home.

Sugar

LOCATION	GATHERED WITH	USES
Crafted item	Crafted from Sugar Cane	Baking, Horse treats

You can make Sugar by crafting a single piece of Sugar Cane into raw Sugar. Sugar is then used to bake Cakes or Pumpkin Pie. It's also an ingredient in Potions of Swiftness.

Feed Sugar to Horses to help with taming them. It also helps heal injured Horses and helps them grow from Foals into adult Horses.

RECIPE

INGREDIENTS	CRAFTING RECIPE	RESULT
Sugar Cane		Sugar

Wheat

LOCATION	GATHERED WITH	USES
Farms	Any tool	Making Bread, animal breeding

Wheat is grown on Farmland. Use Hoes to till Dirt or Grass blocks, plant Seeds on them, and ensure a Water block is within four blocks so the Wheat grows as quickly as possible. Keep light on the area at all times, with sun, Torches, or Redstone Lamps, and harvest your Wheat when it gets tall and turns slightly brownish.

POTIONS

Awkward Potion

LOCATION	GATHERED WITH	USES
Brewing item	Brew a Water Bottle and Nether Wart	This is the core Potion that leads to all useful Secondary and Tertiary Potions

Awkward Potions don't do anything neat by themselves, but they're the foundation of brewing. Create a garden of Nether Wart to provide ingredients, and then brew as many Awkward Potions as you can with your surplus Nether Wart.

Awkward Potions are then used as ingredients for more complex Potions. The number of effects is impressive: healing, harming, health regeneration, poison, faster movement, resistance to fire, breathing underwater, etc. Everything related to brewing comes from Awkward Potions. Brew them. Love them!

Mundane Potion

LOCATION	GATHERED WITH	USES
Brewing item	Brew a Water Bottle with almost any common brewing ingredient	Can make a Potion of Weakness

Mundane Potions aren't of any use. They can be brewed again to make a Potion of Weakness, but that's not a great value either. You need to get Nether Wart and make Awkward Potions to get into serious brewing.

Mundane Potion (X)

LOCATION	GATHERED WITH	USES
Brewing item	Brew a Water Bottle and Redstone	Can make an Extended Potion of Weakness

This Potion doesn't do anything important, but it shows off the core power of Redstone in brewing (i.e., to extend the duration of Potions).

Potion of Fire Resistance

LOCATION	GATHERED WITH	USES
Brewing item	Brew an Awkward Potion with Magma Cream	Protects against Lava, fire, and burning damage

If you're working around Lava frequently or fighting monsters in Nether Fortresses, it's great to have a Potion of Fire Resistance around. Blazes are much easier to handle when their attacks don't burn you.

Potion of Harming

LOCATION	GATHERED WITH	USES
Brewing item	Brew a Potion of Healing or Poison with a Fermented Spider Eye	Deals instant damage to a target

Potions of Harming are excellent weapons against heavily armored targets. These Potions are also great in PvP combat against players with enchanted Diamond armor!

Potion of Healing

LOCATION	GATHERED WITH	USES
Brewing item	Brew an Awkward Potion with Glistering Melon	Heals living targets instantly

Potions of Healing restore health as soon as they're used. Drinking them is fine, but Splash Potions of Healing are even faster because they work as soon as you throw them onto yourself—and they heal friends if you throw them at allies or NPCs. Bring these along when you fight Withers, Ender Dragons, or other players.

TOOLS, RESOURCES, AND CONSUMABLES

Potion of Invisibility

LOCATION	GATHERED WITH	USES
Brewing item	Brew a Potion of Night Vision with a Fermented Spider Eye	Turns you invisible

Potions of Invisibility are fun for sneaking or avoiding conflict. Your weapons and armor are still visible, so you have to remove them if you want to be completely undetectable. Use these Potions around other players to sneak into their bases, scout, and cause chaos.

Potion of Leaping

LOCATION	GATHERED WITH	USES
Brewing item	Brew an Awkward Potion with a Rabbit's Foot	Lets you jump higher than ever before

This Potion allows your character to get through rough vertical terrain without having to do as much tunneling and Stair construction. It's most useful when exploring places that you're not going to return to very often. It's also fun if you're arranging free-running races with your friends and want to get an edge (as long as that's allowable by whatever rules you come up with).

Potion of Night Vision

LOCATION	GATHERED WITH	USES
Brewing item	Brew an Awkward Potion with a Golden Carrot	Lets you see well at any light level

Potions of Night Vision are great when you're underground, in the Nether, or hunting the End. You can see well across long distances, pick out strange areas or buildings, and fight against monsters that would otherwise have a big advantage over you. Your success in battles against Withers depends heavily on these Potions, because Withers love to blow up everything around them, including Torches!

Potion of Poison

LOCATION	GATHERED WITH	USES
Brewing item	Brew an Awkward Potion with a Spider Eye	Deals damage over time

Potions of Poison deal consistent damage over time, regardless of the target's armor. They're nasty to use against other players, especially if your target has enchanted Diamond armor. Many monsters are immune or resistant to Poison damage.

Potion of Regeneration

LOCATION	GATHERED WITH	USES
Brewing item	Brew an Awkward Potion with a Ghast Tear	Restores health over time

Potions of Regeneration don't heal you quickly like Potions of Healing, but they add a tremendous amount of health to your character over time. Combine this with a full health bar to ensure that you heal quickly from all minor wounds. Save Splash Potions of Healing to restore yourself almost instantly from more severe injuries.

Potion of Slowness

LOCATION	GATHERED WITH	USES
Brewing item	Brew a Potion of Fire Resistance or Swiftness with a Fermented Spider Eye	Slows movement

Make a Splash Potion of Slowness and throw it at enemies that you're trying to avoid. These Potions are fairly effective against other characters.

Potion of Strength

LOCATION	GATHERED WITH	USES
Brewing item	Brew an Awkward Potion with Blaze Powder	Dramatically increases melee damage output

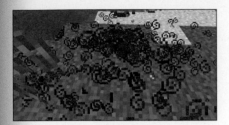

Use these powerful Potions anytime you deal with dangerous enemies. They're ideal when fighting in Nether Fortresses or if you attack Withers, Iron Golems, or any other scary beasts.

Potion of Swiftness

LOCATION	GATHERED WITH	USES
Brewing item	Brew an Awkward Potion with Sugar	Improves movement and jumping speed

Potions of Swiftness are useful when you explore on foot, or if you fight fast creatures and need to maintain a speed advantage against them. They're nice for dealing with some of the Nether's dangerous monsters because many of them possess ranged attacks or high speed.

Potion of Water Breathing

LOCATION	GATHERED WITH	USES
Brewing item	Brew an Awkward Potion with a Pufferfish	You can breathe underwater

Potions of Water Breathing give you several minutes to swim underwater without the fear of drowning. It's nice to have these when you explore deep water, look through underground caves, or if you want to create interesting structures underwater without having to wall off the area ahead of time.

Potion of Weakness

LOCATION	GATHERED WITH	USES
Brewing item	Brew a Water Bottle with a Fermented Spider Eye	Reduces damage output

Potions of Weakness reduce your damage output for a moderate period. They're useful only if you brew them into Splash Potions of Weakness to use against other targets, and even then they aren't especially important.

Thick Potion

LOCATION	GATHERED WITH	USES
Brewing item	Brew a Water Bottle with Glowstone Dust	Brewing Potions

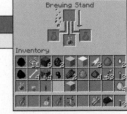

This is a precursor Potion to a Potion of Weakness. To accomplish more powerful brewing, make an Awkward Potion and move up from there.

Water Bottle

LOCATION	GATHERED WITH	USES
Brewing item	Add water to a Glass Bottle	Brewing Potions

Fill a Glass Bottle with water to create the most basic "Potion." Use either a water source or a Cauldron to put water into these bottles. These items become the starting point for Potions, as explained in **Chapter 6**.

TOOLS

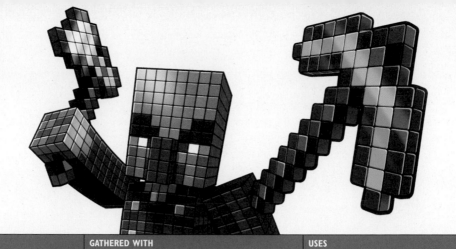

Axe

LOCATION	GATHERED WITH	USES
Crafted item	Crafted	Harvesting Wood

Trees and other wooden objects can be broken with any tool or object, but Axes carve through these blocks faster than anything. Use Wooden Axes early in the game, but upgrade to Stone as soon as you can. Iron Axes are never required, but they're quick to get the job done, and they look nice too.

In a pinch, Axes are decent weapons. They lose more durability when they're used to kill monsters, but if you don't have a Sword, these tools offer your best form of defense.

RECIPE

INGREDIENTS	CRAFTING RECIPE	RESULT	
Stick (2), Metal (3)		Axe	

Bucket

LOCATION	GATHERED WITH	USES
Crafted item	Crafted	Carrying Milk, Lava, or water

Craft a Bucket or two and keep them in your inventory. Use them to carry water over to farming projects or down into the depths. Use that water to irrigate Farmland, to put out Lava and turn it into Obsidian, or to create traps and waterways that carry creatures or goods from one area to another.

Two Buckets are better than one, because two Water blocks can form an infinite water source. Carve out three blocks in the floor to make a trench, and use both Buckets to fill each end of the trench. Now you can gather water from the middle of the trench without needing additional Water blocks. This is quite useful underground or in other dry areas.

If you have a Cow, use a Bucket on it to gather Milk. Milk can remove effects from your character, such as Poison!

RECIPE

INGREDIENTS	CRAFTING RECIPE	RESULT	
Iron Ingot (3)	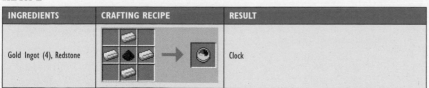	Bucket	

Clock

LOCATION	GATHERED WITH	USES
Crafted item	Crafted	Telling time

Clocks show you the position of either the sun or moon, regardless of where you're standing in the Overworld. This is wonderful if you're worried about getting caught outside in the evening, or if you're underground and still want to stick to a schedule.

RECIPE

INGREDIENTS	CRAFTING RECIPE	RESULT
Gold Ingot (4), Redstone		Clock

Compass

LOCATION	GATHERED WITH	USES
Crafted item	Crafted	Telling time

A Compass is a basic tool you carry around to help you avoid getting lost. It shows the direction you're facing, as long as you stay in the Overworld—Compasses do not work in the Nether or the End.

RECIPE

INGREDIENTS	CRAFTING RECIPE	RESULT
Iron Ingot (4), Redstone	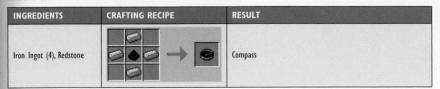	Compass

Empty Map

LOCATION	GATHERED WITH	USES
Crafted item	Crafted	Seeing the world from a bird's-eye view

You can use Empty Maps to create a picture of the world around your character. You can see things near the area where you first use the Map. It's smart to center these on your starting region. However, Maps don't show you very much territory at first. To increase their scope, you need to zoom out, and this involves additional crafting. Use more Paper and your existing Map to see a wider area. You can do this up to four times to get maximum coverage.

If you ever need to copy your Map, use your existing one and a new Empty Map. This creates a clone of your old Map to use as a backup. Or you can give these to other players as a way of sharing knowledge.

INGREDIENTS	CRAFTING RECIPE	RESULT
Paper (8), Compass	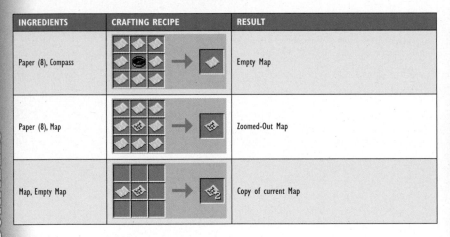	Empty Map
Paper (8), Map		Zoomed-Out Map
Map, Empty Map		Copy of current Map

Fire Charge

LOCATION	GATHERED WITH	USES
Crafted item	Crafted	Ingredient for Firework Stars

Fire Charges are single-use items, so they provide a very costly way to start fires. However, they're often crafted as a precursor to Firework Stars (very fun), or to create dangerous traps. Use Fire Charges and a Dispenser as a way to deal damage to enemies that trigger your trap. This is especially powerful when you fill the target area with flammable objects!

RECIPE

INGREDIENTS	CRAFTING RECIPE	RESULT
Blaze Powder, Gunpowder, Coal/Charcoal	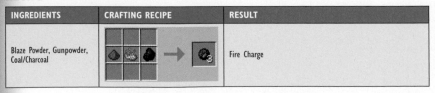	Fire Charge

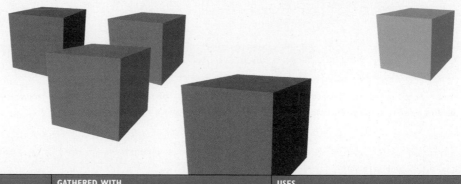

Fishing Rod

LOCATION	GATHERED WITH	USES
Crafted item	Crafted	Gathering materials from water

Fishing Rods are crafted from simple items. Break Wood into Sticks and kill Spiders to get a couple pieces of String early in the game. Once crafted, your Fishing Rod is a decent source of food and occasional treasure.

- **Possible Fish:** Fish, Salmon, Clownfish, Pufferfish (don't eat these)
- **Treasure:** Bow, Enchanted Book, Fishing Rod, Lily Pad, Name Tag, Saddle

RECIPE

INGREDIENTS	CRAFTING RECIPE	RESULT
Stick (3), String (2)		Fishing Rod

Flint and Steel

LOCATION	GATHERED WITH	USES
Crafted item	Crafted	Starting fires

Flint and Steel is a tool for starting fires without much mess or inconvenience. Carry one of these in your inventory, especially if you're killing livestock for food. Set animals on fire to immediately cook their meat; it's a nice time-saver. Or bring Flint and Steel into the Nether so you can relight Nether Portals to return to your home.

Avoid the temptation to set forests on fire. Once started, there's a chance that it can get out of control!

RECIPE

INGREDIENTS	CRAFTING RECIPE	RESULT
Iron Ingot, Flint		Flint and Steel

Hoe

LOCATION	GATHERED WITH	USES
Crafted item	Crafted	Gardening

You don't use Hoes too frequently, so you only need them on your hotbar if you're farming. Use Hoes on Dirt or Grass blocks to turn either of them into Farmland. Farmland is used for planting Seeds, to grow Wheat and other edible crops. Make sure your Farmland has access to water within four blocks to keep it irrigated.

RECIPE

INGREDIENTS	CRAFTING RECIPE	RESULT
Stick (2), Metal (2)		Hoe

Pickaxe

LOCATION	GATHERED WITH	USES
Crafted item	Crafted	Breaking heavy blocks

Pickaxes are possibly the most important tool in *Minecraft*. With these, you can break Stone, Cobblestone, Netherrack, important ores and metals, and so forth. You use these tools constantly when you mine, so they always deserve a place on your hotbar.

You need a certain quality of Pickaxe to mine certain materials. Wood is useful only to harvest your first few pieces of Stone. Stone Pickaxes are faster and stronger, but can't mine better materials, such as Diamond, Redstone, etc. Switch to Iron Pickaxes for most tasks once you're established, and don't look back. Diamond is required only for working on Obsidian blocks.

RECIPE

INGREDIENTS	CRAFTING RECIPE	RESULT
Stick (2), Metal (3)		Pickaxe

Shears

LOCATION	GATHERED WITH	USES
Crafted item	Crafted	Gathering grasses, leaves, and Wool

Shears are a tool that doesn't get constant use, but they're still nice to have in your inventory. This is especially true if you wander the Overworld's surface. Shears safely collect Wool from Sheep, Red Mushrooms from Mooshrooms, String or cobwebs in mine tunnels, and they can hack through leaves like nobody's business.

RECIPE

INGREDIENTS	CRAFTING RECIPE	RESULT
Iron Ingot (2)		Shears

Shovel

LOCATION	GATHERED WITH	USES
Crafted item	Crafted	Digging through Gravel, Dirt, and Sand

Shovels are essential tools that you craft early in the game and never stop creating. A Shovel is the best tool for loose blocks, including Gravel, Dirt, and Sand. Using Axes or Pickaxes for the same tasks damages those tools compared to using them for their normal functions, and it takes much longer.

For this reason, it's smart to keep a Pickaxe, Shovel, and Axe on your hotbar at the same time. Switch between them so you always use the correct tool for the job.

RECIPE

INGREDIENTS	CRAFTING RECIPE	RESULT
Stick (2), Metal		Shovel

WEAPONS AND ARMOR

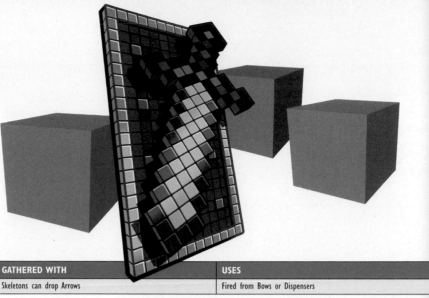

Arrow

LOCATION	GATHERED WITH	USES
Crafted item	Skeletons can drop Arrows	Fired from Bows or Dispensers

Arrows are shot from Bows or Dispensers to deal damage to enemies at range. These attacks inflict 1 to 5 damage, depending on how well-charged the attack is.

Arrows that you fire into regular blocks can be retrieved if you're quick about it. Use this as a way to recover Arrows that you use while practicing, or misses from ranged combat.

Spectral Arrows add the Glowing status effect to anyone they hit. These are primarily used in PvP combat to ensure that someone can be spotted and killed even if they run away or take cover. Glowing lasts for a short time, and causes the target to show up even when they're behind full cover!

Tipped Arrows add the effects of a Lingering Potion to eight crafted Arrows. These can be positive or negative effects, so you can customize whether they're used on friends or enemies (though the base Arrows still do damage, so don't use strong Bows if you're trying to be nice to anyone).

The effects from Tipped Arrows are reduced in strength from their full Potion variants. You deliver about one-eighth of the total result, per shot.

RECIPE

INGREDIENTS	CRAFTING RECIPE	RESULT
Flint, Stick, Feather		Arrows (4)
Glowstone Dust, Arrow		Spectral Arrow (2)
Arrow, Lingering Potion		Tipped Arrow (8)

Boots

LOCATION	GATHERED WITH	USES
Crafted item	Crafted	Damage reduction

Boots are a type of armor. They're made at a Crafting Table by using four pieces of either Leather or metal. Diamond Boots offer the best protection, but Iron Boots are pretty darn good and cost a lot less in terms of time to gather their materials.

Once you make your Boots, go into your inventory to put them on. Your character's appearance changes once they're equipped, and damage you take from physical sources is reduced.

RECIPE

INGREDIENTS	CRAFTING RECIPE	RESULT
Leather or Metal (4)		Boots

Bow

LOCATION	GATHERED WITH	USES
Crafted item	Crafted	Ranged combat

Bows are either crafted or gathered from Skeletons that you defeat (as a rare drop). Gather materials for Bow crafting by breaking Wood into Sticks and by killing Spiders to gather extra String.

Once you complete this weapon, equip it and keep Arrows in your inventory for use. You can deal decent damage at long range, as long as you're good at hitting your targets!

RECIPE

INGREDIENTS	CRAFTING RECIPE	RESULT
Stick (3), String (3)		Bow

Chestplate

LOCATION	GATHERED WITH	USES
Crafted item	Crafted	Damage reduction

Craft a Chestplate to dramatically reduce the damage you take from physical sources. This type of armor requires the most Leather or pieces of metal, so it's costly to craft or replace. However, it also offers the most protection out of all your armor pieces.

Once it's completed, go into your inventory to equip this item and start gaining its benefits. Diamond Chestplates are the best in the game, but Iron Chestplates are suitable for almost all the fights that you encounter.

RECIPE

INGREDIENTS	CRAFTING RECIPE	RESULT
Leather or Metal (8)		Chestplate

Elytra

LOCATION	GATHERED WITH	USES
End Ships	Anything	Gliding

Elytra are Chest items that grant gliding powers to your character. When you're falling, tap the Jump button to start a glide.

These items are repaired using an Anvil and spare Leather, or can be combined with other Elytra to make a single unit that's in better condition.

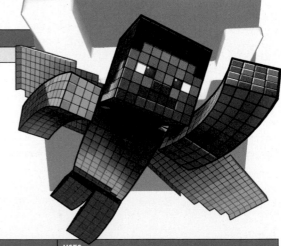

Helmet

LOCATION	GATHERED WITH	USES
Crafted item	Crafted	Damage reduction

Helmets are put together with five pieces of Leather or metal. Go into your inventory to equip them. Using armor reduces the damage you take from physical sources, such as melee attacks, Arrows, and explosions.

RECIPE

INGREDIENTS	CRAFTING RECIPE	RESULT
Leather or Metal (5)		Helmet

Leggings

LOCATION	GATHERED WITH	USES
Crafted item	Crafting	Damage reduction

Leggings are the fourth type of armor. Put together seven pieces of Leather or metal, and use these to protect your character's legs. Go into your inventory, equip them, and enjoy your increased survivability.

RECIPE

INGREDIENTS	CRAFTING RECIPE	RESULT
Leather or Metal (7)		Leggings

Shield

LOCATION	GATHERED WITH	USES
Crafted item	Crafted	Defense

Shields are held in your offhand and are used to block incoming attacks. They're useful against ranged strikes, and can even reduce knockback. Watch out in melee, because these objects only protect your front and enemies can get around behind you. Axe users also have a heavier swing that disables your Shields periodically, so it won't be nearly as effective against them. Damaged Shields can be used to repair each other.

RECIPE

INGREDIENTS	CRAFTING RECIPE	RESULT
Wood Plank (6), Iron Ingot		A protective piece of equipment that's good in melee and amazing against ranged weaponry
Shield (2)		Adds two damaged Shields together to get a single Shield that is in much better repair

Sword

LOCATION	GATHERED WITH	USES
Crafted item	Crafted	Melee attacks

Swords are made with a Stick and two pieces of metal. Early in the game, you're likely to use Stone Swords fairly often, but switch to Iron Swords once you have a couple pieces of Iron Ingots to spare; these improved blades last a long time and kill enemies quickly. You won't need to switch to Diamond Swords for a good while.

Once you have a Sword, use it in close-range combat to kill enemies. Attack them as you retreat to ensure your character gets many attacks in, while your opponents suffer from knockback and miss opportunities to counter.

RECIPE

INGREDIENTS	CRAFTING RECIPE	RESULT
Sticks and Metal (2)		Sword

Creatures Big and Small

This chapter discusses all the monsters, livestock, and anything else you might bump into. We'll show you what items are gathered from *Minecraft*'s beasts and how to safely defeat your enemies. The following list provides basic information for all the creatures in the game. Afterward, we cover each creature in greater depth.

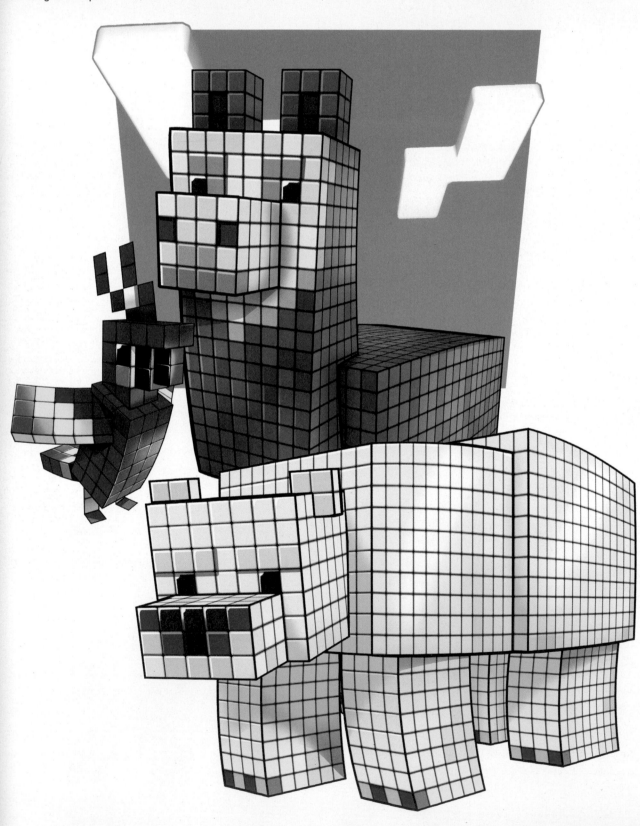

ANIMAL AND MONSTER QUICK LIST

CREATURE	AGGRESSION	SPAWN LOCATION	ITEMS	HEALTH	ATTACK DAMAGE (NORMAL)	EXPERIENCE VALUE	TAMABLE?	RIDEABLE?	NOTES
Bat	Passive	Very low-light areas, deep caves	None	6	None	None	No	No	N/A
Blaze	Aggressive	Nether Fortresses	Blaze Rod, Glowstone Dust (not in PC version)	20	5 at range, 6 up close	10	No	No	Can be damaged by rain, water, or Snowballs
Cave Spider	Neutral	Abandoned Mineshafts	String, Spider Eye	12	2 + Poison	5	No	No	Passive in bright light
Chicken	Passive	Overworld	Feathers, Raw Chicken, Eggs	4	None	1-3	No	No	Produces Eggs over time, and yields Cooked Chicken if slain by fire
Chicken Jockey	Aggressive	Low-light areas	Rotten Flesh, Chicken items	20 for Jockey, 4 for Chicken	3-6 depending on Jockey's health	5 for Jockey, 1-3 for Chicken	No	No	Jockeys do more damage when they get hurt
Cow	Passive	Overworld	Leather, Raw Beef, Milk	10	None	1-3	No	No	Yields Steak if killed by fire, and yields Milk with a Bucket
Creeper	Aggressive	Low-light areas	Gunpowder, Music Disc	20	49 (97 if charged)	5	No	No	Deals more damage if charged by lightning, and yields Music Discs if slain by Skeleton
Ender Dragon	Aggressive	The End	The Overworld Portal, Dragon Egg	200	10	12,000	No	No	Is healed by Ender Crystals
Enderman	Neutral	The Overworld, the End	Ender Pearls	40	7	5	No	No	Attacks when damaged or if you make eye contact
Endermite	Aggressive	Anywhere	None	8	2	3	No	No	Has a 5% chance of spawning each time you throw an Ender Pearl
Evoker	Aggressive	Woodland Mansions	Totem of Undying, Emerald	24	6	10	No	No	Summons Vexes, casts Fang spells, and can color Sheep
Ghast	Aggressive	The Nether, out in the open	Gunpowder, Ghast Tears	10	6 from impact, 17 from explosion	5	No	No	Shots cause an area-of-effect explosion of fire
Guardian	Aggressive	Underwater	Prismarine Crystals, Prismarine Shards, Raw Fish	30	6	10	No	No	Has a ranged attack and defensive spikes
Horse	Passive	The Overworld	Leather	15	None	1-3	Yes	Yes	Also can drop any equipped item when killed (including Saddles, Horse Armor, and Chests)
Illusioner	Aggressive	Must be summoned currently	The equipment they're holding may drop	32	1-4	5	No	No	Uses Bow attacks, casts Blind, and can summon duplicates
Iron Golem	Passive to Villagers	Spawns in Villages	Iron Ingot, Poppy	100	7-21	0	No	No	Attacks players who go after it or its Villagers
Llama	Neutral	Extreme Hills, Savanna	Leather	15-30	1	1-3	Yes	Yes	Can be equipped with Chests for storage
Magma Cube	Aggressive	The Nether	Magma Cream	16	3, 4, or 6 depending on size	4	No	No	Splits into smaller and weaker Magma Cubes as it takes damage
Mooshroom	Passive	Mushroom biomes in the Overworld	Red Mushrooms, Leather, Raw Beef, Milk, Mushroom Stew	10	None	1-3	No	No	Very useful creature, but hard to find
Ocelot	Passive	Jungle biomes of the Overworld	None	10	None	1-3	Yes	No	Creepers are scared of them and run away if one is nearby
Parrot	Passive	Jungles	Feathers	6	None	1-3	Yes	No	Can imitate noises and dance; never feed them Cookies

CREATURE	AGGRESSION	SPAWN LOCATION	ITEMS	HEALTH	ATTACK DAMAGE (NORMAL)	EXPERIENCE VALUE	TAMABLE?	RIDEABLE?	NOTES
Pig	Passive	The Overworld	Raw Porkchop	10	None	1-3	No	Yes	Can be saddled and ridden; drops Cooked Porkchops if killed by fire
Polar Bear	Neutral	Cold biomes	Raw Fish, Raw Salmon	30	6	1-3	No	No	Adult Polar Bears become aggressive if you get close to their cubs
Rabbit	Passive	The Overworld	Rabbit Hide, Raw Rabbit	10	None	1-3	No	No	Can be bred; may appear in an aggressive "Killer Rabbit" variant
Sheep	Passive	The Overworld	Wool	8	None	1-3	No	No	Shearing Sheep yields more Wool than killing them
Shulker	Aggressive	End Cities	Shulker Shell	30	4	5	No	No	Looks like a Purpur block, attacks at range, has an armored shell when being defensive
Silverfish	Aggressive	Spawns inside special blocks or from Monster Spawners	None	8	1	5	No	No	Silverfish blocks take slightly more time to break
Skeleton	Aggressive	Low-light areas of Nether Fortresses or the Overworld	Arrow, Bone	20	1-4	5	No	No	Sometimes drops Bows when killed
Slime	Aggressive	Lower areas of the Overworld	Slimeball	16	0, 2, or 4 depending on size	4	No	No	Breaks into smaller Slimes when damaged
Snow Golem	Passive to players	Created by players	Snowball	4	0 normally	None	No	No	Throws Snowballs that push back targets; these Snowballs can damage Blazes and the Ender Dragon
Spider	Neutral	Low-light areas of the Overworld	String, Spider Eye	16	2	5	No	No	Neutral in brighter light; can climb most blocks
Spider Jockey	Aggressive	Low-light areas of the Overworld	Bone, Arrow, String, Spider Eye	20 for Skeleton, 16 for Spider	3 for Skeleton, 2 for Spider	10 total	No	No	These are rare spawns, so you won't see them often
Squid	Passive	Water blocks in the Overworld	Ink Sac	10	None	1-3	No	No	Can't swim up waterfalls
Vex	Aggressive	Woodland Mansions	Iron Sword (requires Looting)	14	9	3	No	No	Summoned by Evokers to defend them in battle
Villager	Passive	Villages in the Overworld	None	20	None	None	No	No	Traders with varied inventories
Vindicator	Aggressive	Woodland Mansions	Emerald	24	13	5	No	No	Looting enchantments give you more Emeralds when killing Vindicators
Witch	Aggressive	Low-light areas of the Overworld	Glass Bottle, Glowstone Dust, Gunpowder, Redstone, Spider Eye, Stick, Sugar	26	Potions of Poison and Harming	5	No	No	Sometimes drops potions when killed
Wither	Aggressive	Summoned by player	Nether Star	300	8	50	No	No	Created with Soul Sand and Wither Skeleton Skulls
Wither Skeleton	Aggressive	Nether Fortresses	Coal, Bone	20	7	5	No	No	Can drop Wither Skeleton Skulls and Stone Swords
Wolf	Neutral	Forest and taiga biomes of the Overworld	None	8 wild, 20 when tamed	2 wild, 4 when tamed	1-3	Yes	No	Tamed with Bones; healed with food
Zombie	Aggressive	Low-light areas of the Overworld	Rotten Flesh	20	3-6	5	No	No	Does more damage when wounded
Zombie Pigman	Neutral	The Nether	Rotten Flesh, Gold Nugget, Gold Ingot	20	9	5	No	No	Can drop Golden Swords; attacks in packs when provoked
Zombie Villager	Aggressive	Low-light areas of the Overworld	Rotten Flesh	20	3-6	5	No	No	Can be cured with a Splash Potion of Weakness

EXPANDED CREATURE ENTRIES

Passive

Bat

AGGRESSION	SPAWN LOCATION	ITEMS	HEALTH	ATTACK DAMAGE	EXPERIENCE VALUE	TAMABLE?	RIDEABLE?	NOTES
Passive	Very low-light areas, deep caves	None	6	None	None	No	No	N/A

Bats are spawned in dark caverns of the Overworld. You can hear them flying around in these areas, but they don't have any loot to worry about. It's usually best to leave them alone, because they pose absolutely no threat to your character.

Chicken

AGGRESSION	SPAWN LOCATION	ITEMS	HEALTH	ATTACK DAMAGE	EXPERIENCE VALUE	TAMABLE?	RIDEABLE?	NOTES
Passive	The Overworld	Feathers, Raw Chicken, Eggs	4	None	1-3	No	No	Produces Eggs over time, and yields Cooked Chicken if slain by fire

Chickens are very useful to raise for meat and their Feathers. You can breed a fairly large supply of them without much time investment. Pen in a large group of Chickens and periodically walk through your pen to pick up the Eggs that the Chickens lay. If you carry Wheat Seeds in your hand, Chickens will follow you, making it easier to lead them to your barn/pen area.

Use seeds of any type to get Chickens to breed. Feed the seeds to your Chickens as often as every five minutes, and watch them create a new generation of livestock. Another way to spawn Chickens is to throw their Eggs at any creature or hard surface. When they break, there is a 12.5% chance that a Chicken will appear. In very rare cases, multiple Chickens can spawn from a single Egg!

Chicks take 20 minutes to mature and can then be used for breeding, meat, or whatever else you have planned.

Using Hoppers and Dispensers, you can create automated Chicken-breeding facilities.

Cow

AGGRESSION	SPAWN LOCATION	ITEMS	HEALTH	ATTACK DAMAGE	EXPERIENCE VALUE	TAMABLE?	RIDEABLE?	NOTES
Passive	The Overworld	Leather, Raw Beef, Milk	10	None	1-3	No	No	Yields Steak if killed by fire, and yields Milk with a Bucket

Cows are valuable additions to your operation, because they are a source of meat, Leather, and Milk (which can be used to cure Poison). It's always good to build a barn for these creatures as soon as you find them and bring them back to your home.

You find Cows in groups as you explore the Overworld. When you find them, use a Lead or carry Wheat to lure the Cows where you want them to go. Fence them into a safe area, and then bring additional Cows from their herd back to the same place. Once you have a decent group, start your breeding program. Feed Wheat to the Cows to get them to reproduce. You can breed Cows as often as every five minutes. It takes 20 minutes for Calves to grow up and become mature Cows.

To save time with adult Cows that are being slaughtered, use fire to cull them and produce Steak instead of Raw Beef. Flint and Steel work well for this purpose.

Horse

AGGRESSION	SPAWN LOCATION	ITEMS	HEALTH	ATTACK DAMAGE	EXPERIENCE VALUE	TAMABLE?	RIDEABLE?	NOTES
Passive	The Overworld	Leather	15	None	1-3	Yes	Yes	Also can drop any equipped item when killed (including Saddles, Horse Armor, and Chests)

Several types of Horses inhabit the *Minecraft* universe. Horses, Donkeys, and Mules are the normal varieties of these creatures, but using the PC commands can also spawn Undead and Skeletal Horses.

Search for Horses and Donkeys in areas of plains and savannas. Once you find them, you can tame these useful creatures by riding them a few times and then putting a Saddle on them. Horses can be tethered with a Lead to bring them with your character, or ridden if they are saddled.

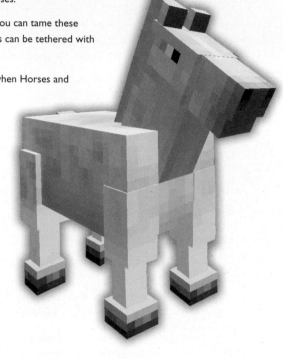

Mules are not found in the Overworld on their own. Instead, these are created only when Horses and Donkeys are used in breeding. Mules are sterile and cannot be used for breeding on their own. Though you can't armor Mules or Donkeys, it is possible to load them with Chests for extra carrying capacity.

The taming process for Horses and Donkeys is somewhat involved. Approach one of these creatures with an open hand and interact with it to ride the creature briefly. They often toss you off pretty soon, but eventually they'll get used to you and display a happy little animation. That's when you can saddle them for long-term use.

Several different foods heal Horses and improve your chances to tame them, as listed here:

FOOD	HEALS	SPEEDS GROWTH BY	IMPROVES TAMING PERCENTAGE BY
Sugar	1	30 sec	3%
Wheat	2	1 min	3%
Apple	3	1 min	3%
Golden Carrot	4	1 min	5%
Bread	7	3 min	3%
Golden Apple	10	4 min	10%
Hay Bale	20	3 min	N/A

Mooshroom

AGGRESSION	SPAWN LOCATION	ITEMS	HEALTH	ATTACK DAMAGE	EXPERIENCE VALUE	TAMABLE?	RIDEABLE?	NOTES
Passive	Mushroom biomes in the Overworld	Red Mushrooms, Leather, Raw Beef, Milk, Mushroom Stew	10	None	1-3	No	No	Very useful creature, but hard to find

Mooshrooms are amazing. They drop and create a wide range of items, making them almost a one-stop shop for food, Poison curing, and crafting goods. The only downside to these beasts is that they're very hard to find. Mooshrooms are a type of cattle that appears only in Mushroom biomes. You can breed them with Wheat and they're easy to take care of, so it's simply a matter of finding a herd. Shear Mooshrooms to collect Mushrooms from them. Use a Bucket on them to get Milk, or a Bowl to get Mushroom Stew. Cull them for Leather and Raw Beef (or Steak if they're killed by fire). You can't go wrong.

Ocelot

AGGRESSION	SPAWN LOCATION	ITEMS	HEALTH	ATTACK DAMAGE	EXPERIENCE VALUE	TAMABLE?	RIDEABLE?	NOTES
Passive	Jungle biomes of the Overworld	None	10	None	1-3	Yes	No	Creepers are scared of them and run away if one is nearby

Ocelots are felines that can be domesticated. Look for Ocelots in jungles around the world. To tame them, use Raw Fish to lure the Ocelot toward your character. Walk until you're roughly ten blocks away from the creature, and then stop moving while holding on to your fish. Give the Ocelot time to notice you and see the fish in your hand.

Be patient to avoid scaring the Ocelot away—let it come to you! Any major movement will scare the Ocelot and reset the taming process. When the Ocelot wanders over, feed the Raw Fish to it. It sometimes takes several feedings to tame your Ocelot. Once the process is complete, the Ocelot changes into a domesticated Cat and gains a new appearance.

Breed Cats by feeding them Raw Fish. As usual, you can breed animals only every five minutes, and their offspring take about 20 minutes to grow to maturity. Be careful with your kitties. They aren't terribly tough, they cannot be armored, and they won't last long in the wild if they're attacked or if they wander into a dangerous location. It's safest to leave your Cats at home so they don't get into too much trouble.

Parrot

AGGRESSION	SPAWN LOCATION	ITEMS	HEALTH	ATTACK DAMAGE	EXPERIENCE VALUE	TAMABLE?	RIDEABLE?	NOTES
Passive	Jungles in the Overworld	Feathers (1-2)	6	None	1-3	Yes	No	Can imitate noises and dance; never feed them Cookies

Parrots are potential pets that you sometimes find when exploring jungles. They are extremely safe to approach and have no attack abilities. They'll fly to get away from danger, but that's their only defense. Other creatures in their areas are nice to them, so players are their only potential predators. If you want to tame a Parrot, use Seeds until they're fully tamed. They'll start to follow you after that point, and can be made to sit by Alt-clicking on them.

As a warning, never feed a Cookie to a Parrot. Cookies are made with Chocolate, and that's very bad for birds. If you do this, you will kill your poor Parrot.

If you move through the same area as one of your tamed Parrots, the Parrot will get up onto your shoulder. You can carry two Parrots at once in this manner. They'll be safe when riding on you and cannot be harmed through normal means, even if you take damage.

Parrots love to imitate noises. This can actually be of use to you. They'll look in the direction of the sound that they've heard as they repeat it. If you hear your Parrot making a monster noise, you get a good idea of where that enemy is hiding.

If you have a Jukebox, play a Music Disc in it to entertain your bird. They'll dance like it's the coolest thing in the world.

Pig

AGGRESSION	SPAWN LOCATION	ITEMS	HEALTH	ATTACK DAMAGE	EXPERIENCE VALUE	TAMABLE?	RIDEABLE?	NOTES
Passive	The Overworld	Raw Porkchop	10	None	1-3	No	Yes	Can be saddled and ridden; drops Cooked Porkchops if killed by fire

Pigs are another type of livestock that you can breed, slaughter for food, or even ride. Several special attributes make these porcine creatures stand out. Lure Pigs back to your farm with Carrots; you also use Carrots to breed Pigs, so a Carrot garden is a must if you want to keep a large number of Pigs. Carrots sometimes drop when you kill Zombies, so hunt the creatures of the night to start your garden.

Once you have Pigs in a nice pen, breed them in the standard timing cycle. It takes five minutes before adults can breed again after their feeding, and 20 minutes for Piglets to grow to adulthood. Consider covering your pen with a roof. Pigs that are struck by lightning turn into Zombie Pigmen, and they aren't quite as edible.

If you have a Saddle and want to ride a Pig, craft a Carrot on a Stick and use it to control the Pig while you ride it. Few things in the world offer as much fun as charging around the wilderness with your trusted Pig mount.

Rabbit

AGGRESSION	SPAWN LOCATION	ITEMS	HEALTH	ATTACK DAMAGE	EXPERIENCE VALUE	TAMABLE?	RIDEABLE?	NOTES
Passive	The Overworld	Rabbit Hide, Raw Rabbit, Rabbit Foot	10	None	1-3	No	No	Can be bred; may appear in an aggressive "Killer Rabbit" variant

Rabbits are normally peaceful animals that hop around meadows. They'll avoid you if attacked, and can be harvested for Hides, food, or sometimes a Rabbit's Foot (useful in Potion making). Breed them using Dandelions or Carrots to create a nice population of these animals, and give them about 20 minutes for new Rabbits to grow up.

Killer Rabbits have a more aggressive look; they have different eyes and a bold, white pelt. They'll jump toward your character and attack quite viciously. They have a mean streak a mile wide, but can be fought off if you stay calm, face them, and smack them each time they get close to your character.

Sheep

AGGRESSION	SPAWN LOCATION	ITEMS	HEALTH	ATTACK DAMAGE	EXPERIENCE VALUE	TAMABLE?	RIDEABLE?	NOTES
Passive	The Overworld	Wool	8	None	1-3	No	No	Shearing Sheep yields more Wool than killing them

Sheep aren't the most useful livestock in *Minecraft*. They cannot be used for food, so Wool is all you get from them. Sheep drop Wool when slain, but this isn't a very efficient process; you get only one Wool per Sheep this way. Instead of killing the little guys, keep them in a barn and shear them. Shears are crafted with Iron, and they let you clip Sheep safely. You get far more Wool per Sheep, even on the first clipping, and their Wool regrows as long as the Sheep have access to grass for food.

You can dye Wool with any dyeing agent, but you can also dye the Sheep itself so that all of the Wool from its next clipping matches the dye's color. Future clippings revert to the Sheep's natural color, which varies between several shades.

Squid

AGGRESSION	SPAWN LOCATION	ITEMS	HEALTH	ATTACK DAMAGE	EXPERIENCE VALUE	TAMABLE?	RIDEABLE?	NOTES
Passive	Water blocks in the Overworld	Ink Sac	10	None	1-3	No	No	Can't swim up waterfalls

Squid appear in large bodies of water and are peaceful creatures. They happily swim around and don't cause any trouble, despite their dangerous appearance. The only items they drop are Ink Sacs, which are used to create a dark dye. Hunt Squid when you need these items, but otherwise it's fine to leave them alone.

Squid cannot swim up waterfalls, so there are numerous ways to trap them in large groups, where they can be killed later, used as decoration, or whatever else you have in mind.

Villager

AGGRESSION	SPAWN LOCATION	ITEMS	HEALTH	ATTACK DAMAGE	EXPERIENCE VALUE	TAMABLE?	RIDEABLE?	NOTES
Passive	Villages in the Overworld	None	20	None	None	No	No	Traders with varied inventories

Villagers appear in small towns located in some of the Overworld's plains, savannas, and deserts. These Villages offer exploration and places to trade for characters, and you won't be attacked unless you start trouble. In that event, Iron Golems often defend Villagers who are under attack.

Interact with Villagers to trade with them. They accept Emeralds as payment, but those are rare gems. Most of the time, you'll do well by giving items to Villagers and trading their goods around until you get the items you want. There are several types of Villagers: Farmers, Librarians, Priests, Blacksmiths, Butchers, and regular Villagers. The items each Villager carries are determined by their profession. Interact with Villagers by clicking on them to see what they're carrying and their profession.

To gain Emeralds without mining Extreme Hills for hours at a time, you need to trade Villagers items that they require. Do not purchase generic items that you already have; the cost is very high in terms of time you invest gathering Emeralds. Instead, save your Emeralds and wait for special items to become available, including Diamond tools, Chainmail, Bottles of Enchanting, Pumpkins (only if you haven't found them yet), and so forth.

Villagers have children if their towns start to lose too many people, often to Zombie attacks. If you want a town to increase its population, add Doors to buildings in the Village. The more Doors there are, the more people want to live in that town. That's just how Villagers are.

As of Version 1.8, Villagers who are struck by lightning turn into Witches. Watch out! They've also learned how to harvest crops, so you can't always rush into town and find an entire field of free goodies to steal (a pity that, but Villagers have to eat too!).

Snow Golem

AGGRESSION	SPAWN LOCATION	ITEMS	HEALTH	ATTACK DAMAGE	EXPERIENCE VALUE	TAMABLE?	RIDEABLE?	NOTES
Passive to players	Created by players	Snowball	4	0 Normally	None	No	No	Throws Snowballs that push back targets; these Snowballs can damage Blazes and the Ender Dragon

Snow Golems are creatures that you create! Stack two Snow blocks and place a Pumpkin on top of the stack. These creatures use Snowballs to defend the area from hostile monsters. Their attacks are ranged but don't do any damage to most targets; they hurt Blazes because Snowballs always damage Blazes. This is also true for the Ender Dragon.

Instead of killing targets, Snow Golems act as more of a distraction. They push enemies back and draw their attention. Place them at your property's outer edges so monsters stay near your perimeter instead of coming forward to harass your main buildings.

Snow Golems take damage over time when they're in warmer areas.

Iron Golem

AGGRESSION	SPAWN LOCATION	ITEMS	HEALTH	ATTACK DAMAGE	EXPERIENCE VALUE	TAMABLE?	RIDEABLE?	NOTES
Passive to Villagers	Spawn in Villages	Iron Ingot, Poppy	100	7	0	No	No	Attacks players who go after it or its Villagers

Iron Golems are defensive creatures, just like Snow Golems. The difference is that these creatures are much tougher, can damage their enemies, and can even hurt your character. If you attack a Village protected by Iron Golems, you'll get their attention. They'll chase after your character and attack if they get close. Run away to lose their interest, and then return at leisure—Iron Golems have short memories.

To create an Iron Golem, you need either a Village or a ton of Iron. To create one directly, forge four Iron blocks and place them in a T-formation: one block on the ground with three blocks horizontally above it. Then add a Pumpkin to the top of the T. This is expensive but makes a strong Iron Golem that loves to attack monsters. If a Village is nearby, simply wait for Iron Golems to appear on their own. This costs you nothing! They can then be farmed for their Iron, making it possible to generate Iron over time without having to mine. That's nifty.

Iron Golems can't be drowned, but regular battle damage and Lava kill them just fine. Or you can suffocate them in Gravel or Sand. This is slower but gets the job done.

Neutral

Cave Spider

AGGRESSION	SPAWN LOCATION	ITEMS	HEALTH	ATTACK DAMAGE	EXPERIENCE VALUE	TAMABLE?	RIDEABLE?	NOTES
Neutral	Abandoned Mineshafts	String, Spider Eye	12	1 + Poison	5	No	No	Passive in bright light

Cave Spiders are tiny monsters that live in the darkness below the Overworld. They fight and move much like regular Spiders, but they have poisonous bites (on most difficulty levels) and can squeeze through any gap in buildings, walls, etc. You have to completely block off an area to ensure they don't get into your safe rooms.

In the case of both types of Spiders, you should retreat while you fight these creatures. Attack them while backing up to limit their number of attacks against you. Having Milk around is useful in case you get poisoned, and keep yourself well-fed so you regenerate health as quickly as possible after the fight.

Lure Cave Spiders away from tight areas, mineshafts with cobwebs, and other difficult places to navigate. Fight them in a place where you can get your back against a wall and force the enemies to come toward you in a straight line. Thus, you won't be overwhelmed by multiple creatures.

Enderman

AGGRESSION	SPAWN LOCATION	ITEMS	HEALTH	ATTACK DAMAGE	EXPERIENCE VALUE	TAMABLE?	RIDEABLE?	NOTES
Neutral	The Overworld, the End	Ender Pearls	40	7	5	No	No	Attacks when damaged or if you make eye contact

Endermen are dark beings from a world beyond our own! They spawn heavily in a place called the End, but they can appear in the Overworld as well. Though they're neutral by default, Endermen are easy to antagonize, and they attack your character viciously if you hit them or even look them in the eyes. Avoid this by staring at Endermen's feet or by wearing a Jack-o'-Lantern on your head so Endermen don't know where you're looking.

Ranged attacks don't work against Endermen; they blink out of existence for a moment and reappear somewhere else—behind you as often as not. This, combined with their higher damage and health, makes them incredibly dangerous opponents when you aren't accustomed to fighting them. For the greatest chance of victory, wear armor and take consistent swings to chop your Enderman target to ribbons. Attacking an Enderman's legs prevents it from teleporting, so this secures your kill while protecting your character from teleportion attacks to your back.

When they're not being attacked, Endermen wander around the world, pick up blocks and move them around, and just kind of act like weirdos. Their ability to teleport allows them to spawn in strange places. You might find them down in your mines, outside, or even within your own home! That's scary stuff. If you hear something moving around indoors, it's probably one of them. Endermen come inside most often when it rains; water hurts them, so they teleport anywhere safe. If your house is nice and dry, it makes a good target.

Llama

AGGRESSION	SPAWN LOCATION	ITEMS	HEALTH	ATTACK DAMAGE	EXPERIENCE VALUE	TAMABLE?	RIDEABLE?	NOTES
Neutral	Extreme Hills, Savanna	Leather (0-2)	15-30	1	1-3	Yes	Yes	Can be equipped with Chests for storage

Llamas are great pack animals that you find in Extreme Hills and the Savanna. Both areas have Llamas with similar properties, but you can distinguish the breeds by their coloration (which is lighter in the Hills and tan in the Savanna). Alt-click on wild Llamas to begin taming them. They appreciate Wheat and Hay Bales if you want to speed up the process, or if you need to heal them. If you keep trying to impress them, they'll eventually be tamed, but the time this takes is heavily influenced by the temper of the individual Llama. If you use Hay Bales on groups of tamed Llamas, you can get them to breed.

Llamas can't do too much damage, but they spit at any attackers that come after them; they'll even take the initiative and go after untamed Wolves aggressively.

Llamas are wonderful for carrying around extra gear. You can decorate these creatures with Carpets, or you can put Chests on them to carry more items. Llamas have varying amounts of strength, and that determines how many items they can hold (3-15 items per Llama). Using a Lead, you can bundle together an entire group of Llamas, even ones that aren't tamed yet. Up to ten Llamas can move with you in this way. Using additional Leads, you can keep even larger groups together.

Polar Bear

AGGRESSION	SPAWN LOCATION	ITEMS	HEALTH	ATTACK DAMAGE	EXPERIENCE VALUE	TAMABLE?	RIDEABLE?	NOTES
Neutral	Cold biomes	Raw Fish, Raw Salmon	30	6	1-3	No	No	Adult Polar Bears become aggressive if you get close to their cubs

Polar Bears appear in Ice Mountains, Ice Plains, and Ice Spikes. You either encounter one adult alone, or an adult with a single cub. Though neutral by default, Polar Bears get aggressive if you come anywhere near a cub. Don't get close to these creatures unless you're ready for a fight. Their drops aren't very powerful or useful, so there isn't a good reason to start a fight with Polar Bears unless you're doing some big-game hunting.

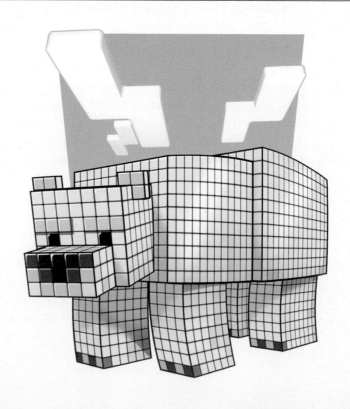

Spider

AGGRESSION	SPAWN LOCATION	ITEMS	HEALTH	ATTACK DAMAGE	EXPERIENCE VALUE	TAMABLE?	RIDEABLE?	NOTES
Neutral	Low-light areas of the Overworld	String, Spider Eye	16	2	5	No	No	Neutral in brighter light; can climb most blocks

Like many Overworld monsters, Spiders appear during nighttime and thunderstorms, wherever illumination falls to extremely dim levels. Spiders don't burn up in sunlight, though they become more docile and won't attack characters unless provoked. Though they aren't terribly dangerous as single attackers, Spiders are still tricky customers. They fit through single-block openings, can climb over your walls, and make a general nuisances of themselves even if they can't get inside. They can also get into your farm field, crush your plants, and must be cleared out manually later on.

Back away from Spiders and fight them while retreating so they can't jump on you as easily. They take only a few hits to kill, so that's a plus. It's easiest to fight these enemies in narrow areas where they can't get around to your sides. Make them come through a tunnel or doorway to get to you so it's easier to hit them.

If you're desperate for food early in a game, Spider Eyes are poisonous, but edible. Spiders also drop String, which can be used to make a Fishing Rod, allowing you to get more food from any body of water.

Wolf

AGGRESSION	SPAWN LOCATION	ITEMS	HEALTH	ATTACK DAMAGE	EXPERIENCE VALUE	TAMABLE?	RIDEABLE?	NOTES
Neutral	Forest and taiga biomes of the Overworld	None	8 wild, 20 when tamed	2 wild, 4 when tamed	1-3	Yes	No	Tamed with Bones; healed with food

One can find Wolves in several areas: forests and various taiga biomes. Growling Wolves are hostile and must be treated carefully. Other Wolves may be wild but are friendly enough to approach. Unless attacked, peaceful Wolves will not attack your character.

Hunt Skeletons for Bones if you'd like to tame a Wolf. Feeding Bones to friendly Wolves is how you tame these creatures. Sometimes the first Bone does the trick, but it might take several more to earn the Wolf's loyalty. You can tame more than one Wolf, so feel free to establish an entire pack for yourself. After they're tamed, Wolves get more health and can deliver more damage, and they won't attack you even if you accidentally hit one of them. They're sweetie pies.

Increase the size of your pack by feeding raw meat to your Wolves. Like most livestock, feeding them causes breeding behavior, as long as two or more Wolves are fed together. Bring spare food to give to the offspring to grant them more health. Note that any type of raw meat does the trick, including Rotten Flesh.

Zombie Pigman

AGGRESSION	SPAWN LOCATION	ITEMS	HEALTH	ATTACK DAMAGE	EXPERIENCE VALUE	TAMABLE?	RIDEABLE?	NOTES
Neutral	The Nether	Rotten Flesh, Gold Nugget, Gold Ingot	20	9	5	No	No	Can drop Golden Swords; attacks in packs when provoked

In most versions of the game, Zombie Pigmen spawn near Nether Portals or, more commonly, inside the Nether. They're involved with the Nether Reactor in the Pocket Version. It's possible for lightning to turn a regular Pig into a Zombie Pigman, though this is not a common occurrence.

Zombie Pigmen don't attack your character on sight. They're surprisingly chilled out for rotting, undead monsters. As long as you don't hurt them or stand nearby when they take damage from fire, you'll be okay. Give them some space and avoid trouble. Hurting Zombie Pigmen causes them to become aggressive, and they bring every other Pigman in the area with them. This produces large battles that pose substantial risk to your character unless you retreat to a safe corridor and fight defensively. Be wary! Zombie Pigmen are fast runners, so it's hard to escape from them once they're angry. Sprint toward safety and hope for the best.

Zombie Pigmen drop a variety of golden items when they die, so farming them has value if you need Gold Nuggets, Gold Ingots, or a rare armor drop. Zombie Pigmen can pick up and equip weapons and armor, so don't leave anything useful on the ground unless you want to arm a local militia of undead piggies. For maximum safety, you can kill groups of Zombie Pigmen by walling yourself into a tunnel and shooting outward at enraged targets.

Aggressive

Blaze

AGGRESSION	SPAWN LOCATION	ITEMS	HEALTH	ATTACK DAMAGE	EXPERIENCE VALUE	TAMABLE?	RIDEABLE?	NOTES
Aggressive	Nether Fortresses	Blaze Rod, Glowstone Dust (not in PC version)	20	5 at range, 6 up close	10	No	No	Can be damaged by rain, water, or Snowballs

Blazes are ranged monsters that live in the Nether. Their fire attacks shoot in bursts of three, giving you several seconds afterward to dash between cover or to charge your opponent. Take cover when you see a Blaze, and ready a Bow or some Snowballs to throw at your target. Pop out from cover, shoot, and hide again. Repeat this process unless the Blaze gets close to your area, at which point you should switch to your Sword and ambush it for the kill.

Don't trade blows with a Blaze. Their attacks hit extremely hard and deal fire damage to your character. Fire Resistance makes such battles easier, but you still need to be quite careful around these opponents. Put up a barrier of Cobblestone so Blazes can't hit you even if they attack in an open walkway. Make it so Blazes have no choice but to give up their ranged advantage.

Also, watch your sides. Blazes fly, which means they're happy to suspend themselves over large drops so you can't get to them. Block all angles of fire to know where the Blazes will move.

Chicken Jockey

AGGRESSION	SPAWN LOCATION	ITEMS	HEALTH	ATTACK DAMAGE	EXPERIENCE VALUE	TAMABLE?	RIDEABLE?	NOTES
Aggressive	Low-light areas	Rotten Flesh, and Chicken items	20 for Jockey, 4 for Chicken	3-6 depending on Jockey's health	5 for Jockey, 1-3 for Chicken	No	No	Jockeys do more damage when they get hurt

Tiny Zombies sometimes spawn on top of a Chicken. They ride the Chicken around like a mount and attack your character as aggressively as they can. It's a funny sight, but you still have to be careful and avoid serious damage.

As usual, a fighting retreat is a good response when a Chicken Jockey attacks. They don't have too much health, so you have to hold them back for only a short time. Don't try to turn around and flee, because these guys chase you fast and far. Fight it out and get your kill. The good news is that you aren't likely to see any more on their way, because they're so rare in the first place.

Creeper

AGGRESSION	SPAWN LOCATION	ITEMS	HEALTH	ATTACK DAMAGE	EXPERIENCE VALUE	TAMABLE?	RIDEABLE?	NOTES
Aggressive	Low-light areas	Gunpowder, Music Disc	20	49-97	5	No	No	Deals more damage if charged by lightning; yields Music Discs if slain by a Skeleton

Perhaps the most iconic monster in *Minecraft*, Creepers are nasty pieces of work. They don't attack you directly. Instead, they move toward your character and then explode when they get close enough. You know one is in the area when you hear an occasional kind of grunty noise. Once Creepers start their explosive attack, you hear a distinct hiss. If you hear this noise and can't see the Creeper, *run forward immediately.* The farther you get from the blast, the lower the damage you take.

Creepers are afraid of Ocelots and Cats, so having one around offers some protection against these surprise attackers. Even without that, vigilance is your best friend against Creepers. They're somewhat slow-moving, and spotting them at range makes it much easier to avoid the enemies, kill them with Arrows, or set up a cautious melee ambush. If you're extremely careful, hit-and-run methods work well against Creepers. Knock them back with a single attack, and retreat to prevent them from detonating; they stop their explosion if you get far enough away before the point of no return.

Lure Creepers into Lava or bodies of water to kill or isolate them. Their explosions don't damage blocks if the Creepers are submerged, so this makes them much easier and safer to fight, even if your character is still at risk. At a minimum, stay away from your house and fields when Creepers are near, or stay away from the walls at night, even if you don't see a Creeper. One explosion can kill you or obliterate whatever you have nearby. Either of these outcomes is horrible to deal with.

In really special cases, you might see a Creeper with a strange aura around it. This is a Creeper that has been struck by lightning. Charged Creepers produce much deadlier explosions. Don't try to detonate one manually, even on Easy difficulty. Use a Bow and be safe.

Ender Dragon

AGGRESSION	SPAWN LOCATION	ITEMS	HEALTH	ATTACK DAMAGE	EXPERIENCE VALUE	TAMABLE?	RIDEABLE?	NOTES
Aggressive	In The End	The Overworld Portal, Dragon Egg	200	10	12000	No	No	Healed by Ender Crystals

The Ender Dragon is a unique monster that appears only in the End, a special world that you can't access until you complete a number of goals. Our explanation for getting to the End appears in our chapter titled **You Can Do Anything With a Little Practice**.

Fighting the Ender Dragon is difficult. You face an opponent with massive health, mobility, and damage output. Endermen in the area attack you if you look at them during the fight. To make matters worse, crystals in the End heal the Ender Dragon, making it practically impossible to kill until you destroy the crystals. Wow.

Avoid the Ender Dragon's charge attack, and know that it can dive through or destroy most blocks. You can't hide from this sucker! Dodge its charges and use the time between them to get to those crystals. Once they're trashed, shoot at the Ender Dragon from behind after it passes you in a charge. Keep your health topped off as best you can. There are many tricks for making this process easier (use exploding Beds for massive damage, keep a Bucket of Water in case you get knocked into the air and need a soft landing, etc.). These are discussed in the full write-up about the End.

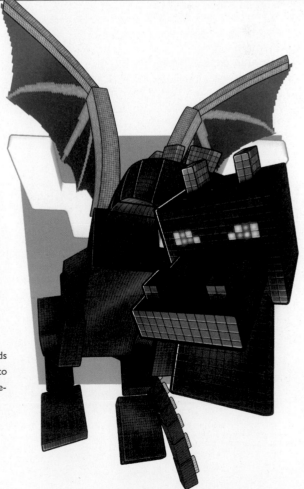

Endermite

AGGRESSION	SPAWN LOCATION	ITEMS	HEALTH	ATTACK DAMAGE	EXPERIENCE VALUE	TAMABLE?	RIDEABLE?	NOTES
Aggressive	Anywhere	None	8	2	3	No	No	Has a 5% chance of appearing after you throw an Ender Pearl

Endermites are monsters that were added in the 1.8 update to *Minecraft*. They're incredibly small but nasty little things. You find them after throwing Ender Pearls, but there isn't a very high chance for them to appear (only 1 in 20). So you don't have to worry about them often. They don't take much damage, so cut them down as soon as you can.

Evoker

AGGRESSION	SPAWN LOCATION	ITEMS	HEALTH	ATTACK DAMAGE	EXPERIENCE VALUE	TAMABLE?	RIDEABLE?	NOTES
Aggressive	Woodland Mansions (Roofed Forest biomes)	Totem of Undying, Emerald	24	6	10	No	No	Summons Vexes, casts Fang spells, and can color Sheep

Evokers live in secluded forest houses, way out in the middle of nowhere. These Woodland Mansions are only found in Roofed Forest biomes, and even there the buildings aren't common. Inside of them, you find a considerable amount of danger (and loot as well). Evokers are like minibosses for these places; you find them here and there throughout the structure, and they have powerful spells to defend themselves. Expect them to summon ghostly Vexes and to damage you directly with Fang spells. If you hang back and try to fight cautiously, you actually end up in more danger. Evokers' low health pools mean it's better to rush and kill them. This doesn't give them much time to summon allies, so you can cut them down quickly in melee, flee, and then clean up additional creatures that are after you.

When they're not in combat, Evokers have a spell that changes Sheep's Wool color (from blue to red, if there are any blue Sheep nearby). It's unknown why they do this, but it's obviously an important part of Evoker culture. This doesn't pose any threat to you, so it's more a matter of flavor.

Evokers drop Totems of Undying. These items are quite useful, because they can save you from death. Equipped in either hand, they drop lethal damage from killing your character. You're left with almost no health, but the Totem gives you Regeneration II and then is destroyed.

CREATURES BIG AND SMALL

Ghast

AGGRESSION	SPAWN LOCATION	ITEMS	HEALTH	ATTACK DAMAGE	EXPERIENCE VALUE	TAMABLE?	RIDEABLE?	NOTES
Aggressive	The Nether, out in the open	Gunpowder, Ghast Tears	10	17	5	No	No	Shots cause an area-of-effect explosion of fire

Ghasts live in the Nether. They're flying white balls of fluff that fire explosive shots at your character. Their damage output is very good, and their area-of-effect fire blasts set tons of Netherrack on fire, making it hard to move safely when you fight Ghasts.

These monsters also have great vision. They spot you from far away, so sneaking past them isn't easy. You usually have to hit them with Bow attacks instead. Kill them by aiming around their tentacles. If you're really lucky and brave, use a melee attack to bounce Ghasts' fireballs back at them. This is effective but hard to pull off without substantial practice.

Never get close to Zombie Pigmen while dealing with Ghasts. The explosions from these fire attacks can enrage the Zombie Pigmen, and they'll blame you for their suffering!

Guardian and Elder Guardian

AGGRESSION	SPAWN LOCATION	ITEMS	HEALTH	ATTACK DAMAGE	EXPERIENCE VALUE	TAMABLE?	RIDEABLE?	NOTES
Aggressive	Underwater	Prismarine Crystals, Prismarine Shards, Raw Fish	30	6	10	No	No	Has a ranged attack and defensive spikes
Aggressive	Underwater	Prismarine Crystals, Prismarine Shards, Raw Fish	80	8	10	No	No	Has a ranged attack and defensive spikes

Guardians are aquatic creatures that have powerful laser attacks, and vicious spikes that wound anyone who attacks them in melee. The spikes retract when Guardians are swimming, so you can attack them safely at that time, but it's hard to sneak up on them unless you're invisible. During battle, Guardians look directly at their intended target, charge their laser eyes, and then fire after a few seconds. This attack does strong damage if you don't have any armor, but is quite survivable as long as you have decent gear.

Water Breathing, enchanted armor, and patience are all useful for killing these pesky targets. They're dangerous to burn down quickly because of the spikes. It's better to fight near obstacles so that you can block the laser and come out for free hits afterward.

Guardians can drop a variety of fish, depending on your Luck. This is similar to the effects of fishing, so it's random which type of fish you receive.

Elder Guardians have higher stats and inflict Fatigue on players who get too close to them (this has a 50-block range and occurs once per minute to an individual target). Elder Guardians only appear near and within underwater monuments, so if you're hit with Fatigue, you know that you're getting close to a monument and should find the body of water that it's in. Once you kill the three Elder Guardians that protect each underwater monument, they're gone forever. Bring friends, or use Potions and higher-end equipment to kill the Elder Guardians as best you can. They'll be in different sections of the monument, so you won't get rushed by the entire trio. The standard layout is to find an Elder Guardian at the top of each monument and then another in each of the two wings of the Temple.

Illusioner

AGGRESSION	SPAWN LOCATION	ITEMS	HEALTH	ATTACK DAMAGE	EXPERIENCE VALUE	TAMABLE?	RIDEABLE?	NOTES
Aggressive	Special *	Bow	32	1-4	5	No	No	Can only be spawned with the / summon command at the time of writing

Illusioners are still not fully implemented into the game as we write this book. You can, however, use the /summon command to bring them into the world and test out their abilities. Illusioners are aggressive casters that use Bow attacks and spells to give you some serious trouble. They cast Blind when initially attacking a target, leaving the victim much more vulnerable for 20 seconds. If you're affected by this attack, move away from the enemy while zigzagging to make yourself a trickier target to hit until you recover.

Illusioners then create mirror images of themselves. The real Illusioner turns invisible, while four duplicates appear. You need to guess the actual location of the Illusioner and aim for that spot. Successful attacks cause the duplicates to collapse in on the Illusioner for a brief moment, so it's always clear when you land a shot. Continue to aim at that area and bring the enemy down.

Magma Cube

AGGRESSION	SPAWN LOCATION	ITEMS	HEALTH	ATTACK DAMAGE	EXPERIENCE VALUE	TAMABLE?	RIDEABLE?	NOTES
Aggressive	The Nether	Magma Cream	16	6	4	No	No	Splits into smaller and weaker Magma Cubes as it takes damage

Magma Cubes are Slimes from the Nether. They are fairly slow, hopping creatures that do damage by bouncing into you. They split into smaller monsters when they take damage, making it harder to defend against the whole bunch.

Focus on individual, smaller Magma Cubes to weaken their force. Don't try to kill everything at once, or you're forced to fight a number of smaller Magma Cubes without a break. Bow attacks are much safer against Magma Cubes; the monsters don't dodge well. However, it is fun to use your Sword on them if you're cautious and a little gutsy. This cuts down on Arrow use dramatically, because Magma Cubes have quite a bit of total health to shoot through.

Shulker

AGGRESSION	SPAWN LOCATION	ITEMS	HEALTH	ATTACK DAMAGE	EXPERIENCE VALUE	TAMABLE?	RIDEABLE?	NOTES
Aggressive	The End (End Cities and End Ships)	Shulker Shell	30	4	5	No	No	Very well armored, has a ranged attack

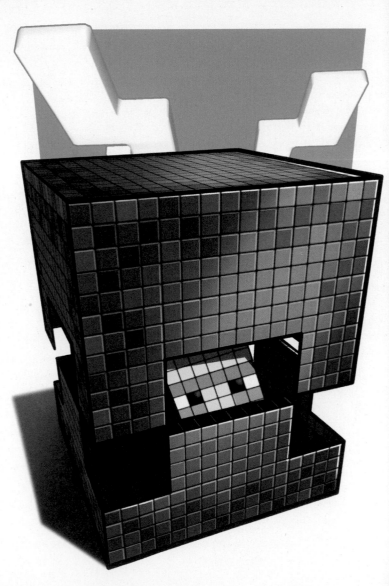

Shulkers are only found in the End, in the cities and ships located in that realm. These enemies look like Purpur blocks most of the time. They have purple armored shells that blend in well. They peek out of their shells periodically, looking for targets. If they see something, they'll attack from range. You have to hit them back while they're still out of their shells. Otherwise, they have tons of armor and laugh off missile attacks. Wait them out and punish the nasty little things just before they attack.

Shulker attacks are slower than most ranged weapons, but they have limited tracking and can hit mobile targets. Block these with shields, attack the projectiles with melee weapons, or dodge behind heavy cover at the last moment. If you're struck by a Shulker, your character starts to levitate for a short time. This is dangerous, because you can get pounded by many other enemies in the area while you're sitting there helplessly levitating.

Silverfish

AGGRESSION	SPAWN LOCATION	ITEMS	HEALTH	ATTACK DAMAGE	EXPERIENCE VALUE	TAMABLE?	RIDEABLE?	NOTES
Aggressive	Spawns inside special blocks or from Monster Spawners	None	8	1	5	No	No	Silverfish blocks take slightly more time to break

Silverfish are hidden monsters that live inside fake blocks. They're found deep inside the Overworld, waiting for you to mine them. Blocks that seem to take longer than usual to mine are actually Silverfish. Once they're uncovered, they attack and cause other Silverfish in the area to break out of their blocks and charge you. This sometimes leads to large and dangerous battles.

Retreat to a defensible area when a Silverfish appears. You can get onto a two-block pillar and kill the Silverfish safely up there. Or you can lure them into a spot in a narrow corridor that is somewhat safe. As long as all the Silverfish are on one side of the passage, it's fairly easy to dispatch them. Getting surrounded is the main thing to avoid when you fight these pests.

Skeleton

AGGRESSION	SPAWN LOCATION	ITEMS	HEALTH	ATTACK DAMAGE	EXPERIENCE VALUE	TAMABLE?	RIDEABLE?	NOTES
Aggressive	Low-light areas of the Overworld	Arrow, Bone	20	3	5	No	No	Sometimes drops Bows when killed
Aggressive	Ice Plains, Ice Mountains, Ice Plains Spikes	Arrow, Bone, Arrow of Slowness	20	3	5	No	No	Can drop Bows and Arrows of Slowness
Aggressive	Nether Fortresses	Coal, Bone, Wither Skeleton Skull	20	8	5	No	No	Hunt these to get materials for summoning a Wither

Skeletons are the biggest annoyances in the Overworld when you're topside, and they're pretty frustrating down in the mines as well. Skeletons have ranged attacks that are fast, accurate, and painful. Their Arrows push you back, making it harder to reach the Skeleton and possibly knocking you off ledges, into Lava, or otherwise giving you problems.

Whenever you can, use cover to lure Skeletons toward you. Up close, they're fairly weak and easy to kill. They also drop great treasure; Bones are used to tame Wolves and grow crops, and the free Arrows sure aren't bad either. Sometimes Skeletons even drop their Bows. So, they're valuable enemies to fight, even if they are jerks.

Don't stand on narrow ledges or near dangerous obstacles when you face Skeletons. If you hear their Bows twang, immediately find cover and figure out where the enemy is firing from. Use your Bow to counter them if they don't come forward, such as when they're across a chasm. Alternatively, tunnel into the rock, come around to a safe area, and approach them that way. They can't shoot through solid blocks!

Shields are extremely effective at protecting you from Skeleton attacks. Ready your Shield and stay behind it while you're approaching Skeletons. Once you're close, attack them and get behind your Shield again until you're ready to repeat the assault.

The absolutely worst fight with a Skeleton is in water when you have only a Sword. The water slows you down, and this, combined with the pushback from a Skeleton's ranged attacks, can effectively keep you from getting to your enemy. At this point, it's best to retreat and wait for a better situation.

Strays are Skeletons that spawn in icy areas. Their Arrows have a tendency to cause Slowness, which makes it even harder to fight the darn things. Otherwise, they're standard archers like their cousins.

Wither Skeletons are only seen in the Nether, and they're different beasties altogether. Look for their individual entry to get tips for killing them.

Slime

AGGRESSION	SPAWN LOCATION	ITEMS	HEALTH	ATTACK DAMAGE	EXPERIENCE VALUE	TAMABLE?	RIDEABLE?	NOTES
Aggressive	Lower areas of the Overworld	Slimeball	16	4	4	No	No	Breaks into smaller Slimes when damaged

Slimes appear in swamps (often at night) or in deeper sections of the Overworld. You hear them from great distance because of the telltale squishing noises they make when they jump around. The Slimeballs they drop are pretty useful, so Slime hunting is periodically a worthwhile pursuit. If you find Slimes at a location once, you'll likely bump into them again there in the future. They are somewhat predictable in their spawns, so mark these areas well and return later for more hunting.

To kill Slimes, use Arrows at range, or approach them carefully with your Sword out. Attack several times in melee, back off, and repeat the assault when you see how the Slime splits apart. Kill smaller Slimes before dealing with larger ones, because you don't want to coat the entire area with little hopping menaces; that increases the chance of taking damage.

Slimes spawn even if it's light in the area, so well-lit Dungeons can have spawns if the conditions are right for Slime growth.

Spider Jockey

AGGRESSION	SPAWN LOCATION	ITEMS	HEALTH	ATTACK DAMAGE	EXPERIENCE VALUE	TAMABLE?	RIDEABLE?	NOTES
Aggressive	Low-light areas of the Overworld	Bone, Arrow, String, Spider Eye	20 for Skeleton, 16 for Spider	3 for Skeleton, 2 for Spider	10 total	No	No	These are rare spawns, so you don't see them often

Chicken Jockeys are cute and a little dangerous. However, Spider Jockeys aren't cute at all—they're just creepy. You have to deal with a Skeleton that has greater mobility and a Spider that's ready to attack you as well. It's a mean duo.

The Spiders can move on their own, so these Jockeys move like Spiders. The Skeletons only control their ranged attacks, which are as accurate as ever. To play it safe, sprint toward cover and ready your best melee weapon. Eat while you wait if you need to, and then ambush the Spider Jockey when it turns the corner. At close range, you can kill these guys somewhat reliably. Still, expect to take damage, so don't even try this fight if your health is low, your armor is poor, or if you're nervous.

Vex

AGGRESSION	SPAWN LOCATION	ITEMS	HEALTH	ATTACK DAMAGE	EXPERIENCE VALUE	TAMABLE?	RIDEABLE?	NOTES
Aggressive	Created by Evokers	Iron Sword	14	9	3	No	No	Created in groups by Evokers

Vexes are created by Evoker spells. They appear in clusters of three and fly toward their targets to attack in melee. They cause a fair amount of damage and are a real threat if you let them swarm you. Evokers continue to summon more Vexes during these battles, so you can eventually end up with more than three of them buzzing around if you take too long to kill everything. As with all Evoker encounters, your goal is to get the Evoker down immediately and then focus on everything else in the room. With the potential for reinforcements removed, the remaining Vexes won't be a very serious threat. They're simple melee attackers; back through a doorway so that they can't flank you. Then take them out one by one as they rush up to your chokepoint.

Vindicator

AGGRESSION	SPAWN LOCATION	ITEMS	HEALTH	ATTACK DAMAGE	EXPERIENCE VALUE	TAMABLE?	RIDEABLE?	NOTES
Aggressive	Woodland Mansions	Emerald	24	13	5	No	No	High-speed and high-damage enemy, but with no tricks

Vindicators protect Woodland Mansions. They're heavy-damage attackers that sprint up to their targets and assault them directly. They're easy to defeat at range, and are somewhat safe in melee too as long as you don't get jumped by additional targets while you're focusing on the Vindicator. Always keep your armor on when exploring Woodland Mansions, because you take tons of damage if anything lands against exposed flesh.

Killing Vindicators is an excellent way to pick up Emeralds. These are difficult to gather normally, so an entire mansion can pull in a king's ransom of these gems. It's a smart idea to use the best Looting-enchanted items that you have whenever you find one of these areas, because the potential haul of Emeralds gets even higher.

Witch

AGGRESSION	SPAWN LOCATION	ITEMS	HEALTH	ATTACK DAMAGE	EXPERIENCE VALUE	TAMABLE?	RIDEABLE?	NOTES
Aggressive	Low-light areas of the Overworld	Glass Bottle, Glowstone Dust, Gunpowder, Redstone, Spider Eye, Stick, Sugar	26	Potions of Poison and Harming	5	No	No	Rarely drops Potions when killed

You don't see Witches as frequently as many monsters in the Overworld, and that's a good thing. These humanoids have Potions that can hurt you, poison your character, or protect the Witch from harm. Witches can heal themselves and speed their movement, so they have a little bit of everything. Good weapons are important when you fight a Witch; they have enough health that any damage improvement makes a big difference. Iron Swords, or even better gear, are advised!

Because Witches use Harm and Poison attacks, you want to kill them quickly. The longer the fight, the bigger your disadvantage becomes. If you can't take out a Witch quickly and you become poisoned, mount a sprinting retreat to put cover between your character and the Witch, so additional Potions don't hit you.

If you have really good timing, lure a Witch toward a corridor or house with a Door. Keep the Door closed until the Witch is nearby. Open the Door, hit the Witch, and close the Door. Wait a moment and then repeat the process. Witches take a moment to unleash their Potion attacks, so this technique is fairly reliable if you have good reflexes.

Wither

AGGRESSION	SPAWN LOCATION	ITEMS	HEALTH	ATTACK DAMAGE	EXPERIENCE VALUE	TAMABLE?	RIDEABLE?	NOTES
Aggressive	Summoned by player	Nether Star	300	8	50	No	No	Created with Soul Sand and Wither Skeleton Skulls

Withers are major enemies, much like the Ender Dragon. Don't go up against these guys unless you're ready for a serious fight and know what you're doing. For a full strategy on killing these guys, look in our section covering the Nether.

One can summon Withers by creating an altar of Soul Sand in a T-formation. Place a Wither Skeleton Skull on all three upper blocks of Soul Sand. When you do this, the altar summons a Wither. Make sure to avoid fighting these monsters near your home; they do horrific damage to the land around them. We strongly recommend fighting them deep underground or far away from home.

Wither Skeleton

AGGRESSION	SPAWN LOCATION	ITEMS	HEALTH	ATTACK DAMAGE	EXPERIENCE VALUE	TAMABLE?	RIDEABLE?	NOTES
Aggressive	Nether Fortresses	Coal, Bone	20	7	5	No	No	Can drop Wither Skeleton Skulls and Stone Swords

Wither Skeletons guard Nether Fortresses, special areas within the Nether. Unlike generic Skeletons, these undead foes favor melee weapons. They're extremely deadly, dealing high damage up front and causing a damage-over-time effect as well. You need solid armor, full health, and hopefully a full hunger bar to go against Wither Skeletons.

Arches that are only two blocks high are too small for Wither Skeletons to pass through. If you see a Wither Skeleton ahead, place blocks behind you to form a barrier that provides just enough room for your character to run through. Shoot at the Wither Skeleton, bring it to the low arch, and then keep hitting it with Arrows. Hit-and-run attacks also work, if you're careful. Another classic move is to attack while backing up. This is effective against many monsters, and works well against Wither Skeletons, as long as you don't fall off a ledge or get attacked by Blazes and/or other Wither Skeletons.

Keep equipment off the ground when you traverse Nether Fortresses. Wither Skeletons are quite happy to pick up Bows or Swords, and they're evil when they get their bony hands on either.

Zombies, Zombie Villagers, and Husks

AGGRESSION	SPAWN LOCATION	ITEMS	HEALTH	ATTACK DAMAGE	EXPERIENCE VALUE	TAMABLE?	RIDEABLE?	NOTES
Aggressive	Low-light areas of the Overworld	Rotten Flesh, Iron Ingot, Carrot, Potato	20	3-6	5	No	No	Does more damage when wounded
Aggressive	Low-light areas of the Overworld	Rotten Flesh	20	1-6	5	No	No	Can be cured with a Splash Potion of Weakness
Aggressive	Desert, Desert Hills, Desert Mountains	Rotten Flesh, Iron Ingot, Carrot, Potato	20	3-6	5	No	No	Not hurt by sunlight, applies Hunger when attacking

There are several types of Zombies in *Minecraft*, though the techniques to deal with them are similar. Zombies, Baby Zombies, and Zombie Villagers are all pretty much mindless, undead horrors. They move toward your character, moaning and trying to kill you with slow melee attacks. Baby Zombies have higher walking speed, but that and their short stature are the only significant distinctions.

Zombies can spawn with equipment or pick up things they find. Well-equipped Zombies are more dangerous, so watch out for them. Kill those Zombies first when you fight a group. And speaking of groups, it's rare to encounter a single Zombie. They often appear with several allies, so back off until you see where all your enemies are standing. Force them to line up for the fight by retreating until all the Zombies are somewhat close together. Then attack and retreat as you thin their ranks. Zombies with helmets are lucky; sunlight doesn't cause them to burst into flames (until the helmet itself is destroyed). Pumpkins serve the same role.

Villagers killed by Zombies have a chance of turning. If they rise as Zombie Villagers, there is still some hope. A Splash Potion of Weakness leaves the Zombie Villager in a vulnerable state. Feed it a Golden Apple afterward and wait a moderate amount of time; the Zombie Villager will return to life.

Zombie Husks are desert variants of the standard Zombie. They have similar stats, but look and sound slightly different. They're immune to sunlight, so watch out during the day for these wandering pests. When they attack, they inflict Hunger on your character, making them more costly to defeat.

Building Bigger and Better Things

Minecraft scales as much as you want it to. You can build entire countries within it, or you can make a log cabin and live out a hermit's life. Or do both. Whatever you like, do it. In this chapter, we go over more challenging construction projects. Pyramids, cities, massive rail systems, and mountain kingdoms are examples of this style of larger builds.

Searching the Internet, you can find countless examples of works from your favorite fantasy worlds and history alike. Some of these have taken multiple people years to create, and that proves how boundless *Minecraft*'s extremes can be.

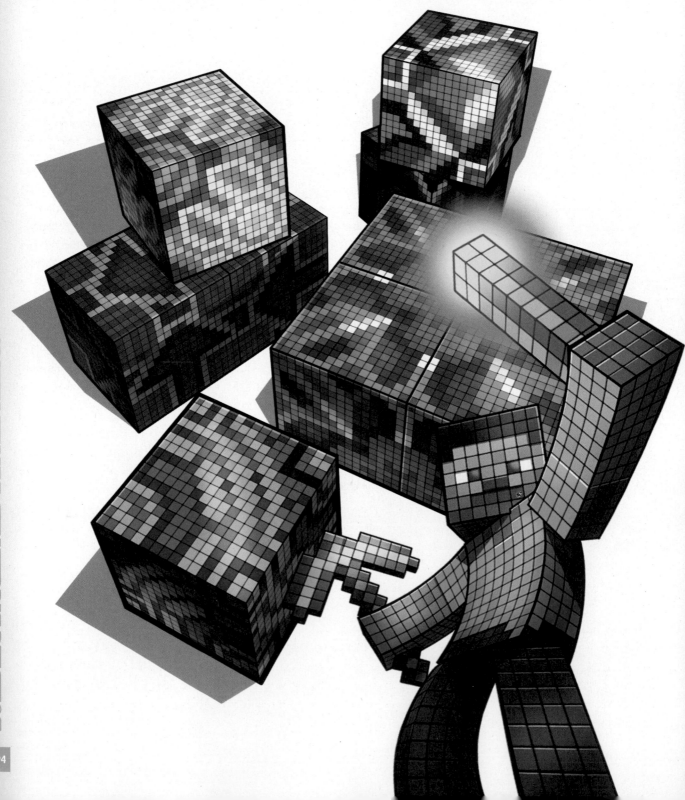

SAMPLE PROJECT: CHICHÉN ITZÁ

Let's give a good example of larger buildings. We've chosen a fairly simple project for our first one. While the build is large, we wanted to show something that could be done in a single day with about four to eight hours of work. That's a big enough time commitment to give you an idea of the principles of larger builds, without getting too daunting.

A classic building, El Castillo of Chichén Itzá presents an impressive and recognizable image. A number of people have created this building before in *Minecraft*, so it's a kind of "Hello World" for people who want to try out larger buildings.

First, let's go over a little history!

HISTORY OF CHICHÉN ITZÁ

In ancient times, Chichén Itzá thrived as one of the largest Mayan cities in the Yucatán Peninsula of Mexico. The Mayan civilization was the greatest power of the early Mesoamerican region, and at their height, the Mayans controlled a third of Mesoamerica. They are known for their calendar system, art, and architecture. They also recorded their history, with language found on the walls of their cities and temples, on pottery, and in screenfold books, although most of those were destroyed.

Chichén Itzá (translated name "At the mouth of the well of the Itzá") was originally settled somewhere between 415 and 455 CE, but the city grew to prominence around 600 CE. At this time, much of the Mayan civilization was in decline, but it remains a mystery as to why (although long-term drought certainly played an important role). Nonetheless, people were fleeing their established homes to the south and flooding into Chichén Itzá, which boasted a plentiful water source. Because of this influx, Chichén Itzá became a huge political and cultural center, with the city-state dominating the local area.

The second settlement of Chichén Itzá occurred when it was conquered in the tenth century by the Toltecs, under the King of Tula, Ce Acatl Topiltzin Quetzalcoatl. The Toltecs were not benevolent conquerors; they subjugated the local population with such ferocity that even their ruling descendants regarded them with both awe and terror. The Mayans themselves were not a gentle civilization, so this must have been quite harrowing.

As an example, the Toltecs believed in human sacrifice, and although this was probably done by the Mayans occasionally, it was rarely, if ever, practiced by Chichén Itzá residents before the Toltecs took them over.

After the conquest of Chichén Itzá, the city architecture became a fusion of Mayan and Toltec elements (called Maya-Yucatec). One of the prime examples of this style is the central pyramid that dominates the city, rising above the surroundings. This pyramid is called El Castillo, and it's a temple dedicated to Kukulkan, a serpent deity closely linked to the Toltec/Aztec god Quetzalcoatl.

We encourage you to examine other monuments in Chichén Itzá, most notably the Temple of the Warriors, which is surrounded by a huge number of impressive stone pillars called the Group of a Thousand Columns; El Caracol, which may have been an early astronomic observatory; and the Cenote Sagrado, which is a natural sinkhole filled with water that was used as a sacred pilgrimage site and sacrificial center.

What caused the end of Chichén Itzá as a thriving city is unknown. However, by the thirteenth century, there was no new construction. When the Spanish conquistadors arrived in Chichén Itzá, they found a small local population, but certainly no grand metropolis. Most of the city itself had been claimed by the surrounding wilderness. By 1588, Spain had taken all of the Yucatán, and Chichén Itzá became a (admittedly impressive) cattle ranch. It wasn't until 1841 that the site was excavated, revealing its archeological importance.

Today, Chichén Itzá is owned by the state of Yucatán, and the site's stewardship is maintained by Mexico's Instituto Nacional de Antropología e Historia (National Institute of Anthropology and History). An estimated 1.2 million tourists visit the ruins every year, making it the second most-visited archaeological site in Mexico. The pyramid of Chichén Itzá conjures fantasies of forgotten ancient ruins buried in the jungle, and we're sure that it will continue to inspire creators for many years to come.

Preparation and Research

The early stages of a build are quite important. Plunging directly into your construction can waste hours because of awkward measurements, poor materials, or myriad other mistakes. Taking an hour or two to figure out what you're doing is well worth the time. The bigger the project, the better your planning needs to be. This is true with single-player builds, and even more accurate when other players join the process. Having multiple people work together can be tricky, since it's easy for someone to accidentally end up using the wrong number or incorrect types of blocks.

So, sit down and look at the types of buildings that inspire you. In our case, we're doing the classic pyramid of El Castillo. There are tons of pictures of the real building to peruse, so that's where we began. We also read through a wiki about the building, which provided the proper dimensions of the structure. You don't have to follow the proper scale of anything, but doing so makes it easier to recreate a building that exists in the real world. You're less likely to have the dimensions feel off in the final product. While making our building, we left pictures of El Castillo up in our browser, and frequently alt-tabbed back and forth to make sure that things looked decently similar. This helped tremendously while working on the upper temple. Our original looked bland and didn't approximate some of the outer features at all. With some thought, we found a few ways to create additional elements that came much closer to those of the real temple. Inverted staircases really made the upper roof pop, and then we used Andesite blocks above the openings to mirror the darker highlights.

El Castillo measures 24 meters high and 55.3 meters across on its sides, with nine tiers and a six-meter temple on top. We can't make these measurements perfectly within *Minecraft*, but we can do a decent job of it.

To come close, we're going to make each level three blocks high. That gives us 27 blocks of rise, which will feel close to the 24 meters of the actual building. *Minecraft* blocks take two on top of each other to equal the height of a fully grown person, so saying that they're about a meter high feels adequate. Thus, for reference, we're saying that *Minecraft* blocks are a cubic meter.

Writing your measurements down on paper, or in an electronic document, really helps to set this stage. Graph paper is awesome because it's exactly what people use when they're building something with specific dimensions. There are free downloadable pieces of graph paper that you can print, so you won't need a trip to the store unless you want to go out.

After our research, we write down that our levels are three blocks high, with nine total tiers. Then we decide to make the sides 60 blocks each. Again, that isn't exactly the same as El Castillo's 55.3-meter sides, but it's close and even.

Our foundation will thus be a large square measuring 60x60 blocks of whatever material we decide to use. To build this out fully, we'd use 3600 blocks of material. However, we have options there. It's possible to build over open air in *Minecraft*, so we can create the outer foundation and leave the interior of the pyramid empty. Or we could make interior rooms, just for fun.

Another option, for people who want to make a building more realistically, is to create the outer sections of your building with special materials (we'll use Diorite for our exterior), but use Cobblestone or another ultra-common material for non-visual structures. It's a way to save on your best materials if you're building in Survival Mode.

CREATIVE OR SURVIVAL MODE?

There isn't a right or wrong answer regarding builds in Creative or Survival Mode. It's obviously a more challenging task to work in Survival Mode. You have to contend with monsters, limited resources, and the time it takes to gather all the things you need. For any build, there is a massive feeling of accomplishment when you finish your work in Survival Mode.

However, Creative Mode has a strong place as well. Though easier to work with (by far), it allows people to come together and experiment with all the blocks in the game without needing to worry about the hours it takes to mine everything. Make gigantic cathedrals of Diamond and Obsidian; it's just as easy in Creative as making a wall of dirt. But in Survival, that type of undertaking is brutal, even with multiple people working together.

Go with whatever motivates you the most. Almost all of our work is done in Survival, though recreating El Castillo was done in Creative due to time constraints.

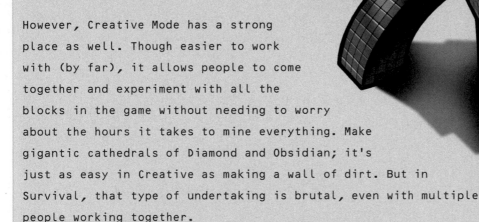

Sticking to Your Measurements

Even with a plan in place, you need to be rigorous about laying your foundation. Our plan of a pyramid with 60x60 sides is a rather easy one to stick to, but lose count when you're setting things up, and suddenly you're lopsided. To help avoid this, use milestones when making runs that are relatively large. Every 10 or 20 blocks, place a Torch. This makes it much easier to quickly assess your distances in the future. That comes in handy even after the blocks are on the ground, so leave your markers up until the project is entirely done. For example, you can easily end up with your staircases off-center if you don't carefully find the middle point of your walls. Having the Torches makes it much faster to figure out where to start placing those elements.

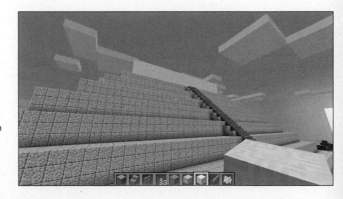

Counting is a powerful way to stay on your measurements while putting down blocks. If you're easily distracted, go back and recount the final product to ensure that you didn't get a bit creative with the math. It's slower this way, but it prevents you from looking at your finished building and saying, "That wall is three blocks too long. Oh, crud. This will take forever to fix." In tiny builds, a correction takes seconds, so who cares if you do something wrong? But the larger the build, the more time it'll take to correct mistakes.

Our Actual Build

We chose Diorite as our primary building material because it gives the closest visual look to El Castillo. The color is very good, and the texture of the rock is closer to the rather smooth stone of the pyramid. The temple on top has a different appearance, so we switched to Chiseled Quartz blocks there. This sets the temple off and avoids having a samey feel to the structure. For an Egyptian pyramid, we'd probably go with a traditional Sandstone set, unless we're adding the limestone cap that the pyramids had back in the old days. For those, Nether Quartz might work best—it's so nice and bright.

Let's take a moment to talk about the problems we faced, even with a relatively simple project like this. El Castillo was a one-day project, and we estimate that almost an hour was wasted on small mistakes, inefficient construction, and only decent planning. There's always room for improvement.

What did we do right, and what did we do wrong?

We failed to check our Torch milestone markers when making a staircase, so it ended up off-center. The thinking involved: "This looks like the middle, and it's right next to a Torch." However, it was the wrong Torch. We decided to leave that staircase in, because it's a great example of what happens when you get fast and free with your measurements.

But all in all, the final product was almost exactly what we wanted to make. The overall appearance of the building is quite nice, the dimensions feel solid, and the pyramid is great for walking around and exploring. We were especially happy with the Stairs, once we widened them a little.

To keep things uniform, we show all of our screenshots without Resource Packs or Shaders installed, but El Castillo looks amazing when you add in proper shadows and watch the sunset.

That is just one of our projects. Now it's time to talk about another—one that's even more ambitious!

NEXT UP: A MOUNTAINOUS UNDERTAKING!

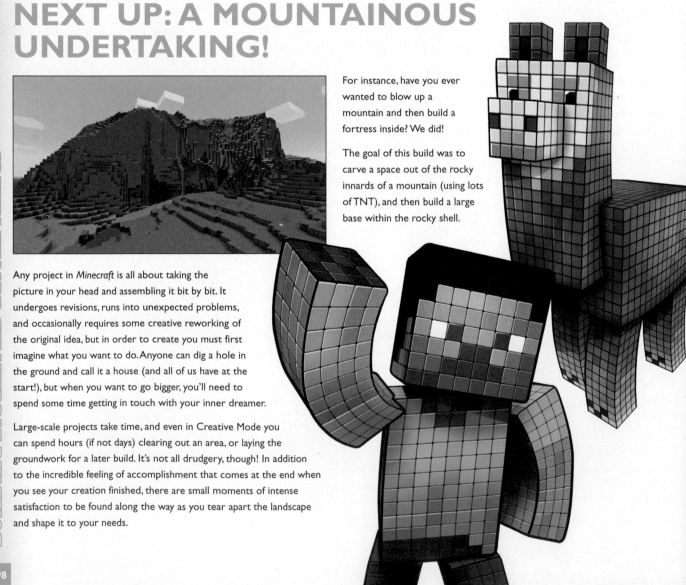

Any project in *Minecraft* is all about taking the picture in your head and assembling it bit by bit. It undergoes revisions, runs into unexpected problems, and occasionally requires some creative reworking of the original idea, but in order to create you must first imagine what you want to do. Anyone can dig a hole in the ground and call it a house (and all of us have at the start!), but when you want to go bigger, you'll need to spend some time getting in touch with your inner dreamer.

Large-scale projects take time, and even in Creative Mode you can spend hours (if not days) clearing out an area, or laying the groundwork for a later build. It's not all drudgery, though! In addition to the incredible feeling of accomplishment that comes at the end when you see your creation finished, there are small moments of intense satisfaction to be found along the way as you tear apart the landscape and shape it to your needs.

For instance, have you ever wanted to blow up a mountain and then build a fortress inside? We did!

The goal of this build was to carve a space out of the rocky innards of a mountain (using lots of TNT), and then build a large base within the rocky shell.

Demolitions and Groundwork

The first step in hollowing out this mountain was getting a handle on the size. Creative Mode is incredibly useful for a build of massive size. Not only do you get access to all the building materials you could possibly want, but you can destroy any block without specialized tools or waiting for it to break. You also gain access to the single most useful tool in all of *Minecraft*: the ability to fly. This lets you get all sorts of different perspectives on your creation, and lets you reach all of the little nooks and crannies speedily. You don't have to use it, but it will make your life a LOT easier.

Taking to the air gave a better perspective on the mountain that would influence the build. In this case, a flyover revealed that while the mountain was tall, it was also kind of skinny (for a mountain).

Any build inside this mountain would have to incorporate a lot of vertical building. The original idea was to hollow it out, then build a fortress inside, but the skinniness of the mountain meant that a sprawling horizontal build would be a lot harder to pull off. However, a build that rose from the bottom of the mountain to the top would offer lots of space to work with.

Swinging around to the back of the mountain revealed that it had two large hollows already present. This gave a way into the interior and a way to start hollowing it out.

When planning a large build, think about how much you'll have to alter the existing landscape. For instance, it's one thing to say, "I'm going to hollow out a mountain," and another to spend hour after hour removing rock and dirt from your build site before you can even lay down a block. Carefully examining the site for potential problems at the start can really save time later.

It didn't look like there were any further geographical complications visible from the outside. So this is where we decided to begin our work.

Let the blasting commence!

Potions of Night Vision are incredibly useful in this sort of work. You'll have to light up the area later, but during the build itself, keep that little bottle handy in your hotbar!

An idea of how much stone is actually involved here becomes apparent during the drill to the top of the mountain. Widening the initial hole may be accomplished by carefully spiraling outward, or you could use TNT to blast your way to a better, more open future.

As the hole widens, layer by layer, the clock ticks away. People have limited amounts of endurance when it comes to crafting, and during a large-scale build, you need to be careful to take breaks and save. It's all about finding that line where you're doing more harm than good! Every build has a point where you want nothing more than to set fire to the whole thing, and when you're working with TNT, there will absolutely be times when the urge to keep filling a room with more and more explosives becomes nigh overpowering.

Save the game, make a copy of your world, and take a deep breath. Then light the fuse! You have to be able to blow off some steam during a big build, so take some time to revel in destruction. Just make sure you save first, in case you end up trashing your work! Backing up your save files is quite valuable, especially if you reach particularly important milestones in the project. "I can always fall back to this later if things don't work out."

Construction Begins

With a large area now successfully carved out of the mountain, construction can begin. It's time to start thinking about building materials and light sources!

We wanted to use the Sea Lanterns for lighting, as they provide as much light as Glowstone and Redstone Lamps. They don't really work as flooring, though. Glowstone doesn't look good as a flooring material either (especially with the Sea Lanterns as an additional light source), so we went with Gold blocks. The solid color and strong contrast worked well in the end. It gives the place a Hall of the Mountain King feel, and that's pretty cool.

A strong central feature can really unite the build. The mountain has a lot of vertical space, so creating a central feature that everything else can wind around will pull it all together.

There are a lot of options, like a central Lava fall or light fixture, or a massive stalactite or stalagmite. However, the Gold block flooring provided an unforeseen bonus—it allowed for the construction of a Beacon!

Beacons send a column of light into the sky (as well as providing other passive bonuses), which seemed ideal to use as a centerpiece that united the rest of the room. A Beacon needs to be built on a pyramid of Gold, Diamond, Emerald, or Iron blocks; with a floor made entirely of Gold blocks, that won't be an issue.

Beacons need an unobstructed view of the sky in order to turn on. A quick flight to the top of the mountain removes the last few blocks that were in the way. A few Glass blocks later, and the Beacon was lit!

Lighting the rest of the interior was a matter of stringing Sea Lanterns on the walls, and building vertical spirals of Sea Lanterns to the ceiling on Dark Oak Fence posts.

Setbacks and Problems

Midway through the build, an unexpected problem arose. There were WAY too many monsters wandering around the build. Even in Creative Mode, it's a good idea to figure out how they're getting in and then clear them out.

Use the flying ability to investigate. In this case, there turned out to be lots of little nooks and crannies in darkness where the monsters could spawn, as well as several small holes in the retaining walls—a result of getting overzealous with the TNT and blowing holes that were a bit too big for our needs. In addition, several open holes in the ceiling and sides were allowing monsters from the outside world to simply wander in!

Three hours of work later, all outside holes were sealed, and any spot not well-lit was a sheer drop to the floor. That means anything that spawned in the dark places would have nowhere to go but down a straight drop to a sudden stop.

This is an instance where more forethought would have made a difference in the initial demolitions. Dark areas spawn monsters, and you need a lot of light to deal with such large, open spaces. However, during demolitions and construction, if you're using Potions of Night Vision constantly, the area appears brightly lit (regardless of the actual light level). In this case, it was easy for the problem to slip under the radar until late in the build.

This is also a good example of how getting a little TNT-happy during demolitions has consequences. Patching the holes in the walls isn't as much fun as making new ones with TNT, but in the long run, it's better to deal with those issues as they come up, rather than waiting until later. Putting off these types of relatively small problems often means you're forced to stop everything mid-build at some point!

Stairway to Progress

With the Beacon lit and the lighting poles in place, construction resumed. The next step was to build a spiraling Wood staircase around the Beacon, following the light toward the ceiling. At regular intervals, platforms would be constructed to allow for living spaces. Dark Oak was the best Wood for the purpose, as it provided a strong contrast with the Sea Lanterns and Gold floor.

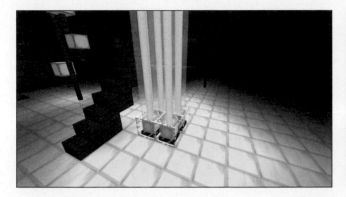 

The first platform would be the living platform. Every fortress needs a place for the lord of the castle to sleep, so a bed was a foregone conclusion. However, it looked lonely by itself on such a large platform!

A nice red carpet added a touch of color, and a variety of Chests and Crafting Tables guaranteed that anyone who lived in this fortress would have everything they needed to expand if they wanted to switch to Survival Mode later on. It was a touch too dark, so a few more Sea Lanterns completed the platform.

SWITCHING FROM CREATIVE TO SURVIVAL

In the PC version of the game, you can switch a world to LAN Mode so that you can open things to your friends and others. While doing this, you can also change the game's mode. This is a viable way to transition to Survival Mode after a major build is completed.

A few more turns on the staircase, and it was time for another platform. This would be the library platform, with an Enchanting Table and lots of Bookcases. The red carpet worked so well on the previous platform that we maintained the theme with this one.

Moving up a few more turns led to the third platform, which would be all about Potions and brewing. A Brewing Stand, Cauldron, and plenty of Chests ensured that anyone who wanted to make Potions would have all the materials at hand!

None of these platforms took too long, because of all the preparation that had gone on before. This was a result of having a strong idea in mind for each one, plus all the required materials and space. At that point, all that was needed was to make a few measurements, keep the widths consistent, and watch everything click into place!

The Final Platform

The last platform would be a bit different. Initially, it was going to be an observation deck at the very top of the mountain, but during the staircase construction, that idea morphed—it would be the perfect place for a garden. Most gardens end up on the ground level of a build, but there was no real reason why it couldn't be on top, and the proximity to the surface meant it would be extremely easy to knock a hole in the ceiling to let in additional light.

Besides, everyone needs fresh vegetables, even people who live inside mountain fortresses!

The platform for the garden was extra thick so that a water channel could be built (and so that it wouldn't leak). Because the top of the mountain was so near at hand, it was a simple matter to knock out a hole and use Glass blocks to provide natural light.

Shortly after the platform was finished, the Water blocks started freezing. The top of the mountain was a chilly, snow-covered place, and the water was freezing from the cold! The quickest solution was to put Sea Lanterns beneath each Water block to make sure it stayed melted.

With the water flowing and the crops flourishing, the final platform was complete!

Home, Sweet Mountain Home

The platforms were all complete, the Sea Lanterns were pushing back the darkness, and everything looked good! There were tons of ways to expand on the mountain fortress—underground railways, secret dungeons, and so forth—but this was the core of the build.

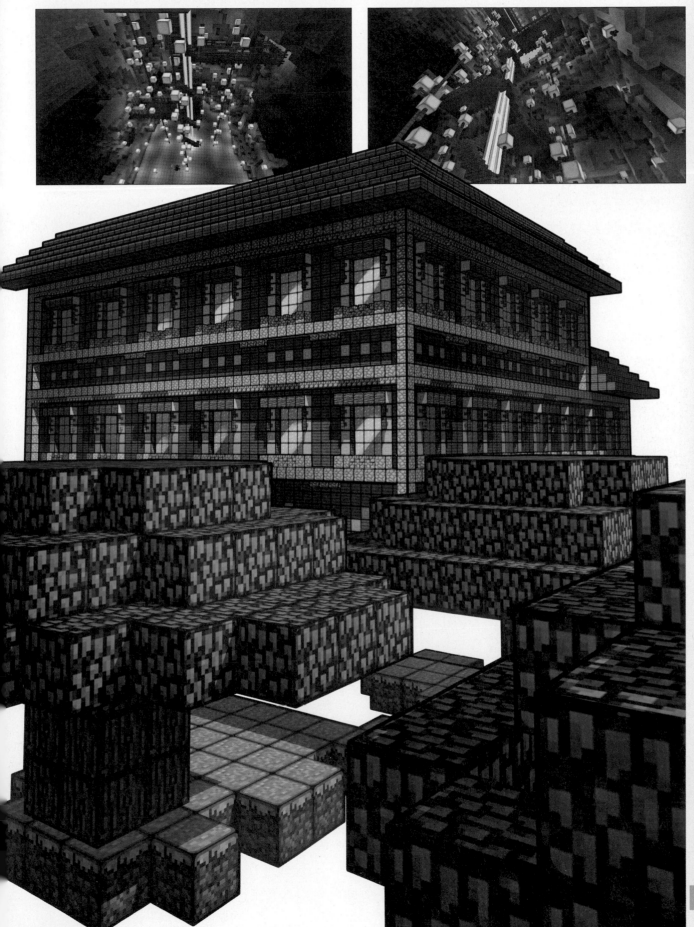

OTHER PEOPLE'S COOL PROJECTS

We've collected neat examples of other things that people have made with *Minecraft*. Take a look and see what you think of these larger builds.

All of Denmark Recreated in Minecraft

The Danish Geodata Agency took on an incredibly ambitious project; they made a 1:1 scale recreation of Denmark within *Minecraft*. It's a four-trillion-Brick build, and the save file for it weighs in at an entire terabyte. Phew. That's one heck of a download.

The project was accomplish using the agency's own elevation model of the region. Here are a few things we asked them about their work!

I've read that you were trying to raise interest and awareness in spatial data. Could you tell me more about that?

On January 1, 2013 the Danish spatial data was bought free and became available for everybody. It opens great opportunities, but in order to use them, people need to know they are there. So we made Denmark in *Minecraft*, mainly to raise interest among children and teachers, but also in general--for example, among game developers, because *Minecraft* is a good showcase of the opportunities.

Why did you decide on *Minecraft* as a tool to make people more excited about this?

Very many people know *Minecraft*, so it was a good but different way of getting our message out. And it was fun!

Was it a difficult task to create such a massive area in the game? Even the file size for the completed work is huge!

It actually didn't take us that long, because the spatial data that we used have such high quality.

Is there anything that you'd like to say about your project and its reception?

We are still grateful that so many people got excited about this and decided to share our work. We got much more attention than expected, and we are so proud of our Denmark in *Minecraft*. It really was great fun to work on this project!

Minecart Interstate

SirCrest, on YouTube, put out a video of his Minecart Interstate in the early days of the game. This brought attention to the game and to some of the cool things that everyone could work on. We tracked him down to ask a few questions! Take a look at his work in 1440P to really get a smile.

How much time have you put into Minecart Interstate (each one, or all in total)?

For the original V3.0 video (which at the time was just the third video of the same track, which had been extended), I think I told most viewers I spent about 24-26 hours on the build itself. This was spread over perhaps two to three months. And I would be playing the game at the time, not solely placing blocks. The video aspect, I couldn't even tell you. it's been nearly five years since I released that video.

As for the V3.0 remake, likely over 100 hours. Even though the track was technically already made, there was a significant amount of work for updating the map file for use in the then-latest version of *Minecraft*. Loading it in Alpha, then Beta for it to convert, then Release for it to convert again. I had to rotate the entire track in some mapping tools so that the sun and moon were in the correct position compared to the original video. Then, due to certain mods not being updated in years and with how certain mechanics with the engine had changed, I had to use those same mapping tools to replace parts of the track to keep the same speed, and thus the same timing in the video. I'm boiling it down, but this process took a week or two to do.

The recording, editing, and processing of the resulting video took another 30-40 hours, chief of which was just waiting for the video to render at various stages. In order to create the very clean, high-fidelity visuals, you need to be a very patient person, or own a tablet to watch stuff on.

Was the construction more a matter of time or planning? Inspiration or perspiration?

Construction was purely time; for a portion of the track the resources were manually gathered, believe it or not. I had a huge hole I dug in the first few hours of owning the game in July of 2010, I had Chests full of Cobblestone, and I ended up using most of that for the track. You can see this hole in some of my follow-up videos in 2010 where I talk about the project. To finish the track, though, I had to start using some inventory editor tools. This was before the days of MCedit or mods for giving items. You had to use a save file editor, close the game, find the inventory for that item, type in the amount of blocks, save it, and reload the game and keep building. Very tedious, but to the best of my knowledge I didn't have an alternative.

Do you scan through the areas well ahead of time to judge if everything is going to be scenic, or just start tunneling to see what comes up?

I am still adamant that Alpha had the best world generation. Yes, you only had really one biome; however, that one biome was so well-generated. At the time I used the phrase "highly realistic, but low-resolution." So because of that, I didn't plan anything for V3; I just kept building, because, to be honest, I knew it would look interesting and would move well past the view.

For V4, I did use a flycam to scout out the track a few times to see where I'd have problems. But eventually I landed on generation that I liked.

Do you have any suggestions for other large builders out there? Any tips for doing crazy stuff?

Research your tools. There may be something out there which can automatically do what you want to do manually. While I often enjoy the brute-force methods in some of my video projects, that is not always the smartest route. And frankly, I use these video projects as an excuse to try out these methods of video creation. Don't be afraid to sit down and browse forums or do some Internet searches for a few hours before starting on a project; you may find some information to inspire a change, or you might find someone did something similar and you can learn from their experience. And that applies to anything in life.

Any closing comments?

Only thing I think I'd close with is that, as silly as it sounds, the V3.0 Interstate video changed my life. That video got me interviews with websites and some TV networks like this. I got thousands upon thousands of emails and comments and messages talking about that video. It jump-started my "real" YouTube career, as well as all the experience in editing and video production that I have now. If that video didn't go viral, video editing and production would still just be a weird hobby I have, rather than my career and passion.

TAMING THE WILDS!
MASTERING MINECRAFT
FOURTH EDITION

Written by Michael Lummis
Cover Illustration by Keith Lowe
Interior Illustrations by Daz Tibbles

DK/Prima Games, a division of
Penguin Random House LLC
6081 East 82nd Street, Suite #400
Indianapolis, IN 46250

ISBN: 978-0-7440-1891-2

Printing Code: The rightmost double-digit number is the year of the book's printing; the rightmost single-digit number is the number of the book's printing. For example, 18-1 shows that the first printing of the book occurred in 2018.

21 20 19 18   4 3 2 1

001-310097-Mar/2018

Printed in the USA.

Credits

Senior Product Manager
Jennifer Sims

Production
Beth Guzman

Book Designers
Brent Gann
Jeff Weissenberger

Copy Editor
Serena Stokes

Prima Games Staff

Publisher
Mark Hughes

Digital Publisher
Julie Asbury

Licensing
Paul Giacomotto

Marketing Manager
Jeff Barton

NOT AN OFFICIALLY LICENSED MINECRAFT® PRODUCT

FREE eGUIDE!

Enter this code at primagames.com/code to unlock your FREE eGuide:

V3WP-9ZSX-MUD6-XXGK

CHECK OUT OUR eGUIDE STORE AT PRIMAGAMES.COM

All your strategy saved in your own personal digital library!

Mobile Friendly: Access your eGuide on any web-enabled device.

Searchable & Sortable: Quickly find the strategies you need.

Added Value: Strategy where, when, and how you want it.

BECOME A FAN OF PRIMA GAMES!

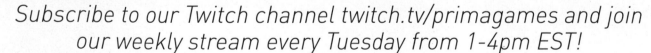

Subscribe to our Twitch channel twitch.tv/primagames and join our weekly stream every Tuesday from 1-4pm EST!

*Tune in to **PRIMA 365** on our YouTube channel youtube.com/primagamesvideo for a new video each day!*

www.primagames.com